AF856130

TRUTH COMMISSIONS AND COURTS

To Gérard Cohen-Jonathan

TRUTH COMMISSIONS AND COURTS

THE TENSION BETWEEN CRIMINAL JUSTICE AND THE SEARCH FOR TRUTH

Edited by

WILLIAM A. SCHABAS
Irish Centre for Human Rights
National University of Ireland
Galway, Ireland

And

SHANE DARCY
Transitional Justice Institute
University of Ulster
Northern Ireland

Reprinted from *Criminal Law Forum*, Volume 15, Nos. 1–2, 2004

A.C.I.P. Catalogue record for this book is available from the Library of Congress

ISBN 1-4020-3223-4

Published by Kluwer Academic Publishers,
P.O. Box 990, 3300 AZ Dordrecht, The Netherlands

Sold and distributed in North, Central and South America
by Kluwer Academic Publishers,
101 Philip Drive, Norwell, MA 02061, U.S.A.

In all other countries, sold and distributed
by Kluwer Academic Publishers,
P.O. Box 322, 3300 AH Dordrecht, The Netherlands

Printed on acid-free paper

All Rights Reserved
© 2004 Kluwer Academic Publishers
No part of the material protected by this copyright notice may be reproduced or utilized in any form or by any means, electronic or mechanical, including photocopying, recording or by any information storage and retrieval system, without written permission from the copyright owner

Printed in the Netherlands

Table of Contents

Truth Commissions and Courts
The Tension between Criminal Justice and the Search for Truth

WILLIAM A. SCHABAS

INTRODUCTION

Criminal justice for human rights abuses committed during periods of political repression or dictatorship is one of the great challenges to post-conflict societies. In many cases, there has been no justice at all. Sometimes serious political concerns that efforts at accountability might upset fragile peace settlements have militated in favour of no action and no accountability. In many cases, the outgoing tyrants have conditioned their departure upon a pledge that there be no prosecutions.

But thinking on these issues has evolved considerably in recent years. Largely driven by the view that collective amnesia amounts to a violation of fundamental human rights, especially those of the victims of atrocities, attention has increasingly turned to the dynamics of post-conflict accountability. At the high end of the range, of course, sit the new international criminal justice institutions: the *ad hoc* tribunals for the former Yugoslavia and Rwanda, the Special Court for Sierra Leone, the various "hybrid" tribunals in Kosovo, East Timor and Cambodia, and the new International Criminal Court. But in terms of sheer numbers, the most significant new institutions are truth and reconciliation commissions. Of variable architecture, depending upon the prerogatives of the society in question and the features of the past conflict, they have emerged as a highly popular mechanism within the toolbox of transitional justice.

In some cases, the truth commission is held out as an alternative to criminal justice. Transitional states often may simply refuse to contemplate the criminal justice option, and offer the truth commission as a modest alternative. In others, a dynamic is created between the truth commission process and criminal courts, whereby those who participate in the truth commission process are in some way sheltered from prosecution.

But with the emergence of international criminal justice, either through dedicated institutions or the exercise of universal jurisdiction, it has become more difficult to adequately address the relationship between these accountability mechanisms. Even if truth commissions fit within some acceptable domestic compromise, they cannot

Criminal Law Forum **15:** 1–2, 2004.
© 2004 *Kluwer Academic Publishers. Printed in the Netherlands.*

be insulated from prosecution in other jurisdictions, including the international ones. This situation increasingly promises to become the rule, as the numbers of States parties to the Rome Statute of the International Criminal Court grows. In joining the Court, States in effect renounce to any option about the presence of criminal justice in a post-conflict environment. How the new International Criminal Court will relate to truth and reconciliation commissions remains a question for the future. Its answer may well depend upon the personality and vision of the Court's independent prosecutor.

The drafters of the Rome Statute of the International Criminal Court were regularly confronted with the issue of how such a body would relate to national approaches to accountability falling short of full-blown criminal prosecution. The Statute might seem to suggest that the Court will act when national courts fail to prosecute, but many observers feel that it would be loathe to intervene if an effective and credible indigenous process is contributing to peace.

Perhaps the greatest difficulty in the relationship concerns the reuse of materials developed within a truth and reconciliation commission process for the purposes of subsequent criminal prosecution. It is a source of concern that a truth and reconciliation commission might find itself reduced to some sort of inquiry chamber or pre-trial investigative body for the courts. This seems to devalue the whole exercise, and may ultimately compromise the operations of such commissions, discouraging participation and cooperation with them, especially by perpetrators.

The papers in this special issue of *Criminal Law Forum* were initially produced for an international conference on the interrelationship between truth commissions and criminal courts, held at the Irish Centre for Human Rights at the National University of Ireland, Galway, in late 2002. In addition to the Irish Centre for Human Rights, two organizations with profound involvement in transitional justice issues, the International Centre for Transitional Justice and the United States Institute of Peace, co-sponsored the event.

The contributions review the experience of several of the major truth commissions in recent years: Peru, Guatemala, El Salvador, Ghana and East Timor. The Sierra Leone experience is addressed not with an article but with a judgment, the November 2003 ruling by the President of the Special Court for Sierra Leone concerning the relationship between the Court and the Truth and Reconciliation Commission. In addition, there are thoughtful overview pieces by Tristram Hunt and Martin Imbleau, and a report on an analogous body, the Saville inquiry into "Bloody Sunday" in Northern Ireland.

WILLIAM A. SCHABAS*

A SYNERGISTIC RELATIONSHIP: THE SIERRA LEONE TRUTH AND RECONCILIATION COMMISSION AND THE SPECIAL COURT FOR SIERRA LEONE

Sierra Leone's Truth and Reconciliation Commission was a product of the *Lomé Peace Agreement* of 7 July 1999, a negotiated truce between the Government of Sierra Leone and the rebel Revolutionary United Front.[1] A truth commission had been on the agenda for several years at that point, and had also been proposed in an earlier and subsequently aborted peace settlement to the war that was reached in Abidjan in November 1996.[2] As originally conceived, there was never any thought of defining how the Sierra Leone Truth Commission would relate to criminal prosecutions. The model driving all discussion at the time, that of the South African Truth and Reconciliation Commission,[3] had placed the institution within a dynamic based on a parallel regime of criminal justice, in that witnesses were encouraged to testify in exchange for amnesty or immunity from prosecution. But the Sierra Leone peace settlement promised a full amnesty to combatants on all sides. The Truth Commission was presented as an alternative to prosecutions, not a complement to them.

But this all changed a year later, and well before the Truth Commission was formally established. A resurgence in the conflict

---

* Professor of human rights law, National University of Ireland, Galway, and Director, Irish Centre for Human Rights; <william.schabas@nuigalway.ie>. The author was a member of the Sierra Leone Truth and Reconciliation Commission. This article was written in his private capacity and does not necessarily reflect the views of the other commissioners or of the Commission.

[1] *Peace Agreement between the Government of Sierra Leone and the Revolutionary United Front of Sierra Leone*, Lomé, 7 July 1999, art. XXVI.

[2] *Peace Agreement between the Government of the Republic of Sierra Leone and the Revolutionary United Front of Sierra Leone (RUF)*, 30 November 1996.

[3] There is a great deal of literature on the South African Commission. For a personal account by its vice-president, see: ALEX BORAINE, A COUNTRY UNMASKED (2000).

Criminal Law Forum **15:** 3–54, 2004.
© 2004 *Kluwer Academic Publishers. Printed in the Netherlands.*

prompted Sierra Leone's President to request that the United Nations establish an international criminal tribunal. The concept was immediately endorsed by the Security Council, which instructed the Secretary General to negotiate an agreement between the United Nations and the Government of Sierra Leone for the establishment of a court. The preamble to the Security Council resolution acknowledged the truth commission's position within the overall context of post-conflict justice, noting 'the steps taken by the Government of Sierra Leone in creating a national truth and reconciliation process, as required by Article XXVI of the Lomé Peace Agreement (S/1999/777) to contribute to the promotion of the rule of law'.[4] The Security Council subsequently referred to the complementary role of the Truth and Reconciliation Commission within the overall context of post-conflict justice in Sierra Leone in its correspondence with the Secretary-General concerning establishment of the Special Court.[5] The Secretary-General shared the view that the Commission was a complementary institution to the Court, writing in a 2001 report that '[t]hese two institutions are mutually reinforcing instruments through which impunity will be brought to an end and long-term reconciliation may be achieved'.[6] In a letter to the United Nations Security Council, dated 12 January 2001, the Secretary-General said that 'care must be taken to ensure that the Special Court for Sierra Leone and the Truth and Reconciliation Commission will operate in a complementary and mutually supportive manner, fully respectful of their distinct but related functions'.[7]

Nearly two more years were to pass before the two organisations became operational. As preparations progressed, much attention was devoted to defining the 'relationship' between the Truth Commission and the Special Court. But when activities actually began, more or less at the same time for both institutions, in July 2002, how exactly the two bodies were to interact was unresolved. For about 18 months – the lifespan of the Truth and Reconciliation Commission – the two

[4] UN Doc. S/RES/1315 (2000).

[5] 'Letter dated 22 December 2000 from the President of the Security Council addressed to the Secretary-General', UN Doc. S/2000/1234, p. 1; 'Letter dated 31 January 2001 from the President of the Security Council addressed to the Secretary-General', UN Doc. S/2001/95.

[6] 'Eleventh report of the Secretary-General on the United Nations Mission in Sierra', UN Doc. S/2001/857, para. 66.

[7] 'Letter dated 12 January 2001 from the Secretary-General addressed to the President of the Security Council', UN Doc. S/2001/40, para. 9.

institutions operated in parallel. By sheer coincidence, they were located in neighbouring premises on Freetown's Jomo Kenyatta Road. Operating from different perspectives, both institutions attempted to investigate and understand the complex conflict that brought Sierra Leone to its knees during the 1990s. In the end, they never clarified the relationship between the two bodies, at least in a formal sense. Yet they worked for most of the 18 months without major incident, and with a public profile of cordiality. Both repeatedly explained to the people of Sierra Leone that there was no cooperation between the two bodies, but that they respected the role of the other institution and appreciated its contribution to post-conflict justice.

In the final months of the Truth Commission's activities, in late 2003, three prisoners who had been indicted by the Court asked to testify in a public hearing before the Truth and Reconciliation Commission. The Prosecutor opposed the request, and ultimately the issue was litigated before judges of the Court. On 28 November 2003, the President of the Appeals Chamber, Geoffrey Robertson, gave each side 'half a loaf', ruling that the accused could testify, but not publicly.[8] His judgment now represents the principal judicial examination of the relationship between truth commissions and criminal prosecutions and will doubtless influence future efforts at transitional justice where truth commissions and courts operate simultaneously.

That the two bodies concluded the period of their parallel operation with tension and conflict gives a misleading impression of the nature of their relationship. The final report of the Commission probably does not assist in this regard either, as it is the product of compromises within the organisation between those with different assessments of the significance of the two institutions to post-conflict justice and reconciliation. In fact, the quarrel over testimony by indicted prisoners was the only significant dispute between the Truth Commission and the Special Court. And it showed that when issues did arise between the two institutions, an appropriate mechanism and procedure could be devised to resolve differences. The real lesson of the Sierra Leone experiment is that truth commissions and courts can work productively together, even if they only work in parallel. This complementary

[8] *Prosecutor* v. *Norman* (Case No. SCSL-2003-08-PT), Decision on Appeal by the Truth and Reconciliation Commission for Sierra Leone ('TRC' or 'The Commission') and Chief Samuel Hinga Norman JP Against the Decision of His Lordship, Mr Justice Bankole Thompson Delivered on 30 October 2003 to Deny the TRC's Request to Hold a Public Hearing With Chief Samuel Hinga Norman JP, 28 November 2003. The ruling is reproduced in full at pp. 247–272 of this volume.

relationship may have a synergistic effect on the search for post-conflict justice as part of the struggle against impunity.[9]

I. ESTABLISHMENT OF THE TRUTH AND RECONCILIATION COMMISSION

The *Lomé Peace Agreement* of 7 July 1999 pledged that the Truth and Reconciliation Commission (TRC) was to be established within 90 days. Although efforts were soon directed to this task,[10] legislation for the purpose was not adopted by Sierra Leone's Parliament until 22 February 2000.[11] On 5 October 2004, the Truth and Reconciliation Commission presented its multi-volume report to the President.[12] It had been more than a year in preparation, although the

---

[9] The author has developed some of these ideas in earlier publications, to which the reader is referred for a more thorough examination of these issues: William Schabas, 'The Relationship Between Truth Commissions and International Courts: The Case of Sierra Leone', (2003) 25 *Human Rights Quarterly* 1035; William Schabas, *"Internationalised" Courts and their Relationship with Alternative Accountability Mechanisms: The Case of Sierra Leone*, in PROCEEDINGS OF THE 31ST ANNUAL CONFERENCE OF THE CANADIAN COUNCIL ON INTERNATIONAL LAW 322–350 (2004); William Schabas, *Addressing Impunity in Developing Countries: Lessons from Rwanda and Sierra Leone*, in LA VOIE VERS LA COUR PÉNALE INTERNATIONALE: TOUS LES CHEMINS MÈNENT à ROME 159–178 (Hélène Dumont & Anne-Marie Boisvert, eds., 2004); William Schabas, *Truth Commissions and Courts Working in Parallel: The Sierra Leone Experience*, [2004] AM. SOC. INT'L L. PROC. 189; William Schabas, *Internationalised Courts and their Relationship with Alternative Accountability Mechanisms: The Case of Sierra Leone*, in INTERNATIONALISED CRIMINAL COURTS AND TRIBUNALS, SIERRA LEONE, EAST TIMOR, KOSOVO AND CAMBODIA 157–180 (Cesare P.R. Romano, André Nollkaemper & Jann K. Kleffner, eds., 2004); William Schabas, *Conjoined Twins of Transitional Justice? The Sierra Leone Truth and Reconciliation Commission and the Special Court for Sierra Leone*, 2 J. INT'L CRIM. J. forthcoming (2004).

[10] See Richard Bennett, *The Evolution of the Sierra Leone Truth and Reconciliation Commission*, in TRUTH AND RECONCILIATION IN SIERRA LEONE 37–51 (2001).

[11] *Truth and Reconciliation Commission Act 2000*, Supplement to the Sierra Leone Gazette Vol. CXXXI, No. 9.

[12] The final report of the Commission was formally presented to the President of Sierra Leone on 5 October 2004. Although a published version, consisting of four volumes, was handed over, the Commission did not subsequently release the full report to the general public. The publishers of the report had not done a satisfactory job, and the volumes were riddled with errors and inconsistencies. By 2 November 2004, the Commission disseminated a final version of two sections of the report, entitled 'Findings' and 'Recommendations' (available at www.nuigalway.ie/human_rights). It is expected that the full version of the report will not be issued until some time in 2005.

actual activities of the Commission lasted less than eight months. The operations of the Commission consisted of two distinct periods, a statement-taking phase, from December 2002 until March 2003, and a hearings phase, from April 2003 until the first days of August of that year. Trials before the Special Court did not actually begin until June 2004, well after the completion of the activities of the Commission. But during 2003, while the Commission was at the height of its activities, the Court was engaged in investigation, indictments, arrests and preliminary judicial proceedings. Any attempt to summarise the Commission's Report in a few lines or paragraphs risks oversimplifying ideas and conclusions of considerable complexity. Readers are urged to consult the Report as a whole, or at the very least Volume II, which consists of a 25-page 'Executive Summary', a section entitled 'Findings' and another entitled 'Recommendations'.

Although it was a national institution, established by Act of Parliament, the TRC had an international dimension because of the participation of the Special Representative of the Secretary-General and the High Commissioner for Human Rights in its establishment. These two senior United Nations officials were responsible for recommending the appointment of the three members of the Commission who were not citizens of Sierra Leone.[13] Virtually the entire financing for the Commission came from international donors, with the Office of the High Commissioner assuming principal responsibility for fund-raising.[14] Initially budgeted at $10 million,[15] poor donor response resulted in a reduction to less than $7 million. In the end, the TRC received less than $4 million, a disappointing result that seemed to indicate an indifference to its mission, despite grand statements to the contrary.[16]

It may be that the failure to raise adequate funds for the Commission was a consequence of donor enthusiasm for the Court. Some of the participants in the Commission process may even have felt

---

[13] *Truth and Reconciliation Commission Act 2000*, *supra* note 11, s. 3.

[14] This is discussed in detail in the 2003 Annual Report of the Office of the High Commissioner for Human Rights.

[15] 'Fourteenth report of the Secretary-General on the United Nations Mission in Sierra Leone', UN Doc. S/2002/679, para. 27.

[16] As a result of inadequate financial resources, many of the activities that had been planned had to be scaled down or simply eliminated. The TRC did not have the robust team of internationally qualified researchers and investigators, with vehicles, travel funds and other appropriate resources, that had been planned and expected. Because of funding and cash flow issues, salaries were often left unpaid for unacceptably long periods, with obvious consequences in terms of employee morale.

upstaged by the Court. Possibly donors saw the Commission as the compromised offspring of the Lomé Agreement, with its distasteful amnesty, something with which the Court was untainted. But the Court, too, suffered from donor indifference. Besides contending for a fair share of scarce financial resources from donors, the two institutions were also in competition for trained personnel. In practice, there was almost no real difficulty, although there were a couple of skirmishes. At one point, an investigator left the Commission to take up employment with the Court, which, to be fair, offered better salaries and greater job security. This gave grist to the mill of those who argued that the Commission and the Court were in some kind of sinister partnership, and that information accumulated by the Commission in the course of its investigations was being handed over to the Court. The problem had not been anticipated, and might easily have been addressed by requiring employees to sign a restrictive covenant in which they would undertake not to work for the other organisation within a specified time frame.

The Commission's mandate had both fact-finding and therapeutic dimensions. According to Solomon Berewa, who had been Attorney General of Sierra Leone when the TRC legislation was enacted, 'far from being fault-finding and punitive, it is to serve as the most legitimate and credible forum for victims to reclaim their human worth; and a channel for the perpetrators of atrocities to expiate their guilt, and chasten their consciences. The process has been likened to a national catharsis, involving truth telling, respectful listening and above all, compensation for victims in deserving cases.'[17] The 'Memorandum of Objects and Reasons', which was attached to the *TRC Act*, noted that the Peace Agreement 'envisaged the proceedings of the Commission as a catharsis for constructive interchange between the victims and perpetrators of human rights violations and abuses'.

The TRC's mandate, set out in section 6(1), was to prepare an historical record of the country from 1991, when the war began, until the *Lomé Peace Agreement* of 7 July 1999. However, the *Act* also required the Commission to investigate and report on the 'antecedents' of the 'conflict'.[18] Moreover, the TRC was also charged with addressing impunity, responding to the needs of victims, promoting healing and reconciliation and preventing a repetition of the

---

[17] Solomon Berewa, *Addressing Impunity using Divergent Approaches: The Truth and Reconciliation Commission and the Special Court*, in TRUTH AND RECONCILIATION IN SIERRA LEONE 59 (1999).

[18] *Truth and Reconciliation Commission Act 2000*, *supra* note 11, s. 6(2)(a).

violations and abuses suffered. This aspect of the mandate had no precise temporal framework. It seemed, therefore, that the TRC could inquire into events both prior to 1991 and subsequent to 7 July 1999, although the 'impartial historical record' that it was to prepare had a beginning and an end that was clearly defined by the statute. In practice and without any incident or fanfare, the TRC took evidence of post-Lomé events during its public hearings, and also inquired into pre-1991 events, all as if there were no temporal limitations in a jurisdictional sense. The 'Findings' and 'Recommendations' in its final report, issued 5 October 2004, indicated that the Commission was in no way constrained by the temporal parameters of the enabling legislation and that it saw its task as a general inquiry into the context of conflict in Sierra Leone as a whole, past, present and future.

The TRC's mandate referred to 'violations and abuses of human rights and international humanitarian law related to the armed conflict in Sierra Leone'. Paragraph 6(2)(a) of the Act indicated that the functions of the Commission included investigating 'the role of both internal and external factors in the conflict'. The TRC was to inquire into whether the conflict was 'the result of deliberate planning, policy or authorisation by *any* government' (italics added). Finally, it was empowered 'to request information from the relevant authorities of a foreign country and to gather information from victims, witnesses, government officials and others in foreign countries'.[19] The scope was broad indeed, with the only 'territorial' requirement being a relationship with the armed conflict in Sierra Leone. At the very least, the TRC was clearly mandated to consider the situation of war refugees in camps outside the country.[20] In practice, it organised research visits to neighbouring countries, and explored the role of external actors, such as Muammar Ghadaffi of Libya and Charles Taylor of Liberia.

The Truth and Reconciliation Commission was not engaged in prosecution, and so it is hardly appropriate to speak of 'personal jurisdiction'. The *Act* referred in several places to 'victims and perpetrators', suggesting that these two groups made up the Commission's principal constituency. Special attention was focussed on children, including child perpetrators, as well as victims of sexual abuse.[21] It is

[19] *Ibid.*, s. 8(1)(f).

[20] On violations of the human rights of refugees from Sierra Leone committed in neighbouring States, see for example: 'Refugee Women in Guinea Raped', Human Rights Watch Press release, 13 September 2000.

[21] *Truth and Reconciliation Commission Act 2000*, *supra* note 11, s. 7(4).

often claimed that the TRC had a special mandate to investigate issues relating to women, but in fact there was no such reference anywhere in the *Act*. Nevertheless, the Commission made it clear that it considered violations and abuses directed against women to be a major part of its mandate, and an entire chapter in the final report was devoted to this. The Commission was also given a role in determining responsibilities, of identifying the 'causes'[22] and the 'parties responsible',[23] and here its attention was directed to 'any government, group or individual'.[24]

At the core of the Commission's mandate was the concept of 'human rights violations and abuses'. The *Act* seemed to suggest that these might be committed by individuals as well as governments, and the Commission approached matters as if this were indeed the case. Responsibilities might have extended, for example, to transnational corporations or private security organisations. In the chapter of the final report dealing with the mining industry, the Commission explored this aspect of the question, although it did not in any way condemn the transnational corporations involved in the international diamond trade.[25] Be that as it may, the Commission is evidence of a trend within international human rights law to include non-state actors as perpetrators of human rights violations. It would be no surprise if, in the future, the legislation creating the Commission and the work of the Commission itself are cited as examples of an evolving State practice in this respect.

The Truth and Reconciliation Commission was charged with examining 'violations and abuses of human rights and international humanitarian law'. It was mandated to 'create an impartial historical record' of such violations and abuses[26] and to 'investigate and report on the causes, nature and extent' of the violations and abuses.[27] The *Truth and Reconciliation Commission Act 2000* provides no further guidance on the scope of the terms 'human rights' and 'international humanitarian law'. The Commission took a broad view of the concept of human rights, in keeping with United Nations doctrine on the

[22] *Ibid.*, s. 6(2)(a).

[23] *Ibid.*, s. 7(1)(a).

[24] *Ibid.*, s. 6.

[25] L. Sanders, *Rich and Rare Are the Gems they War: Holding De Beers Accountable for Trading Conflict Diamonds*, 24 FORDHAM INT'L L. J. 1402 (2001); William A. Schabas, *Enforcing International Humanitarian Law: Catching the Accomplices*, 83 INT'L REV. RED CROSS 439 (2001).

[26] *Truth and Reconciliation Commission Act 2000*, *supra* note 11, s. 6(1).

[27] *Ibid.*, s. 6(2).

indivisibility of human rights. Accordingly its researchers and investigators took evidence of violations of economic, social and cultural rights, as well as that of the more 'classic' civil and political rights involving attacks on bodily integrity and property. Some may have felt that this broad approach deprived the Commission of an appropriate focus. In fact, this helped to direct the Commission towards an understanding of the causes of the conflict and towards answers to the problems of Sierra Leone.

II. REPORT OF THE TRUTH AND RECONCILIATION COMMISSION

Michael Ignatief has famously said that '[a]ll that a truth commission can achieve is to reduce the number of lies that can be circulated unchallenged in public discourse'.[28] Probably they can do more than that, but if the Report of the Sierra Leone TRC does no more than debunk some of the myths of the conflict, it will have made a useful contribution. There are two widespread explanations for the conflict in Sierra Leone, one that largely blames external forces – Liberia's Taylor, Libya's Ghadaffi, and the international diamond smuggling mafias – and the other that focuses on internal causes – corruption, bad governance and the lingering legacies of colonialism. The Commission unequivocally opted for the second of these two visions in explaining the civil war's origins and causes. The Report explains that rebellion, driven by the country's frustrated and disillusioned youth, was probably the inexorable result of the post-colonial dictatorships. Regrettably, the 'rebels' had little if any ideological underpinning, and they soon fell into the same corrupt, abusive ways as those whom they had condemned and pledged to overthrow. The Report notes that essentially all sides in the conflict were responsible for serious violations of human rights and international humanitarian law.

This should be an unpopular conclusion among the ruling circles of Sierra Leone. The corrupt, morally bankrupt elite that had brought post-colonial Sierra Leone from being a model for others to being listed among the poorest countries in the world, and that set the stage for rebellion (let us recall the preamble of the Universal Declaration of Human Rights: 'Whereas it is essential, if man is not to be compelled to have recourse, as a last resort, to rebellion against

[28] Michael Ignatieff, *Articles of Faith*, 25:5 INDEX ON CENSORSHIP 113 (1996).

tyranny and oppression, that human rights should be protected by the rule of law.') is still essentially running the place. Sierra Leone's oligarchy would have been more than comforted by a view portraying it as the victim of persecution from external actors. Instead, the Commission takes a perspective that is inherently introspective. At the same time, it is a vision that in many ways is full of hope and promise for the country, because internal causes can be fixed by the people themselves.

It would be misleading to suggest that the Report of the Commission shifts the blame for violations and abuses of human rights and international humanitarian law away from the Revolutionary United Front (RUF), which launched the war in 1991. The Commission acknowledged that the majority of atrocities could be laid at the feet of the RUF and its recently deceased leader, Foday Sankoh. But the Commission did not subscribe to the 'just war' theory that has been so fashionable in Sierra Leone's ruling circles, by which any means were acceptable in order to suppress the rebellion. Nor did it denounce the rebellion as an inherently perverse or negative development, given the wretched state of governance in Sierra Leone in the early 1990s. Furthermore, the atrocities committed by the pro-government Civil Defence Forces (CDF), and notably by one sub-group of them known as the *kamajors*, were on a par with the worst the RUF had to offer.

This finding would seem to be in line with the investigations conducted by the Special Court. Significantly, although the Prosecutor of the Special Court is not charged with determining whether the war was just, he is to confine indictments to 'those who bear the greatest responsibility' for serious violations of humanitarian law. Accordingly, leaders of the pro-Government CDF were indicted and arrested,[29] and their trial began in mid-2004. The only unresolved question is why the pro-Kabbah minister responsible for the *kamajors*, Sam Hinga Norman, was arrested and charged with crimes against humanity and war crimes, while President Kabbah himself remained untouched by prosecution.[30]

The 'Findings' of the Truth and Reconciliation Commission debunked other myths about the conflict. The prevailing view among

---

[29] *Prosecutor* v. *Norman* (Case No. SCSL-2003-08-I), Indictment, 7 March 2003; *Prosecutor* v. *Fofana* (Case No. SCSL-2003-11-I), Indictment, 7 March 2003; *Prosecutor* v. *Kondewa* (Case No. SCSL-2003-12-I), Indictment, 24 June 2003.

[30] Like other modern international criminal law instruments, the *Statute of the Special Court for Sierra Leone* codifies principles of liability based upon command or superior responsibility. See *Statute of the Special Court for Sierra Leone*, art. 6(3).

external observers, commentators and non-governmental organisations is that diamonds were at the root of the war in Sierra Leone.[31] The Commission concluded otherwise, noting that the rebel groups did not focus on controlling the diamondiferous regions until the later years of the conflict. Because diamonds are central to the country's economy, they were inevitably a factor in the conflict, but their role has been largely overstated. Indeed, it seems that for much of the conflict, diamond smuggling remained under the control of the corrupt Freetown elite, where it had always been. This again shifts the focus of attention in terms of understanding the causes and solutions: the conflict was brought on by internal contradictions, not greedy outsiders.

The 'Recommendations' section is pregnant with implications, because the legislation creating the Commission bound the Government to implement them. According to section 17 of the *Act*, '[t]he Government shall faithfully and timeously implement the recommendations of the report that are directed to state bodies and encourage or facilitate the implementation of any recommendations that may be directed to others'. Many of the Recommendations are dramatic and far-reaching, carefully crafted to be free of significant economic consequences and therefore conceived in such a way as to be subject to immediate implementation. The government cannot invoke cost implications so as to avoid them. They are largely inspired by the big issues in contemporary human rights.

For example, the Commission calls for the abolition of the death penalty as well as the immediate commutation of all outstanding death sentences. Capital punishment, generally imposed for the crime of treason, has been used by the Sierra Leone government as a means of intimidating political opponents since the time of independence (of course, it was used for the same purpose prior to independence by the British colonisers). In the last few years, Sierra Leone has been condemned by both the Human Rights Committee and the African Commission of Human and Peoples' Rights as a result of the abusive use of capital punishment by the Kabbah regime at the height of the conflict.[32] The Commission also called for the immediate release of

---

[31] IAN SMILLIE, LANSANA GBERIE & RALPH HAZELTON, THE HEART OF THE MATTER: SIERRA LEONE, DIAMONDS AND HUMAN SECURITY (2000).

[32] *Mansaraj* et al. v. *Sierra Leone* (Nos. 839, 840 & 841/1998), UN Doc. CCPR/C/64/D/839, 840 & 841/19; *Forum of Conscience* v. *Sierra Leone* (No. 223/98), 28th Ordinary Session of the African Commission of Human and Peoples' Rights, Cotonou, Benin, 23 October to 6 November 2000.

prisoners currently being held without charge in Freetown's Pademba Road Prison. A significant number – perhaps twenty or more – of sympathisers with the rebel Revolutionary United Front (RUF) have been detained in Freetown's Pademba Road prison since May 2000; they have never been indicted, and they have been constantly denied access to either legal counsel or to their families. Their release can be ordered by the executive, and the Kabbah regime will be in violation of the *Truth and Reconciliation Commission Act 2000* if it refuses to comply immediately with this mandatory recommendation. The Commission also demanded the repeal of legislation concerning sedition and defamatory libel. The laws are holdovers from the repressive colonial period, and have no place in a contemporary democratic society.

With respect to children, the Commission recalled the particular suffering they endured during the war, calling for the prohibition of all forms of corporal punishment of children, both in schools and in the home. Implicitly, at any rate, the Report seemed to draw a link between brutal children and children who had been brutalised. Children were the backbone of the combatant forces. Their immaturity made them particularly vulnerable to manipulation by the adult leaders of different groups. The use of narcotic drugs may have contributed to the process, although the role of such substances in the conflict was probably exaggerated. Evidence before the Commission indicated that the older military leaders of both the RUF and the pro-government militias had begun their careers as child soldiers themselves. They had been recruited to British colonial forces in the 1950s, when they were in their early teens. Apparently it was the British who coined the term 'Small Boys Units', which was used in Sierra Leone in the 1990s as a label for combat units of children as young as 10.[33] This is not to excuse the conduct in Sierra Leone – recruitment of child soldiers is now recognised as a war crime[34] – but it certainly helps account for the origins of the practice.

---

[33] There is even a trace of this in the case law of the European Commission on Human Rights. In 1968, the Commission dismissed an application against the United Kingdom filed by parents of 15 and 16-year old boys who had enlisted in the British Navy for periods of service of 8–12 years. The Commission held that this did not constitute 'servitude' within the meaning of article 4(1) of the European Convention on Human Rights. Application Nos. 3435-3438/67, 11 *Yearbook of the European Convention on Human Rights* 562, 596 ff.

[34] *Statute of the Special Court of Sierra Leone*, art. 4(c). See: *Prosecutor* v. *Norman* (Case No. SCSL-2004-14-AR72(E)), Decision on Preliminary Motion Based on Lack of Jurisdiction (Child Recruitment), 31 May 2004.

The most celebrated truth commissions have operated not only when the conflict was over but when the transition, in a social sense, was well underway. The South African Truth and Reconciliation Commission did not need to recommend that the causes of its country's own suffering, *apartheid* and racial discrimination, be prohibited. This was all well understood and could remain unsaid. Similarly, Chile's truth commission did not have to argue that democracy was a better alternative to dictatorship. Sierra Leone is different. The end of the conflict was little more than a ceasefire, not a decisive victory by one side over the other, and above all no triumph of a progressive social vision over the perverse values and practices of the past. The Commission's Report attempted to point the way to a broad social transition, one that would be dependent on the political will and values of Sierra Leoneans rather than upon the largesse of foreign donors, who for too long have been held out as those with the resources and wherewithal to fix the ills of this most miserable and unfortunate of countries. Only time will tell whether Sierra Leone is prepared to address the underlying causes that led desperate young men and women to take up arms, and that brought on the decade-long war.

III. ESTABLISHMENT OF THE SPECIAL COURT FOR SIERRA LEONE

The peace established by the *Lomé Agreement* was built on a fragile power-sharing scheme. In many ways, it was more of a ceasefire between combatant factions than a roadmap for a transition to stability. Nobody was surprised when fighting broke out in May 2000. Tensions involving UN peacekeepers culminated in a hostage-taking of blue-helmeted Kenyans by the RUF in the Sierra Leonean hinterland, and this in turn led to a violent political crisis within Freetown itself. When the unrest settled, the RUF had been isolated and its leaders arrested. The Government of Sierra Leone 'reassessed'[35] its position with respect to the amnesty. Sierra Leone's President Kabbah wrote to the Security Council requesting that it establish an international tribunal to prosecute members of the Revolutionary United Front.[36] He explained that '[t]he purpose of such a court is to

[35] Solomon Berewa, *supra* note 17, at p. 56.

[36] 'Letter dated 9 August 2000 from the Permanent Representative of Sierra Leone to the United Nations addressed to the President of the Security Council', UN Doc. S/2000/786, annex.

try and bring to credible justice those members of the Revolutionary United Front (RUF) and their accomplices responsible for committing crimes against the people of Sierra Leone and for the taking of United Nations peacekeepers as hostages'. President Kabbah made explicit reference to the amnesty in the Lomé Agreement:

> As you are aware, the atrocities committed by the RUF [Revolutionary United Front] in this country for nearly 10 years in its campaign of terror have been described generally as the worst in the history of civil conflicts. In July 1999, my Government and the leadership of the RUF signed the Lomé Peace Agreement. The aim of this Agreement was to bring peace and a permanent cessation to those atrocities and the conflict. As a prize for such peace, my Government even conceded to the granting of total amnesty to the RUF leadership and its members in respect of all the acts of terrorism committed by them up to the date of the signing of that Peace Agreement.[37]

But he added that the Revolutionary United Front had 'since reneged on that Agreement'. Attached to the letter was a proposed 'Framework for the special court for Sierra Leone'. It, too, stressed that the mandate of the court would be to prosecute members of the Revolutionary United Front:

> The mandate of the court could be designed to be narrow in order to prosecute the most responsible violators and the leadership of the Revolutionary United Front. This could result in the numbers being limited to the dozens. This will also allow the court to be quick and efficient in its tasks of doing justice while at the same time breaking the command structure of the criminal organization responsible for the violence.[38]

Nowhere did President Kabbah attempt to clarify whether the Court was to be confined to post-Lomé offences, thereby respecting the amnesty provision in the Lomé Agreement, or whether he intended for it to override the amnesty.

The Security Council responded positively to Kabbah's request. On 14 August 2000, in Resolution 1315, the Council instructed the Secretary-General to negotiate an agreement with the Government of Sierra Leone with a view to establishing a special court. The Resolution's preamble noted that 'the Special Representative of the Secretary-General appended to his signature of the Lomé Agreement a statement that the United Nations holds the understanding that the amnesty provisions of the Agreement shall not apply to international

---

[37] *Ibid.*

[38] *Ibid.*

crimes of genocide, crimes against humanity, war crimes and other serious violations of international humanitarian law'.[39] But although the Resolution addressed a number of specific details concerning jurisdiction and related matters, it did not speak specifically to the issue of the amnesty, nor did it propose the temporal jurisdiction of the new tribunal (something which would have, indirectly, indicated a position on the amnesty issue, because had the Council states that the court would have jurisdiction over pre-Lomé offences this would have implied a retraction of the amnesty). The Resolution '[r]ecogniz[ed] that, in the particular circumstances of Sierra Leone, a credible system of justice and accountability for the very serious crimes committed there would end impunity and would contribute to the process of national reconciliation and to the restoration and maintenance of peace'.[40] Significantly, the Council once again flagged the significance of the Truth and Reconciliation Commission (it had also done this in its August 1999 resolution welcoming the Lomé Agreement), which had been created largely in response to the amnesty.[41] There was no reference to the Revolutionary United Front in the Security Council Resolution, despite the suggestion in President Kabbah's letter that it be the sole target of prosecutions. Instead, the Security Council said that the proposed court should have jurisdiction over all perpetrators, whatever their political affiliation: '*Recommends further* that the special court should have personal jurisdiction over persons who bear the greatest responsibility for the commission of [crimes against humanity, war crimes and other serious violations of international humanitarian law], including those leaders who, in committing such crimes, have threatened the establishment of and implementation of the peace process in Sierra Leone.'[42]

Following talks between the United Nations and the Government of Sierra Leone, in early October 2000 the Secretary-General proposed a draft statute for the special court. It was presented within a lengthy report that discussed the relevant issues in detail. The Secretary-General's Report noted that in negotiations about the draft statute of the special court, the Government of Sierra Leone had 'concurred with the position of the United Nations and agreed to the inclusion of an amnesty clause which would read as follows: "An amnesty granted to any person falling within the jurisdiction of the

---

[39] UN Doc. S/RES/1315 (2000), preamble, para. 5.

[40] *Ibid.*, preamble, para. 7.

[41] *Ibid.*, preamble, para. 4.

[42] *Ibid.*, operative paragraph 3.

Special Court in respect of the crimes referred to in articles 2 to 4 of the present Statute shall not be a bar to prosecution.'"[43] The Secretary-General's Report clarified the position of the Government of Sierra Leone with respect to the amnesty. Consequently, noted the Secretary-General, '[w]ith the denial of legal effect to the amnesty granted at Lomé, to the extent of its illegality under international law, the obstacle to the determination of a beginning date of the temporal jurisdiction of the Court within the pre-Lomé period has been removed'.[44]

The Secretary-General's Report considered the possible interaction between the proposed court and the Truth and Reconciliation Commission:

> Since the present report is limited to an analysis of the legal framework and the practical operation of the Special Court, it does not address in detail specifics of the relationship between the Special Court and the national courts in Sierra Leone, or between the Court and the National Truth and Reconciliation Commission. It is envisaged, however, that upon the establishment of the Special Court and the appointment of its Prosecutor, arrangements regarding cooperation, assistance and sharing of information between the respective courts would be concluded and the status of detainees awaiting trial would be urgently reviewed. In a similar vein, relationship and cooperation arrangements would be required between the Prosecutor and the National Truth and Reconciliation Commission, including the use of the Commission as an alternative to prosecution, and the prosecution of juveniles, in particular.[45]

Sierra Leone had argued that the Court should have jurisdiction over offenders aged 15 and more, and this rankled with the United Nations. The Convention on the Rights of the Child requires States parties to establish a minimum age of criminal responsibility, but does not set out what this should be,[46] and there are many states with ages below 15. But faced with the same issue, the drafters of the Rome Statute of the International Criminal Court decided that 18 should be the minimum age for international prosecution.[47] In an attempt to finesse the issue, the Secretary-General suggested that the

[43] 'Report of the Secretary-General on the establishment of a Special Court for Sierra Leone', UN Doc. S/2000/915, para. 24.

[44] *Ibid.*, para. 24.

[45] *Ibid.*, para. 8.

[46] *Convention on the Rights of the Child*, GA Res. 44/25, Annex (1989), art. 40(3)(a).

[47] *Rome Statute of the International Criminal Court*, UN Doc. A/CONF.183/9, art. 26.

TRC might be a better forum for addressing the problem of adolescent criminality during the conflict.[48] Along the same lines, the President of the Security Council wrote: 'The members of the Council continue to believe it is extremely unlikely that juvenile offenders will in fact come before the Special Court and that other institutions, such as the Truth and Reconciliation Commission, are better suited to address cases involving juveniles.'[49]

The Statute was agreed to by the United Nations and the Security Council in January 2002,[50] and operations of the Court began in about July, at roughly the same time as the Truth Commission was beginning its activities.[51] The Parliament of Sierra Leone enacted legislation concerning implementation of the Statute, but this did not

---

48 'Report of the Secretary-General', *supra* note 43, paras. 33, 36.

49 'Letter dated 31 January 2001', *supra* note 5. Also: 'Letter dated 22 December from the President of the Security Council addressed to the Secretary-General', UN Doc. S/2000/1234. See: D.M. Amann, *Calling Children to Account: The Proposal for a Juvenile Chamber in the Special Court for Sierra Leone*, 29 PEPPERDINE L. REV. 167 (2002); Stephanie Bald, *Searching for a Lost Childhood: Will the Special Court for Sierra Leone Find Justice for its Children?*, 18 AM. U. INT'L L. REV. 537 (2002).

50 *Agreement between the United Nations and the Government of Sierra Leone on the Establishment of a Special Court for Sierra Leone*, Freetown, 16 January 2002.

51 The establishment of the Court is discussed in some detail in *Prosecutor* v. *Kallon* et al. (Case Nos. SCSL-2004-15, 16 and 17-AR72-E), Decision on Constitutionality and Lack of Jurisdiction, 13 March 2004. On the Court, there is now a considerable literature: Micaela Frulli, *The Special Court for Sierra Leone: Some Preliminary Comments*, 11 EUR. J. INT'L L. 857 (2000); Giorgio Bosco, *The Special Court for Sierra Leone and the Extraordinary Chambers for Cambodia*, 15 RIVISTA DELLA COOPERAZIONE GIURIDICA INTERNAZIONALE 15 (2003); Robert Cryer, *A 'special court' for Sierra Leone?*, 50 INT'L & COMP. L. Q. 435 (2001); Suzannah Linton, *Cambodia, East Timor and Sierra Leone: Experiments in International Justice*, 12 CRIM. L. FORUM 185 (2001); Avril McDonald, *Sierra Leone's Shoestring Special Court*, 84 INT'L REV. RED CROSS 121 (2002); S. Beresford & A.S. Muller, *The Special Court for Sierra Leone: An Initial Comment*, 14 LEIDEN J. INT'L L. 635 (2001); Melron C. Nicol-Wilson, *Accountability for Human Rights Abuses: The United Nations' Special Court for Sierra Leone*, [2001] AUSTRALIAN INT'L L.J. 159; Celina Schocken, *The Special Court for Sierra Leone: Overview and Recommendations*, 20 BERKELEY J. INT'L L. 436 (2002); Abdul Tejan Cole, *The Special Court for Sierra Leone*, 14 INTERIGHTS BULLETIN 37 (2002); J. Cerone, *The Special Court for Sierra Leone: Establishing a New Approach to International Criminal Justice*, 8 ILSA J. INT'L & COMP. L. 379 (2002); Nicole Fritz & Alison Smith, *Current Apathy for Coming Anarchy: Building the Special Court for Sierra Leone*, 25 FORDHAM INT'L L.J. 391 (2001); C. Denis, *Le Tribunal special pour la Sierra Leone – Quelques discussions*, [2001] REVUE BELGE DE DROIT INTERNATIONAL 236; Marissa Miraldi, *Overcoming Obstacles of Justice: The Special Court of Sierra Leone*, 19 N.Y.L. SCH. J. HUM. RTS. 849 (2003).

touch on the amnesty issue.[52] The purpose of the legislation was to provide a legal framework for the activities of the Court within Sierra Leone, and to impose obligations upon the Government of Sierra Leone to cooperate with the Court. Sierra Leone, like most common law countries based on English law, is dualist, and international agreements are not directly enforceable before its courts in the absence of such implementing legislation.

The Special Court is an international organisation in its own right, created by treaty between the Government of Sierra Leone and the United Nations.[53] Institutionally, it largely resembles the *ad hoc* tribunals for the former Yugoslavia and Rwanda, although the latter were created by the Security Council and are therefore blessed with the international enforcement powers that this entails. Like the TRC, the Special Court is funded by voluntary contributions from international donors, and its budget has also been scaled down from an amount that originally exceeded $100 million to about $60 million over 3 years. There is no prescribed lifespan for the Court, but it is not expected that trials will continue much beyond the 3-year period. While the Special Court may deliver 'truth-seeking', 'catharsis', 'expiation of guilt' and so on, its mission is essentially punitive: 'to prosecute persons who bear the greatest responsibility for serious violations of international humanitarian law and Sierra Leonean law committed in the territory of Sierra Leone since 30 November 1996, including those leaders who, in committing such crimes, have threatened the establishment of and implementation of the peace process in Sierra Leone'.[54]

In early May 2002, the Secretary-General appointed David Crane of the United States as Prosecutor of the Special Court, and Robin Vincent of the United Kingdom as Acting Registrar (he was subsequently confirmed in this position by the judges). On 26 July 2002, the Secretary-General announced the appointment of eight judges and two alternates for the Special Court. The judges took their oaths of office in December 2002. In March 2003 eight indictments were issued against several obvious and well-known suspects, including former Revolutionary United Front leader Foday Sankoh, former junta leader Johnny Paul Koroma, and incumbent deputy defence minister

[52] *Special Court Agreement (Ratification) Act 2002,* Supplement to the Sierra Leone Gazette Vol. CXXX, No. II dated 7th March 2002.

[53] *Agreement between the United Nations and the Government of Sierra Leone on the Establishment of a Special Court for Sierra Leone*, Freetown, 16 January 2002.

[54] *Ibid.*, art. I(1).

Sam Hinga Norman. Preliminary defence motions were filed in mid-2003, and trials began in mid-2004. Like the counterparts in The Hague and Arusha, the trials are proceeding excessively slowly. Much of the evidence being led by the Prosecutor consists of background material rather than direct proof of atrocities. Defence counsel make frequent objections, and the judges consider these in patient and almost painstaking detail. They will probably last much longer than is expected.

To a large extent, the Special Court – like the Truth and Reconciliation Commission - was a response to the amnesty granted by the *Lomé Peace Agreement*. Because of the amnesty, the national courts that would ordinarily have jurisdiction over offences committed in Sierra Leone have been prevented from prosecuting offenders. The date at which the temporal jurisdiction of the Special Court begins, 30 November 1996, coincides with the signature of the *Abidjan Peace Agreement*, reached between the Government of Sierra Leone and the rebel Revolutionary United Front (RUF).[55] There is no end-point to its temporal jurisdiction, although of course the Statute can always be amended by agreement of the two parties.[56] The reference in article 1 of the Statute to jurisdiction over those who have 'threatened the establishment of and implementation of the peace process in Sierra Leone' should be a warning that the Court may continue to exercise jurisdiction over events until the completion of the 'peace process'.[57]

The Secretary-General had recommended that 30 November 1996 be chosen as the beginning of the temporal jurisdiction so as not to impose a 'heavy burden' on the Court, although the conflict is generally agreed to have begun on 23 March 1991, when the RUF first invaded Sierra Leone from neighbouring Liberia. In mid-2001, the Government of Sierra Leone unsuccessfully requested the United Nations to extend the temporal jurisdiction to the beginning of the conflict in 1991. The explanation given by the United Nations for limiting the jurisdiction is not very convincing. Perhaps the United Nations is itself uncomfortable with involvement in pre-Abidjan

[55] *Peace Agreement between the Government of the Republic of Sierra Leone and the Revolutionary United Front of Sierra Leone*, Abidjan, 30 November 1996.

[56] *Vienna Convention on the Law of Treaties*, (1979) 1155 UNTS 331, art. 39.

[57] In a recent report, the Secretary-General listed a number of benchmarks that need to be accomplished as part of the 'peace process'. 'Fifteenth report of the Secretary-General on the United Nations Mission in Sierra Leone', UN Doc. S/2002/987, para. 13. The issue of the end-point for the Special Court was discussed by the Secretary-General in 'Report of the Secretary-General', *supra* note 43, para. 28.

prosecutions because it did not object to the amnesty provisions at the time, in contrast with the position it took three years later at Lomé.

Article 1(1) of the *Statute of the Special Court* refers to violations 'committed in the territory of Sierra Leone'. The judges may have to rule on the extent to which they are prepared to extend the territorial jurisdiction to cover acts and omissions that take place outside the country if these produce significant effects on the territory of Sierra Leone. Article 6(1) of the *Statute* allows prosecution of any person who 'planned, instigated, ordered, committed or otherwise aided and abetted in the planning, preparation or execution of a crime'. Such secondary participation or inchoate crime may well have taken place outside Sierra Leone. The judges will undoubtedly be guided by the wealth of comparative criminal law authorities that already exist on these complex matters.

The Special Court's jurisdiction is defined in article 1 of the *Statute* as comprising 'persons who bear the greatest responsibility for serious violations of international humanitarian law and Sierra Leonean law committed in the territory of Sierra Leone since 30 November 1996, including those leaders who, in committing such crimes, have threatened the establishment of and implementation of the peace process in Sierra Leone'. The Secretary-General did not succeed in convincing the Security Council that it was better to refer to the 'persons most responsible'.[58] The January 2002 Planning Mission for the Special Court speculated on prosecutorial strategy, but conceded that the selection of those bearing the greatest responsibility 'necessarily entails a measure of discretion on the part of the Prosecutor both as to the identification of individual indictments and to any priority that may be assigned to them'.[59]

The jurisdiction of the Special Court is in no way limited by the nationality of the perpetrator, although in the case of foreign peacekeeping troops there is a rule of complementarity corresponding to the concept set out in article 17 of the *Rome Statute of the International Criminal Court*. Only when the 'sending State', which is presumably the state of nationality of the peacekeeper suspected of criminal acts, is 'unwilling or unable genuinely' to prosecute may the Special Court exercise jurisdiction.[60] This reduction in the primary jurisdiction of the Court was a response to

[58] 'Report of the Secretary-General', *supra* note 43, paras. 29–31.

[59] "Report of the Planning Mission on the Establishing of the Special Court for Sierra Leone", UN Doc. S/2002/246, para. 29.

[60] *Statute of the Special Court for Sierra Leone*, art. 1(3).

concerns of the Security Council, which felt such prosecutions to be the responsibility of the States that had sent the peacekeeping troops. It had proposed that the Court would only have jurisdiction over peacekeepers if the Security Council were to make a specific determination.[61] In any event, the 'sending States' referred to in article 1(3) of the *Statute of the Special Court* are not parties to the *Special Court Agreement* and are therefore under no treaty obligation to cooperate with the Court.

Unlike the TRC, which could and did examine the responsibility of 'groups', the Special Court's jurisdiction is confined to persons. There will be no determinations about the existence of 'criminal organisations',[62] although the Special Court will surely get at them indirectly by prosecuting the leaders of such bodies. Indeed, its three trials, each involving multiple defendants, are grouped according to the organisations with which the accused were associated. The reference to 'persons' in the *Statute of the Special Court* is not explicitly confined to physical persons, and the possibility of prosecution of corporate bodies cannot be ruled out, should the Prosecutor file additional indictments.

The *Statute of the Special Court* gives it jurisdiction over persons who were at least 15 years old at the time of the crime.[63] The issue provoked considerable controversy during the drafting of the *Statute of the Special Court*.[64] Subsequently, Prosecutor David Crane made several public statements indicating that he was not interested in prosecuting child offenders. The view was frequently expressed by both the Secretary-General and the Security Council that the Truth and Reconciliation Commission was probably a better venue for dealing with child or juvenile offenders, and the final report of the Commission, discussed earlier in this essay, made detailed findings and recommendations on the subject. In an implicit reference to the

---

[61] 'Letter dated 22 December 2000', *supra* note 49, para. 1.

[62] Unlike the situation at Nuremberg. On the usefulness of the concept of 'criminal organisation' for contemporary prosecutions of serious violations of international humanitarian law, see Nina Jorgensen, *A Reappraisal of the Abandoned Nuremberg Concept of Criminal Organisations in the Context of Justice in Rwanda*, 12 Crim. L. Forum 371 (2001).

[63] *Statute of the Special Court for Sierra Leone*, art. 7.

[64] For the Secretary-General's position, see 'Report of the Secretary-General ', *supra* note 43, paras. 32–38; 'Letter dated 12 January 2001', *supra* note 7, paras. 7–9. The Security Council considered it 'extremely unlikely' that juvenile offenders would come before the Special Court: 'Letter dated 31 January 2001', *supra* note 5. Also: 'Letter dated 22 December 2000', *supra* note 49.

TRC's role with respect to child offenders, the *Statute of the Special Court* speaks of 'alternative truth and reconciliation mechanisms'.[65]

A reference to 'international humanitarian law' appears in both the *Truth and Reconciliation Commission Act* and the *Statute of the Special Court*. In the case of the TRC, it was to examine 'violations and abuses' of international humanitarian law, while the Special Court is to prosecute 'serious violations' of international humanitarian law. The somewhat more limited subject-matter jurisdiction of the Special Court is further restrained by the specific enumeration of crimes that it may prosecute. Borrowing the wording used by the Security Council in article 3 of the *Statute of the International Criminal Tribunal for Rwanda*,[66] the *Statute of the Special Court* contemplates 'serious violations' of common article 3 to the Geneva Conventions and of Protocol Additional II. Furthermore, the *Statute* lists three additional 'serious violations': intentionally directing attacks against the civilian population, intentionally directing attacks against peacekeepers, and recruiting child soldiers. These three crimes are drawn from article 8(2)(f) of the *Rome Statute*.[67] But a comparison with the *Rome Statute* indicates clearly that the list of war crimes in the *Statute of the Special Court* does not include all offences in non-international armed conflict that are punishable under international law.

Moreover, it would appear that the Special Court has no jurisdiction over war crimes to the extent that these were committed in an international rather than a non-international armed conflict. The Sierra Leone conflict was obviously an internal armed conflict, so the issue may only be of theoretical interest. There were, nevertheless, significant international dimensions to the conflict.[68] For example, considerable attention has been paid to the role of mercenaries in the Sierra Leone conflict. The issue of mercenaries only arises in international humanitarian law with respect to international armed conflict.[69]

---

[65] *Statute of the Special Court for Sierra Leone*, art. 15(5). On this subject, see: D.M. Amann, *supra* note 49; Stephanie Bald, *supra* note 49.

[66] UN Doc. S/RES/955 (1994), annex.

[67] With some adjustment, due to what the Secretary-General describes as the 'doubtful customary nature' of the Rome Statute provision prohibiting recruitment of child soldiers during non-international armed conflict. See 'Report of the Secretary-General ', *supra* note 43, para. 18.

[68] See, for example: *Guinean Forces Kill, Wound Civilians in Sierra Leone*, Human Rights Watch Press release, 28 February 2001.

[69] *Protocol Additional to the 1949 Geneva Conventions of 12 August 1949, and Relating to the Protection of Victims of International Armed Conflicts*, (1979) 1125 UNTS 3, art. 47.

Accordingly, such matters fall within the remit of the TRC but appear to be outside the scope of the Special Court. The TRC's report did discuss, although in rather summary fashion, the role of mercenaries in the conflict.

The Special Court also has jurisdiction over crimes against humanity and certain specified violations of the laws of Sierra Leone, concerning sexual abuse of girls and destruction of property, that are not normally defined as serious violations of international humanitarian law. There is no direct reference to these offences in the *Truth and Reconciliation Commission Act* although the underlying behaviour likely falls within the rubric of violations and abuses of human rights.

IV. ATTEMPTS TO REGULATE THE RELATIONSHIP BETWEEN TRC AND COURT

The proposal to establish a special court altered the scheme of post-conflict justice and accountability in the *Lomé Agreement*, which was predicated essentially on two elements, the amnesty and the truth commission. It might well have been surmised from President Kabbah's proposal in mid-2000 to establish a court that the truth commission would no longer be necessary, or that its establishment and activities would be postponed, given the new focus on criminal prosecution. But it seems that most of the active forces in the process assumed from the earliest days that the two institutions were compatible with one another, and that they would work simultaneously. Attention soon focussed on the issue of the 'relationship' between the TRC and the Court.

On 2 October 2000, subsequent to the Security Council resolution but even prior to the Secretary-General's first draft, the United States Institute of Peace, the International Human Rights Law Group and two experts, Priscilla Hayner and Paul van Zyl, held an expert round table on how the two bodies would relate to each other.[70] The Secretary-General's report of 4 October 2000, which first set out the draft statute and the reasoning behind it, said that 'relationship and cooperation arrangements would be required between the Prosecutor and the National Truth and Reconciliation Commission, including the use of the Commission as an alternative to prosecution, and the prosecution of juveniles, in particular'.[71] In November 2000, an

[70] Richard Bennett, *supra* note 10, at p. 43.

[71] 'Report of the Secretary-General', *supra* note 43, para. 8.

international workshop organised by the Office of the High Commissioner for Human Rights (OHCHR) and the United Nations Assistance Mission for Sierra Leone (UNAMSIL) proposed establishing a consultative process 'to work out the relationship between the TRC and the special court'.[72]

A spectrum of views emerged, framed by two extreme positions: those who saw criminal prosecution as a threat to peace and a Western intrusion in African accountability mechanisms,[73] and those for whom truth commissions were an inadequate sop that was inconsistent with international legal obligations requiring prosecution and punishment of perpetrators of serious violations of human rights.[74] Those who favoured restorative justice approaches responded by insisting upon the relevance of a strong and dynamic TRC as a complement to prosecution. Those on the other pole suggested the TRC might be a useful adjunct to the court by assisting in information gathering with a view to prosecution. At the same time, there were many more nuanced views of the relationship between the two, driven by a commitment to the viability and importance of both options.

Many believed that because the two bodies were directed to issues of accountability and impunity, it was only logical that their activities be associated. During 2001, in the context of discussions on the content of the draft statute of the Special Court, several of the relevant issues in the relationship between the two bodies were considered. There were frequent proposals for a 'relationship agreement' between the two institutions. In 2001, the Secretary-General reported that UNAMSIL and the OCHCR would be preparing 'general guidelines' for the relationship between the TRC and the Special Court.[75]

---

[72] 'Situation of human rights in Sierra Leone', UN Doc. E/CN.4/2001/35, p. 13, para. 41.

[73] Okechukwu Oko, *Confronting Transgressions of Prior Military Regimes: Towards a More Pragmatic Approach*, 11 CARDOZO J. INT'L COM. L. 89 (2003).

[74] For example, Amnesty International wrote that the TRC's 'contribution to ending impunity is likely to be extremely weak or non-existent'. Furthermore, it recommended that 'the government of Sierra Leone and the international community should acknowledge that, while the TRC may be able to make an important contribution to establishing the truth about human rights abuses and understanding the nature of the conflict in Sierra Leone, it should not be a substitute for prosecuting those responsible for serious crimes under international law'. *Sierra Leone: Renewed Commitment to End Impunity*, AI index: AFR 51/007/2001, 24 September 2001.

[75] 'Eleventh report', *supra* note 6, para. 47.

In December 2001, as part of its activities to prepare for the establishment of the TRC, the High Commissioner for Human Rights and the Office of Legal Affairs convened an expert meeting in New York City. The meeting was described as follows in the report of the High Commissioner:

The expert meeting on the relationship between the TRC and the Special Court was organised by OHCHR and the Office for Legal Affairs (OLA) of the United Nations in New York on 20 and 21 December 2001. The participants discussed the important issue of an amicable relationship between the two institutions that would reflect their roles, and the difficult issue of whether information could and should be shared between them. The pros and cons of a wide range of possibilities regarding cooperation between the Commission and the Court were examined. Based on those discussions, the participants agreed on a number of basic principles that should guide the TRC and the Special Court in determining modalities of cooperation. These principles include the following:

(i) The TRC and the Special Court were established at different times, under different legal bases and with different mandates. Yet they perform complementary roles in ensuring accountability, deterrence, a story-telling mechanism for both victims and perpetrators, national reconciliation, reparation and restorative justice for the people of Sierra Leone.

(ii) While the Special Court has primacy over the national courts of Sierra Leone, the TRC does not fall within this mould. In any event, the relationship between the two bodies should not be discussed on the basis of primacy or lack of it. The ultimate operational goal of the TRC and the Court should be guided by the request of the Security Council and the Secretary-General to 'operate in a complementary and mutually supportive manner fully respectful of their distinct but related functions' (S/2001/40, paragraph 9; see also S/2000/1234).

(iii) The modalities of cooperation should be institutionalised in an agreement between the TRC and the Special Court and, where appropriate, also in their respective rules of procedure. They should respect fully the independence of the two institutions and their respective mandates.[76]

In addition to the UN-sponsored meetings, some international NGOs developed rather elaborate proposals on the type of provisions that might be governed by a relationship agreement. Although there was consideration of the possibility of joint or common efforts at witness protection, translation and public awareness, most consideration about how the two bodies might cooperate tended to dwell on what was called 'information sharing', something the December expert meeting had agreed was a 'difficult issue'. Nevertheless, what may well be the most difficult problem in the relationship between the

[76] UN Doc. E/CN.4/2002/3, para. 70.

two bodies, which is the question of admissibility in a prosecution of self-incriminating evidence that has been produced before the TRC, was hardly considered. For example, the Human Rights Watch policy paper made no mention whatsoever of the issue of a right against self-incrimination, and instead proposed that self-incriminating testimony given to the TRC might, if given voluntarily, justify a 'reduced sentence' by the Special Court![77]

The debate was fuelled by considerable anecdotal evidence to indicate the importance of concerns by perpetrators inclined to testify before the TRC that such testimony could be used in prosecutions before the Special Court. For example, a 2001 report by the Secretary-General claimed that the Revolutionary United Front (RUF) was 'receptive' to the TRC, but that it expressed 'concern over the independence of the Commission and the relationship between it and the Special Court'.[78] Many people, including NGOs associated with former combatants and participants in the abuses, indicated their willingness to cooperate with the TRC, but only on the condition that this material not be used for criminal prosecution. According to Human Rights Watch, doubt about the ability of the TRC to obtain information in confidence 'could potentially undermine the willingness of persons to come before the TRC to provide testimony'.[79] The International Centre for Transitional Justice referred to a statement by a local NGO that works closely with ex-combatants:

> We have witnessed the negative reaction of ex-combatants about information sharing... Many out-rightly have reversed their initial consent to face the TRC upon hearing about this possibility [of the TRC being compelled to give evidence to the Special Court]. To them, there seems to be evidence that the TRC will be an investigative arm of the Special Court and that whatever is being said at the TRC will be used to prosecute them or point the Prosecutor towards them as potential witnesses against their commanders... From our daily interactions, we know that many are willing to participate with the TRC so long as they can be guaranteed that this will not send them to the Special Court as a defendant or a witness against their commanders.[80]

[77] 'Human Rights Watch Policy Paper on the Interrelationship Between the Sierra Leone Special Court and the Truth and Reconciliation Commission', 18 April 2002. The issue is referred to, but only summarily, in the International Centre for Transitional Justice paper: 'Exploring the Relationship Between the Special Court and the Truth and Reconciliation Commission of Sierra Leone', 24 June 2002, p. 13.

[78] 'Eleventh report', *supra* note 6, para. 44.

[79] 'Human Rights Watch Policy Paper', *supra* note 77, p. 2.

[80] Letter from PRIDE to ICTJ, cited in 'Exploring the Relationship', *supra* note 77, p. 8.

Although much intellectual and political energy was expended by the United Nations and by international and national NGOs on the issue of the 'relationship' ever since the proposal to create a Special Court was first mooted, most of the discussion and the ensuing proposals did not prove to be particularly helpful. In the case of the administrative or practical arrangements by which it was recommended that the two bodies, Special Court and Truth and Reconciliation Commission, share resources, once operational neither of the organisations could see how this might actually work. Confronted with what it saw as a problem of public perception, and a fear that its ability to fulfil its mandate might be compromised by public confusion about the relationship between the two bodies, early in its work the TRC took the position that information given to it in confidence would remain confidential. The seven commissioners, none of whom were involved in the United Nations discussions on the 'relationship' or in the NGO consultations, dismissed the suggestions that there should be sophisticated arrangements providing for sharing of information, along the lines proposed by Human Rights Watch and the International Centre for Transitional Justice. They considered that assurances of total confidentiality were necessary if the Commission were to fulfil one of its objectives, as set out in article XXVI of the *Lomé Agreement*: 'to provide a forum for both the victims and perpetrators of human rights violations to tell their story'. The solution was not entirely satisfactory, because it was central to the mandate of the TRC that perpetrators tell their stories publicly. The Commission received a great deal of confidential testimony, but its real utility to the entire process was not that great.

The Prosecutor of the Special Court has not faced the same difficulties as the TRC, because the concerns of perpetrators have been about prosecution by the Court, and not the other way round. Nobody was worried that evidence given to Special Court investigators might also come to the attention of the Commission, for obvious reasons. But Prosecutor David Crane stated, in numerous interviews, that he intended to prepare his cases using his own resources. On several occasions, he said he had no interest in TRC materials and, in a general sense, helpfully attempted to defuse any anxiety on this issue. There was never any serious suggestion that the Special Court would share information gathered in the course of its own investigations with the TRC. Certainly, the Special Court never offered to provide materials to the TRC. Yet the Special Court did not view the product of its investigations as being entirely confidential. The senior investigator of the Special Court provided a detailed briefing to another 'commission', that established by the Government of the United States to investigate the events of 11 September 2001.[81]

As the TRC hearings progressed during mid-2003, many perpetrators came forward to tell their stories to the Commission and, in some cases, to ask pardon or forgiveness of the victims. Belying most predictions, they did not appear at all concerned about the threat of prosecution by the Special Court. Perhaps they had already understood that the Special Court was only concerned with 'big fish', and realised that their own level of responsibility was more modest or secondary. But even some of the 'big fish' who had been indicted by the Special Court indicated to the TRC that they would be interested in testifying. This was the complete opposite of what anybody had expected. And in an even more bizarre twist, the Special Court actually opposed allowing those who had been indicted and detained to appear before the TRC. In other words, alleged perpetrators wished to testify before the TRC, but the Court opposed this.

4.1. *Self-incriminating Evidence Adduced before the TRC*

The legislation establishing the South African Truth and Reconciliation Commission specified that self-incriminating evidence could not be used in criminal prosecutions before the courts of South Africa.[82] There was a similar provision in Ghana's truth commission statute. But there would appear to be no legal guarantee against self-incriminating evidence presented to the TRC being used against an accused in a prosecution before the Special Court or, for that matter, before the courts of Sierra Leone. It may well be that the Parliament of Sierra Leone did not include a provision dealing with self-incriminating testimony before the TRC when it enacted the enabling legislation because at the time no prosecutions were envisaged, a consequence of the amnesty in the *Lomé Peace Agreement*. The TRC was predicated on the concept that perpetrators as well as victims come forward to tell their story. Absent the threat of self-incrimination because of the amnesty, it was probably thought there was no need to deal with the point directly.

The TRC was forced to address this issue indirectly, relying on a provision in the legislation enabling it to take evidence on a

[81] The power point presentation that was submitted to the 9/11 Commission has been posted on the internet. See: <www.douglasfarah.com/documents.shtml/pdfs/stonesUN.pdf>.

[82] See: Celina Schocken, *supra* note 51, pp. 458–459.

confidential basis. The *Act* stated: 'At the discretion of the Commission, any person shall be permitted to provide information to the Commission on a confidential basis and the Commission shall not be compelled to disclose any information given to it in confidence.'[83] In addition, section 7(4) suggested that the Commission actually had a positive duty to prevent disclosure of certain information, in requiring it to 'take into account the interests of victims and witnesses when inviting them to give statements, including the security and other concerns of those who may wish to recount their stories in public'. The Commission was empowered to implement special procedures to address the needs of children or those who have suffered sexual abuses, matters that may also required some limitation of access to its proceedings. Members and staff of the Commission were prohibited from making private use of or profit from any confidential information gained as a result of their work, and a breach may result in dismissal.[84] At the conclusion of its work, and prior to its dissolution, the Commission was charged with organising its archives and records, and determining which information may be made available to the public and when, and the measures 'necessary to protect confidential information'.[85]

At the outset of its work, the Commission declared that evidence given on a confidential basis would never be made public. There was much public debate on this point, particularly in light of a provision in the *Special Court Act* that seemed to imply a power of the Court to order production of materials in the possession of the Commission, even evidence taken on a confidential basis.[86] The Commission insisted that according to its interpretation of the legislation, the Court did not have such authority. To reinforce this, in the 'Recommendations' section of its final report, the Commission states: 'The Commission recommends that Parliament refrain from passing legislation authorising access by criminal justice mechanisms, either directly or indirectly, to information in the archives of the Commission that was provided on a confidential basis... This is an imperative recommendation.'

The question is still shrouded in uncertainty, however, because whether the Court can actually compel production of confidential materials in possession of the Commission has never been tested.

[83] *Truth and Reconciliation Act 2000*, *supra* note 11, s. 8(3).

[84] *Ibid.*, s. 14(3).

[85] *Ibid.*, s. 19(2).

[86] This is discussed in detail in the next section of this essay.

Because of Prosecutor Crane's insistence on relying upon his own materials, it seems unlikely that any challenge will come from his quarter. However, as the trials proceed, defence lawyers may well attempt to obtain these materials. The task will not be an easy one, as judges of the Court are likely to reject attempts at a 'fishing expedition' in the archives of the Commission. Probably, defence counsel will have to demonstrate with reasonable precision the nature of any evidence that they believe to be in the possession of the Commission before judges would even entertain the issue of breaching the confidentiality of the Commission.

The judges of the Special Court might well decide that confidential testimony is in any case privileged, comparable to information given in confidence to a lawyer, a doctor or a priest. The *Rules of Procedure and Evidence* applicable to the Special Court only address the issue of lawyer-client privilege,[87] but case law of the *ad hoc* tribunals has recognised that a broader set of norms applies to other categories of privilege.[88] International criminal law on this issue continues to evolve. The most recent attempt to clarify the applicable principles appears in Rule 71 of the *Rules of Procedure and Evidence of the International Criminal Court*:

> 1. Without prejudice to article 67, paragraph 1 (b), communications made in the context of the professional relationship between a person and his or her legal counsel shall be regarded as privileged, and consequently not subject to disclosure, unless:
>
> (a) The person consents in writing to such disclosure; or
>
> (b) The person voluntarily disclosed the content of the communication to a third party, and that third party then gives evidence of that disclosure.
>
> 2. Having regard to rule 63, sub-rule 5, communications made in the context of a class of professional or other confidential relationships shall be regarded as privi-

[87] 'Rules of Procedure and Evidence of the International Criminal Tribunal for Rwanda', Rule 97.

[88] *Prosecutor* v. *Simić* et al. (Case No. IT-95-9-PT), Decision on the Prosecution Motion Under Rule 73 for a Ruling Concerning the Testimony of a Witness, 27 July 1999 (concerning information obtained by the International Committee of the Red Cross); *Prosecutor* v. *Delalic* et al. (Case No. IT-96-21-A), Decision on Motion to Preserve and Provide Evidence, 22 April 1999 (concerning evidence of communications between the judges and their legal officers); *Prosecutor* v. *Brdjanin & Talic* (Case No. IT-99-36-A), Decision on Motion to Set Aside Confidential Subpoena to Give Evidence, 15 December 2002 (concerning compellability of a war correspondent).

leged, and consequently not subject to disclosure, under the same terms as in sub-rules 1 (a) and 1 (b) if a Chamber decides in respect of that class that:

(a) Communications occurring within that class of relationship are made in the course of a confidential relationship producing a reasonable expectation of privacy and non-disclosure;

(b) Confidentiality is essential to the nature and type of relationship between the person and the confidant; and

(c) Recognition of the privilege would further the objectives of the Statute and the Rules.[89]

Although not bound by these Rules, the judges of the Special Court would be likely to view them as a helpful and persuasive attempt at codification.

Thus, according to the Rules of the International Criminal Court, three conditions must be satisfied for the Court to respect the claim to confidentiality. All three of them, listed in paragraphs (a), (b) and (c) of sub-rule 71(2), appear to apply to evidence given to the TRC in confidence. TRC testimony given on a promise of confidentiality is certainly given in the course of 'a confidential relationship producing a reasonable expectation of privacy and non-disclosure'. Moreover, the very functions of the TRC require that perpetrators feel comfortable 'bearing their chest' before the Commission, which answers the condition in paragraph (b). And finally, would the Court not conclude that recognition of the privilege furthers its objectives, given the complementarity between TRC and Special Court, and their joint contribution to justice, accountability and healing in Sierra Leone?[90]

But even if the judges were prepared to recognise that TRC testimony given in confidence was privileged, they might also conclude that respect for the privilege entails a breach of the right to a fair trial. And all concerned parties, including the Prosecutor and the TRC, have an interest in fair trials taking place. A truth and reconciliation

---

[89] 'Report of the Preparatory Commission for the International Criminal Court, Addendum, Finalized draft text of the Rules of Procedure and Evidence', UN Doc. PCNICC/2000/INF/3/Add.3.

[90] For a discussion of the interpretation of this provision, see: Donald K. Piragoff, *Evidence*, in The International Criminal Court, Elements of Crimes and Rules of Procedure and Evidence 361 (Roy S. Lee, ed., 2001). Piragoff says such objectives might include protection of the well-being, dignity and privacy of victims, reparation for victims, rehabilitation, and respect for national legal systems, all of which are well within the remit of the Sierra Leone Truth and Reconciliation Commission.

commission will hardly want to contribute to a system of criminal justice where the rights of the accused are compromised. Nor will it want its zealous protection of confidential information to become the justification for a stalemate and ultimate failure of the Special Court, an initiative whose fundamental objective, which is to address impunity, is shared by both institutions. But there seems to be no obvious solution to the dilemma. It is, essentially, the same headache that arises with respect to all privileged information before all criminal courts. In practice, this issue may never really be resolved.

Although some witnesses may never be reassured of some protection against the subsequent use of self-incriminating testimony, many might have been relieved had they been reassured that evidence delivered to the Commission would not then be available for prosecution before the Court. As has already been mentioned, this is the approach taken in South Africa and Ghana. It is easy to realise when both commission and court belong to the same jurisdiction, but the issue becomes more complex when one institution is a national body and the other an international body. Even had the Sierra Leone Parliament thought to include a non-self-incrimination provision in the legislation establishing the truth commission, this would have been ineffective if it was not matched by some comparable provision in the law applicable to the Special Court.

Special Court legislation is certainly alive to the issue of self-incrimination. In what has now become international human rights boilerplate, the *Statute of the Special Court* states that a person accused before the Court has the right '[n]ot to be compelled to testify against himself or herself or to confess guilt'.[91] Even witnesses are protected against self-incriminating testimony, by virtue of Rule 90(E) of the *Rules of Procedure and Evidence* of the International Criminal Tribunal for Rwanda which, pursuant to article 14(1) of the *Statute of the Special Court*, apply *mutatis mutandis*: 'A witness may refuse to make any statement which might tend to incriminate him. The Chamber may, however, compel the witness to answer the question. Testimony compelled in this way shall not be used as evidence in a subsequent prosecution against the witness for any offence other than perjury.'

It would seem reasonable for the Special Court to adopt a similar rule with respect to evidence given to the TRC. The existing Rule 90(E) is justified essentially by concerns of fairness to an accused, and

[91] *Statute of the Special Court for Sierra Leone*, art. 17(4)(g).

there is no reason why the same logic should not apply in the case of TRC testimony. The judges are empowered, by article 14(2) of the *Statute*, to modify the *Rules of Procedure and Evidence*. Alternatively, the *Statute of the Special Court* might have been amended to provide a guarantee against self-incrimination. This could have been accomplished by modification of the Agreement between the Government of Sierra Leone and the United Nations.[92] Article 18(4)(g) of the *Statute* could be amended so as to read: 'Evidence given by an accused person before the Truth and Reconciliation Commission may not be used in a prosecution before this Court for the crimes listed in articles 2 to 5.'

Such an amendment, ensuring that self-incriminating evidence given to the TRC could not be used in a prosecution before the Special Court, would have responded in a relatively thorough and complete manner to the major difficulty that had been raised by perpetrators and potential TRC witnesses. It might also have been an important gesture from the Special Court indicating its respect for the unique but complementary functions of the Truth and Reconciliation Commission. Although this solution was proposed, neither the Special Court nor the two parties to its creation, for whatever reasons, ever took up the matter.

4.2. *Can the Special Court Subpoena Confidential Information from the TRC?*

Naturally, the Special Court is empowered to make orders for the production of evidence. The prospect of an order from the Special Court directed to the Truth Commission itself, or one of its members or staff, for the production of confidential information is certainly a plausible hypothesis. Human Rights Watch took the position that 'the Special Court should subpoena the TRC only as a last resort'.[93] But the question of both the legality of such an order and its enforceability arise.

The *Statute of the Special Court* indicates that it has 'primacy', and some NGOs, like the International Crisis Group, mistakenly suggested that this subordinated the Commission to the Court. But the principle of primacy merely establishes a rule to govern conflicts

---

[92] *Agreement between the United Nations and the Government of Sierra Leone on the Establishment of a Special Court for Sierra Leone*, 16 January 2002, art. 22.

[93] 'Human Rights Watch Policy paper', *supra* note 77.

between courts with concurrent jurisdiction.[94] It is totally irrelevant to the relationship between the Court and the TRC. Any suggestion of a hierarchy would be a great surprise, given the prior statements from a variety of United Nations sources to the effect that the two bodies were mutually supportive and complementary. Nevertheless, a January 2002 discussion paper prepared by the Office of the Attorney General and Ministry of Justice of Sierra Leone, with the technical cooperation of the NGO No Peace Without Justice, insisted that the TRC was subordinate to the Special Court:

> The legal relationship between the Special Court and the Truth and Reconciliation Commission is clear. The Special Court is an international judicial body whose requests and orders require no less than full compliance by the Truth and Reconciliation Commission, as by all Sierra Leonean national institutions, in accordance to [*sic*] the international obligations agreed to by Sierra Leone.[95]

The basis of these obligations, according to the paper, was article 17 of the *Agreement between Sierra Leone and the United Nations*. Article 17 refers to obligations of the 'Government', requiring it to cooperate with the Court and to comply with its requests. It says nothing of the TRC, which is a body independent of the Government of Sierra Leone.

Although it is created by international agreement between Sierra Leone and the United Nations, and not by the Security Council, the model for the Special Court is the International Criminal Tribunal for Rwanda (ICTR). Accordingly, both its *Statute* and its *Rules of Procedure and Evidence* are derived in large measure from those of the ICTR. The ICTR operates, for the purposes of arrest and transfer of suspects, gathering of evidence and similar functions, through requests to national governments for assistance. A broadly similar 'mutual legal assistance' approach exists for the Special Court, at least with respect to Sierra Leone itself.

On 25 April 2002, the national implementing legislation, the *Special Court Agreement (Ratification) Act 2002*, came into force.[96] Confirming the 'mutual assistance' model, the *Act* actually referred to

[94] *Statute of the Special Court for Sierra Leone*, art. 8(1).

[95] Office of the Attorney General and Ministry of Justice Special Court Task Force, 'Briefing Paper on Relationship between the Special Court and the Truth and Reconciliation Commission, Legal Analysis and Policy Considerations of the Government of Sierra Leone for the Special Court Planning Mission', <www.special-court.org/SLMission/PlanningMission/BriefingPapers\TRC_SpCt.html>.

[96] Supplement to the Sierra Leone Gazette, Vol. CXXXIII, No. 22.

'Mutual Assistance between Sierra Leone and Special Court'.[97] It also contemplated the giving of 'Orders' by the Special Court. Any such 'Order' was to have the same effect as if it were issued by a judge, magistrate or justice of the peace of a Sierra Leone court. The *Act* did not specify what matters might be properly included in an 'Order'. 'Orders' are governed by sections 20 to 22, while section 22 refers to a 'forfeiture order'. Given the general application of the 'mutual assistance' approach to relations between Sierra Leone and the Special Court, it would seem that the reference to 'Orders' in sections 20 to 22 ought to be interpreted rather narrowly.

The heart of the difficulty is a mysterious provision, section 21(2) of the *Special Court Agreement (Ratification) Act 2002*, which states: 'Notwithstanding any other law, every natural person, corporation, or other body created by or under Sierra Leone law shall comply with any direction specified in an order of the Special Court.' This provision has been interpreted in several NGO studies as an authorisation by the Special Court to order the TRC to divulge evidence obtained in confidence. For example, Human Rights Watch has concluded summarily that '[b]ecause the TRC is a body created under Sierra Leone law, the Implementing Law creates a duty for the TRC to comply with orders of the Special Court. Because there are no exceptions stated in the Implementing Law, the implications are that the TRC would have to comply with *all* orders of the Special Court.'[98]

It is argued that on a literal reading, the reference to any person or other body must necessarily include the TRC. Moreover, in a related argument it is suggested that section 21(2), as subsequent legislation, implicitly repeals the 'incompatible' confidentiality provisions in section 7 of the *Truth and Reconciliation Commission Act 2000*. These views are supported by use of the terms 'notwithstanding any other law', and by application of the maxim *leges posteriors priores contraries abrogant*. Such an interpretation seems far-fetched and manifestly incorrect, for a number of reasons.

The literal reading of section 21(2) that has been proposed leads to a patent absurdity. Under the 'golden rule' of statutory construction, courts should not follow a construction that gives an absurd or illogical result.[99] The provision in question surely cannot mean that

---

[97] Part. IV.

[98] 'Human Rights Watch Policy paper', *supra* note 77, pp. 1–2. The position of the International Centre for Transitional Justice is only slightly less categorical: 'Exploring the Relationship', *supra* note 77, p. 5.

[99] *Grey* v. *Pearson*, (1857) 6 HLC 61, 106, 10 ER 1216, 1234.

an order from the Special Court would override any previous legislative provision or common law rule that might, in a literal sense, be incompatible with it. In this respect, it is helpful to consider whether the Special Court can also breach the confidentiality of other individuals or bodies in Sierra Leone who are entitled to protection. Several examples come to mind. Cabinet proceedings would be covered by confidentiality. Notes of deliberations of the Supreme Court and the Court of Appeal would also be protected. And what of immunities for diplomats and similar officials which, while subject to international law, depend for their implementation within Sierra Leone upon national legislation, just like the Special Court does? Under the extravagant literal interpretation that is proposed by some, section 21(2) would enable the Court to order the production of the files in the United States Embassy, or those of the Special Representative of the Secretary General.[100] These are all examples of confidentiality that is protected by prior legislation in Sierra Leone, be it statute law or common law, or customary international law. It is preposterous to argue that all of this is implicitly repealed by the Special Court Act, and that such a result was actually intended by Parliament.

The argument then retreats to the suggestion that section 21(2) targets the TRC, rather than all privileges and immunities. But that too is unsustainable, because the provision makes no reference whatsoever to the *Truth and Reconciliation Commission Act 2000*, adopted by the same Parliament less than two years previously. Surely if Parliament had aimed section 21(2) at the TRC, it would have said so more explicitly.

Perhaps the most reliable approach is purposive interpretation. The Special Court was created not to marginalise or incapacitate the TRC, but rather to add a new dimension to the accountability process in Sierra Leone. This was recognised in Security Council Resolution 1370 (2000),[101] and in any number of United Nations documents. Nothing in the United Nations documentation on the Special Court, including reports and letters from the Secretary-General and resolutions of the Security Council, even hints at the idea of conflict, supremacy, paramountcy or anything else that might

---

[100] The United Nations very probably considers that the SRSG and other mission personnel are immune from process of the Special Court: *Prosecutor* v. *Blaskic* (Case No. IT-95-14-T), Decision of Trial Chamber I on the Protective Measures for General Philippe Morillon, Witness of the Trial Chamber, 12 May 1999.

[101] See paragraph 17.

necessitate some special provision for the relationship between Court and TRC. Both bodies involve partnerships with the United Nations and significant international participation. Both are expected to be independent and impartial, and they have provisions in the enabling instruments to ensure this is the case. They are said to be different approaches to the achievement of similar goals. The Special Court was never intended to compromise the efficacy of the TRC, but rather to complement its contribution to the search for justice and accountability, and the campaign against impunity. Thus, in the absence of an explicit statutory provision to the contrary, it must be assumed that the *Special Court Agreement, 2002 (Ratification) Act 2002* has no impact whatsoever upon the *Truth and Reconciliation Commission Act 2000*. Accordingly, the confidentiality provisions of the *TRC Act* have full force and effect. No order from the Special Court can breach such confidentiality.

On the assumption that all of this reasoning is incorrect, and that the alternative interpretation is valid, one would have expected the legislature to provide for the enforceability of an order to produce confidential information directed to the TRC, to its members or to its staff. To put the question differently, what would be the consequence of a refusal by the TRC, or by its members or its staff, to divulge confidential information to the Special Court? The *Truth and Reconciliation Commission Act 2000* protects Commissioners and the TRC staff from any liability for acts carried out within the scope of their duties.[102] Such duties include, *inter alia*, the protection of confidential information. Had the legislature truly meant to facilitate orders from the Special Court directed to Commissioners or to TRC staff, and to make one body prevail over another, it would have provided for some form of enforceability. The absence of such provision is only a further argument against the theory that the Special Court *Act* in effect 'trumps' the *TRC Act*.

4.3. *Decisive Evidence of Guilt or Innocence*

It has been suggested that despite the TRC's decision not to make materials given to it in confidence available to the Special Court, an exception should nevertheless be made in the case of what is sometimes called 'decisive evidence of guilt or innocence'. Surely the TRC would not, it is argued, in the name of a rigorous policy of confidentiality, stand by passively while an innocent person was

[102] *Truth and Reconciliation Commission Act 2000*, *supra* note 11, s. 14(4).

convicted or a guilty one discharged? The United Nations Planning Mission Report saw information 'essential for the conviction or acquittal of the accused' to be a justifiable exception to the general rule of confidentiality for the TRC.[103] One NGO proposed a draft relationship agreement that would govern the determination of such matters.[104]

What exactly such information might consist of has never been easy to determine. Few examples are given. One suggestion has been conflicting testimony: a prosecution witness says one thing before the Court and something else before the TRC. But evidence that somebody has lied can never be 'decisive evidence' of either guilt or innocence. The fact that a witness lied before the TRC does not mean he or she is not telling the truth before the Court, or *vice versa*. All that contradictory testimony proves is that the witness has lied at least once, or perhaps only that the witness is confused!

In reality, this problem is not at all peculiar to the relationship between the TRC and the Special Court. Indeed, the Special Court itself seems to allow for a situation where 'decisive evidence of guilt or innocence' cannot be used. Take the case of a confession of guilt by a witness which in many legal systems would be deemed to be fairly 'decisive' inculpatory evidence. The *Rules of Procedure and Evidence* recognise that a person may, in testimony before the Court, be forced to admit guilt and to provide decisive evidence of it. Yet Rule 90(E) says that such decisive proof of guilt 'shall not be used as evidence in a subsequent prosecution'. Moreover, the Prosecutor may confront the same problem himself. In the course of his work, the Prosecutor, like many prosecutors in legal systems around the world, may find it necessary to make commitments of confidentiality so as to obtain evidence or otherwise facilitate investigation. Rule 70(B) of the ICTR Rules of Procedure and Evidence actually sanctifies the ability of the Prosecutor to guarantee confidentiality, without exception, even in the case of 'decisive evidence of innocence or guilt'.[105] Even the Defence may obtain information that decisively proves guilt or innocence, for example in the course of an interview with the accused. But the Rules say that such evidence is shrouded by lawyer-client privilege.

This concept of 'decisive evidence of guilt or innocence' does not appear to be particularly helpful to the discussion of the relationship

---

[103] 'Report of the Planning Mission', *supra* note 59, para. 55.

[104] 'Exploring the Relationship', *supra* note 77.

[105] Rule 70(B).

between Special Court and TRC. If it were, one would expect to find judicial models for dealing with the issue in other legal systems because, after all, the problem is far from unique. Indeed, this probably explains why those concerned about the 'relationship' between the TRC and the Special Court have had to invent formulae in order to address this issue. To the extent that legal systems recognise the concept of privilege and protections against self-incrimination, they all have to live with the possibility that 'decisive evidence of guilt or innocence' will be occasionally unavailable.

This, by the way, does not in any way suggest indifference towards such difficulties. Should such a situation have arisen, the Truth and Reconciliation Commission – like all others in similar circumstances, who possess information taken in confidence: lawyers, doctors, prosecutors, priests and so on – would have had to balance a number of conflicting concerns in an attempt to reach a solution consistent with fundamental principles of justice and human rights. The fact that it has left nothing in its report on this point is a good indication that the TRC was not aware of anything that might fall within the category of 'decisive evidence of innocence'.

V. THE OPERATIONAL PERIOD: A DISPUTE ABOUT PERPETRATOR TESTIMONY

Witness issues were always at the heart of any real or potential tension between the Special Court and the Truth Commission. Even before the arrival of the Special Court on the scene, there had been widespread concern that perpetrators would not testify before the Commission because it could not offer them amnesty in return. This had been the model for the South African TRC, where amnesty was offered in exchange for full disclosure. But there was no amnesty to grant: it had already been accorded by the *Lomé Peace Agreement*. When the proposal to establish the Court began to pick up momentum, this was seen as yet another complication. If, despite the inability to grant amnesty, any naïve or foolhardy perpetrators were still willing to testify before the Commission, the prospect that their testimony might be used in an eventual prosecution by the Court was thought to deliver the *coup de grâce* to any hope they might come forward. From the TRC's standpoint, there was concern that any threat that the Court might have access to its materials would have a chilling effect on perpetrators who would otherwise have been tempted to cooperate with the Commission, even on a purely confidential basis.[106]

In fact, the actual impact of these factors on the willingness or unwillingness of perpetrators to testify in public before the TRC, or to provide it with information on a confidential basis, is impossible to assess. It is a fact, though, that many perpetrators did come forward and cooperate with the Commission, and this despite either the absence of a carrot or the presence of a stick. The willingness or reluctance of perpetrators to participate in accountability processes – be they truth commissions or courts – may have far less to do with promises of amnesty or threats of prosecution than many may think. Any experienced criminal lawyer can provide no shortage of anecdotal evidence to support the view that some individuals simply want to talk about what they have done. Whether they do this in an entirely honest manner is, of course, another matter.

Just as criminals often confess, despite *Miranda* warnings about the right to silence, not to mention stern admonition from their lawyers, some perpetrators of serious human rights violations may feel the need to unburden themselves, to 'tock dee troot', as they say in Krio, Sierra Leone's lingua franca. Of course, there are also those who are incapable of admitting to what they have done. But even the promise of immunity from prosecution will not be enough to induce them to testify, something that is amply demonstrated by the disappointingly small number of perpetrators who came before the South African Commission. All of this suggests that truth telling may or may not work regardless of the threat of criminal trial. Perhaps the best proof of the danger of oversimplifying these issues was the astonishing initiative, in August 2003, after the TRC had concluded its hearings, by three detainees charged before the Special Court, who asked to testify in public before the Commission.

Not surprisingly, counsel discouraged their clients from testifying before the Commission. From the sole standpoint of the criminal

---

[106] Section 7(3) of the *Truth and Reconciliation Act 2000* states: 'At the discretion of the Commission, any person shall be permitted to provide information to the Commission on a confidential basis and the Commission shall not be compelled to disclose any information given to it in confidence.' But many believed that this provision could not resist a subpoena from the Court, principally because of provisions in the *Special Court Agreement (Ratification) Act 2002*, Supplement to the Sierra Leone Gazette, Vol. CXXXIII, No. 22. See, for example: Office of the Attorney General and Ministry of Justice Special Court Task Force, 'Briefing Paper on Relationship between the Special Court and the Truth and Reconciliation Commission', *supra* note 95.

justice process, defence lawyers understood that there was nothing to gain. The three accused saw this otherwise, perhaps because they are political animals and their own objectives go beyond simply winning in court. The focus here was the man who is perhaps the Court's most celebrated defendant, Chief Sam Hinga Norman. When Norman was arrested in March 2003, he was a member of the current government's cabinet. He was actually arrested in his ministerial office. Norman was charged with respect to his role as National Coordinator of the pro-government militias known as the Civil Defence Forces (CDF). Norman's arrest stunned many Sierra Leoneans who see him as a hero for his role in the war against the Revolutionary United Front. For the Truth Commission, there was nothing shocking in the idea that those responsible for the CDF, either as direct commanders or under the principle of command responsibility, might be indicted. The Commission's report provides ample evidence of CDF atrocities. One of the CDF's hallmarks was the practice of forced cannibalism.

In his position as a member of the cabinet, Norman attended the opening of the TRC's headquarters in February 2003, where he sat alongside representatives of the Special Court, United Nations officials and members of the diplomatic corps, only days prior to his indictment and arrest. Ironically, the TRC's permanent headquarters were situated in a Freetown motel that had been occupied the previous year by the CDF. At the close of the ceremony, a representative of the Commission agreed with Norman to conduct an informal interview.

In May and June 2003, after his arrest, the Commission approached the Special Court to inquire about the possibility of interviewing the detainees. The requests were transmitted to the detainees, via their legal representatives, but none desired contact with the TRC while trials were pending. Norman's legal representative, J.B. Jenkins-Johnston, wrote to the Commission to say he considered it inappropriate for his client to appear before the TRC as long as he was indicted before the Special Court.[107]

After the Commission had completed its hearings phase, which culminated in dramatic testimony by President Kabbah, Norman changed his mind. On 26 August 2003, he wrote to his legal counsel with a view to appearing before the Commission:

---

[107] Letter of 17 June 2003 from Mr. J.B. Jenkins-Johnston, legal representative of Chief Hinga Norman, to the Registrar of the Special Court.

I have long been in receipt of copy of your letter referenced JBJJ/ZYS dated 17 June 2003, expressing the inappropriateness for me (your client) to appear before the Truth and Reconciliation Commission while I remain an indictee before the Special Court.

Well, I was arrested, charged and detained on the 10th March 2003, thinking that by now, 25th August 2003, my trial would have started long ago; but I thought wrongly. Since there is no news about the start of the trial and there are signs that the TRC may soon close its sittings, I would prefer to be heard by the people of Sierra Leone and also be recorded for posterity especially where my boss, The President of Sierra Leone, who appointed me and under whom I served as the Deputy Minister of Defence and National Coordinator of the Civil Defence Force (CDF/SL), has already testified before the Commission.

As my SOLICITOR, I am applying through you and requesting you as a matter of urgency to please inform the necessary parties of my willingness to appear and testify before the TRC without any further delay.

Shortly afterward, the Commission was approached by two other defendants, this time individuals who had been affiliated with the Revolutionary United Front, Augustine Gbao, on 16 September 2003, and Issa Sesay, on 19 September 2003.

After consulting the principals of the Special Court, the Registrar issued a '*Practice Direction on the procedure following a request by a National Authority or Truth & Reconciliation Commission to take a statement from a person in the custody of the Special Court for Sierra Leone*'.[108] The Practice Direction created a procedure whereby the TRC or other body would make an application to a judge of the Special Court in such cases.[109] The application was to set out a list of specific questions to be posed to the detainee.[110] The interview would be 'supervised' by a legal officer of the Court, who would have the authority to intervene to stop specific questions and even bring an end to the interview.[111] The Direction required that all interviews be

[108] Rule 33(D) of the Special Court's Rules of Procedure and Evidence authorises the Registrar 'in consultation with the President of the Special Court, [to] issue Practice Directions addressing particular aspects of the practice and procedure in the Registry of the Special Court and in respect of other matters within the powers of the Registrar'.

[109] 'Practice Direction on the procedure following a request by a National Authority or Truth & Reconciliation Commission to take a statement from a person in the custody of the Special Court for Sierra Leone', 9 September 2003, para. 5.

[110] *Ibid.*, para. 2(g).

[111] *Ibid.*, para. 6.

recorded and transcribed.[112] Transcripts of the interviews were to be handed over to the Prosecutor for use at trial as a matter of course.[113]

The Commission responded to the Practice Direction by letter addressed to the Registrar dated 9 September 2003. Its arguments focussed on the right to take testimony on a confidential basis. In reality, this issue was not central to the issue of testimony by Norman, Gbao and Sesay, who expressly wanted to testify *in public*. At a subsequent meeting, the Registrar agreed to reconsider the Practice Direction in light of the concerns expressed by the Commission. A revised Practice Direction was issued on 4 October 2003.[114] No longer was a transcript of the interview to be forwarded automatically to the Prosecutor. Instead, it would be filed with the Court Management Section (the Registrar), but could subsequently be made available to any party to the criminal proceedings, including the Prosecutor, upon order of the Presiding Judge.[115] The revised Practice Direction also made clearer that there was a presumption in favour of granting requests for interviews with detainees. It said the Presiding Judge was to 'grant approval (conditional or otherwise) if the said judge is satisfied that the detainee agrees to the questioning and has been fully advised... In such circumstances, the request for questioning will only be rejected if the Presiding Judge is satisfied that a refusal is necessary in the interests of justice or to maintain the integrity of the proceedings of the Special Court.'[116]

The Commission was still dissatisfied with the revised Practice Direction, and on 8 October 2003, it reiterated its threat to 'not make use of the Practice Direction, as it is presently formulated, for the purposes of conducting confidential interviews or closed hearings'. It did not object to the provisions concerning public hearings, however, and on 7 October 2003, the TRC submitted an application for a public hearing with Hinga Norman. A second application was submitted on 10 October 2003 to conduct a public hearing with Augustine Gbao. The Prosecutor opposed the applications. In submissions dated 21 October 2003, the Prosecutor argued that such

---

[112] *Ibid.*, para. 8(b).

[113] *Ibid.*, para. 8(c).

[114] 'Revised Practice Direction on the procedure following a request by a State, the Truth and Reconciliation Commission, or other legitimate authority to take a statement from a person in the custody of the Special Court for Sierra Leone'; 4 October 2003.

[115] *Ibid.*, paras. 4(b) and 4(c).

[116] *Ibid.*, para. 5.

hearings would be inappropriate because the case was *sub judice*.[117] He warned that testimony by Norman and Gbao might stir up public feelings and frighten victims and potential witnesses from the Court proceedings.[118] The Prosecutor concluded that peace in Sierra Leone rested upon a 'fragile equilibrium', which could be imperilled by such a hearing.[119]

The application in the Norman case was argued before Judge Bankole Thompson, the Presiding Judge of the Trial Chamber, on 24 October 2003. Five days later, Judge Thompson heard argument on the Gbao application. On 30 October 2003, Judge Bankole Thompson denied the application for a hearing with Chief Hinga Norman.[120] He focussed on a phrase in the Commission's written application, where it attempted to justify the importance of its request by noting that Norman had 'played a central role' in the conflict. Judge Thompson reasoned that the Truth and Reconciliation Commission had prejudged the matter and was therefore violating Hinga Norman's presumption of innocence.[121] It was a strange remark, because nobody in Sierra Leone would quarrel with the Commission's essentially innocuous observation. The Norman indictment by the Court said that 'Samuel Hinga Norman was the National Coordinator of the CDF. As such he was the principal force in establishing, organising, supporting, providing logistical support [for] and promoting the CDF...'[122] The Court had confirmed the indictment, thereby determining 'that the allegations in the Prosecution's case summary would, if proven, amount to the crime or crimes as

[117] See the Inter-Office Memorandum of 21 October 2003 from Desmond de Silva QC, Deputy Prosecutor (on behalf of the Prosecutor), to Judge Bankole Thompson, Presiding Judge of the Trial Chamber; memorandum entitled: 'Samuel Hinga Norman and the TRC' ('Objections of the Prosecutor').

[118] *Ibid.*, para. (b).

[119] *Ibid.*, para. (c).

[120] *Prosecutor* v. *Norman* (Case No. SCSL-2003-08-PT), Decision on the Request by the Truth and Reconciliation Commission of Sierra Leone to Conduct a Public Hearing with Samuel Hinga Norman, 29 October 2003. A few days later, the Gbao application was also dismissed: *Prosecutor* v. *Gbao* (Case No. SCSL-2003-09-PT), Decision on the Request by the Truth and Reconciliation Commission to Conduct a Public Hearing with Augustine Gbao, 3 November 2003. The Gbao legal defence team filed a response to the TRC application setting out several conditions, a move that prompted the Court to rule that Gbao 'was uncertain as to whether to testify before the Commission'.

[121] *Prosecutor* v. *Norman*, *ibid.*, para. 12.

[122] *Prosecutor* v. *Norman* (Case No. SCSL-2003-08-I), Indictment, 7 March 2003; at para. 12.

particularised in the indictment'.[123] But the poor Commission, because it had said that the acknowledged leader of one of the combatant factions had 'played a central role', was now being faulted with having violated the presumption of innocence, with the consequence that its application was denied. In any event, the presumption of innocence was Norman's right, and he was entitled to set it aside if he wished. He had not raised this objection to the TRC's application, which he in fact supported, and the Presiding Judge had no business raising the matter in his place. But Judge Thompson said: 'In the overarching scheme of things, it is the duty of International Judges to safeguard the interest of the International Community that persons charged with international crimes are accorded what may be characterised as "super due process rights" in vindicating themselves regardless of national considerations, however compelling.'[124]

The Practice Direction allowed for an appeal before the President of the Appeals Chamber, a position at the time held by Geoffrey Robertson. The appeal was filed on 4 November 2003. In an exceedingly informal manner, Judge Robertson convened the parties the following day, at Freetown's Bintumani Hotel, for a 'discussion'. Judge Robertson later noted that he was not treating the matter 'strictly as an appeal'.[125] The sensitivity of the whole matter soon became quite apparent.[126] Judge Robertson asked the Prosecutor's representative, Jim Johnson, for certain background details on Hinga Norman including his role in the current government. He asked Johnson whether Hinga Norman had the 'approval of government' and the answer was affirmative. Judge Robertson then asked defence counsel, Tim Owen, whether this would be part of Norman's defence, and he said it would. 'If you establish a prima facie against [President Kabbah], he'll have to appear in the witness box', said Judge Robertson. He inquired whether the TRC would 'make a determination on the guilt or innocence of certain individuals'. When

[123] *Rules of Procedure and Evidence*, Rule 47(E)(ii).

[124] *Prosecutor* v. *Norman*, *supra* note 43, para. 15.

[125] *Prosecutor* v. *Norman*, *supra* note 120, para. 3.

[126] It certainly bears noting that Judge Robertson was appointed to the Court by President Kabbah, in accordance with article 12(1)b) of the Statute. In *Prosecutor* v. *Sesay* (Case No. SCSL-2004-15-PT), Decision on the Defense Motion Seeking Disqualification of Justice Robertson from the Appeals Chamber, 13 March 2004, the Appeals Chamber ruled that he could not sit in cases involving defendants associated with the RUF, because in his book *Crimes Against Humanity*, he had expressed views about the nature of the conflict and the responsibility for the human rights violations that were committed.

representatives of the Commission told him that it would not, because it was not a court, Judge Robertson said it would be preferable if the TRC refrained from making pronouncements on the roles and responsibilities of persons indicted by the Special Court. Musing on the wisdom of having two institutions such as the Special Court and the TRC in parallel operation, he said: 'It may be that our hope of working together and at the same time may not be possible.'

Judge Robertson issued his reasons for judgment on 28 November 2004. He allowed the application in part, authorising Norman to meet with Commission, but he denied the possibility of a hearing.[127] Norman subsequently refused to cooperate with the Commission on such a basis, and the Commission concluded its work without ever meeting with him or hearing what he had to say. In his written reasons, Judge Robertson did not address the substance of the ruling by Judge Thompson of the Trial Chamber, with its bizarre argument about the presumption of innocence. He said: 'It is not normally appropriate for one judge to review another's exercise of discretion, so I have not treated this appeal as a judicial review of the decision of Judge Thompson or strictly as an appeal from his decision, by rather as a fresh hearing in a context where as President, I have the flexibility to explore alternative solutions.'[128]

Judge Robertson described the issue as a 'novel and difficult question', but also 'one that is likely to recur for other indictees and in other post war situations where the local and international community considers that the establishment of both a Special Court and a Truth Commission will assist in the restoration of peace and justice'.[129] Citing its submissions on the motion, which underscored the importance of hearing Hinga Norman, Judge Robertson said: 'I endorse this claim, so far as it goes. The TRC certainly can have the indictee's evidence, if (and only if) he is prepared to take the risk of volunteering it.'[130] But Judge Robertson was most certainly not enamoured with the idea of any public hearing: 'There shall be no public hearing of the kind requested or any other kind prior to the conclusion of the trial.'

What is actually proposed by this application may be described in different ways: it may appear as a spectacle. A man in custody awaiting trial on very serious charges is

[127] *Prosecutor* v. *Norman*, *supra* note 120, para. 41.
[128] *Ibid.*, para. 3. Also, paras. 9–10.
[129] *Ibid.*, para. 2.
[130] *Ibid.*, para 19.

to be paraded, in the very court where that trial will shortly be held, before a Bishop rather than a presiding judge and permitted to broadcast live to the nation for a day or so uninterrupted. Thereafter for the following day or days, he will be examined by a barrister and then questioned from the bench by the Bishop and some five or six fellow Commissioners. In the immediate vicinity will be press, prosecutors and 'victims.' His counsel will be present and permitted to interject but there are no fixed procedures and no Rules of Evidence. The event will have the appearance of a trial, at least the appearance of a sort of trial familiar from centuries past, although the first day of uninterrupted testimony may resemble more a very long party political broadcast. It is not necessary to speculate on the consequences of this spectacle: there may be none. There may be those the Prosecution fears which could lead to intimidation of witnesses and the rally of dormant forces. There may be those that doubtless informed the original advice of his lawyers against testifying – namely fodder for the Prosecution, an adverse effect on public perceptions of his innocence and a consequent disheartening of potential defence witnesses. There will probably, I fear, be this consequence, namely intense anxiety amongst other indictees, especially from rival factions, and concerns over whether they should testify to the TRC as well, or in rebuttal. The spectacle of the TRC sitting in court may set up a public expectation that it will indeed pass judgement on indictees thus confronted and questioned, whose guilt or innocence it is the special duty of the Special Court to determine.

I cannot believe that the Nuremberg Tribunal would have allowed its prisoners to participate in such a spectacle, had there been a TRC in Germany after the war, or that the International Criminal Tribunals for the Former Yugoslavia or Rwanda would readily permit indictees awaiting trial to broadcast in this way to the people of Serbia or Rwanda. If it is the case that local TRC's and international courts are to work together in efforts to produce post-conflict justice in other theatres of war in the future, I do not believe that granting this application for public testimony would be a helpful precedent.[131]

Judge Robertson attempted to summarise what he called 'first principles':

Let me return to first principles. Truth Commissions and International Courts are both instruments for effectuating the promise made by states that victims of human rights violations shall have an effective remedy. Criminal courts offer the most effective remedy – a trial, followed by punishment of those found guilty, in this case of those who bear the greatest responsibility. TRC reports can assist society to move forward and beyond the hatreds that fuelled the war. Truth commissions offer two distinct prospects for victims – of truth, i.e. learning how and why they or their loved ones were murdered or mutilated, and of reconciliation, through understanding and forgiveness of those perpetrators who genuinely confess and regret. It seems to me that these are separate and severable objectives.[132]

---

[131] *Ibid.*, paras. 30–31.

[132] *Ibid.*, para. 33 (reference omitted).

Judge Robertson concluded that '[t]he work of the Special Court and the TRC is complementary and each must accommodate the existence of the other'.[133] The denial of the application for a public hearing was not easy for the Commission to digest, and some saw it as a repudiation. In reality, while reasonable people might disagree with Judge Robertson's ruling, he sought a way to reconcile conflicting concerns and to allow the operations of both bodies to proceed. It was most unfortunate that this quarrel between the Court and the Truth Commission came at the close of what had otherwise been a cordial and uneventful relationship.

VI. THE TRC's ASSESSMENT OF THE SPECIAL COURT

The TRC's mandate to 'address impunity' was an invitation for it to consider issues relating to the amnesty in the Lomé Agreement and the subsequent decision to withdraw it. This necessarily involved it in an assessment of the wisdom and validity of the establishment of the Special Court for Sierra Leone itself. Many witnesses testified before the Commission about matters related to these subjects. According to the Commission's Report,

> It is not clear why unconditional amnesty was accepted by the United Nations in November 1996, only to be condemned as unacceptable in July 1999. This inconsistency in United Nations practice seems to underscore the complexity of the problems at hand. The Commission is unable to condemn the resort to amnesty by those who negotiated the Lomé Peace Agreement. The explanations given by the Government negotiators, including in their testimonies before the Commission, are compelling in this respect. In all good faith, they believed that the RUF would not agree to end hostilities, if the Agreement were not accompanied by a form of pardon or amnesty.
>
> Accordingly, those who argue that peace cannot be bartered in exchange for justice, under any circumstances, must be prepared to justify the likely prolongation of an armed conflict. Amnesties may be undesirable in many cases. Indeed there are examples of abusive amnesties proclaimed by dictators in the dying days of tyrannical regimes. The Commission also recognises the principle that it is generally desirable to prosecute perpetrators of serious human rights abuses, particularly when they rise to the level of gravity of crimes against humanity. However amnesties should not be excluded entirely from the mechanisms available to those attempting to negotiate a cessation of hostilities after periods of brutal armed conflict. Disallowing amnesty in all cases is to deny the reality of violent conflict and the urgent need to bring such strife and suffering to an end.

[133] *Ibid.*, para. 44.

> The Commission is unable to declare that it considers amnesty too high a price to pay for the delivery of peace to Sierra Leone, under the circumstances that prevailed in July 1999. It is true that the Lomé Agreement did not immediately return the country to peacetime. Yet it provided the framework for a process that pacified the combatants and, five years later, has returned Sierra Leoneans to a context in which they need not fear daily violence and atrocity.[134]

These comments do not specifically address the legal issues concerning the objection formulated by the Special Representative of the Secretary General to the amnesty clause. But the Commission Report also raised questions about the wisdom of the objection. It noted that in an earlier peace agreement, reached at Abidjan in November 1996, there was an amnesty clause that was roughly equivalent to the one in the Lomé Agreement. The United Nations had similarly endorsed the Abidjan Agreement, but there was no comparable reservation or objection.[135]

The Commission did not enthusiastically endorse the amnesty, but nor did it condemn it. Whatever the wisdom of actually granting an amnesty, taking it away once it was granted seemed to be a dangerous precedent. According to the Commission's report:

> The Truth and Reconciliation Commission is concerned at the consequences of the withdrawal of the amnesty. In repudiating the amnesty clause in the Lomé Peace Agreement, both the United Nations and the Government of Sierra Leone have sent a message to combatants in future wars that peace agreements containing amnesty clauses ought not to be trusted.
>
> Henceforth, combatant organisations will regard amnesty clauses with suspicion; they will hold them to be uncertain and unreliable. For those who consider that amnesty cannot be granted under any circumstances, this outcome is desirable. However the Commission has already stated that it cannot condemn the grant of amnesty in the Lomé Peace Agreement, taking into account all of the circumstances; nor can it rule out the more general proposition that there will be conflicts in future for whose resolution a trade of peace for amnesty represents the least bad of the available alternatives. By repudiating the amnesty in the Lomé Peace Agreement, the United Nations and the Government of Sierra Leone have inadvertently undermined future peace negotiations where amnesty is contemplated.
>
> Nonetheless the Commission is mindful of the fact that parties to a peace agreement should not be permitted to breach its provisions with impunity. The Commission recommends that future peace agreements in which an amnesty is included should

[134] 3B WITNESS TO TRUTH: REPORT OF THE SIERRA LEONE TRUTH AND RECONCILIATION COMMISSION ch. 6, p. 4 (2004). This reference is to the version of the report presented to the President of Sierra Leone on 5 October 2004.

[135] In *Prosecutor* v. *Kallon*, *supra* note 7, defense counsel made a similar point (see para. 58).

also contain an agreed 'amnesty revocation' clause. Such a clause should, in the event of a breach of the agreement, specifically revoke the protection of amnesty in respect of the party or individuals responsible for that breach. [136]

With respect to the Court itself, the Commission did not attempt to assess whether the decision to create a judicial body was a good one, although its concerns about the withdrawal of the amnesty might be interpreted in this way. The Report of the Commission refers to the difficulties between the two institutions, and elaborates on the litigation before the Court about the testimony of detained witnesses in excruciating detail.

VII. CONCLUSION

In his ruling on the appeal in the Norman case, Judge Robertson seemed to speculate on the wisdom of States allowing the two somewhat different transitional justice institutions – a court and a truth commission – to operate contemporaneously. The same sentiments were often expressed within and outside the Truth and Reconciliation Commission, although the consequences varied depending upon the preference held for one or the other institution. But in fact, there will be less and less choice in the matter. At time of writing the International Criminal Court has 97 States parties. As a result, for not quite half the countries in the world, there is no longer any option about the presence of a court as part of the transitional justice landscape. This is not to say that States will no longer contemplate establishing truth commissions. There seems to be no end to the enthusiasm for the truth commission process.

The recent report of the Secretary-General to the Security Council, presented in August 2004, recognises the role of truth commissions in post-conflict justice:

50. Another important mechanism for addressing past human rights abuses is the truth commission. Truth commissions are official, temporary, non-judicial fact-finding bodies that investigate a pattern of abuses of human rights or humanitarian law committed over a number of years. These bodies take a victim-centred approach and conclude their work with a final report of findings of fact and recommendations. More than 30 such truth commissions have already been established, including those of Argentina, Chile, South Africa, Peru, Ghana, Morocco, El Salvador, Guatemala, Timor-Leste and Sierra Leone. The Commissions of El Salvador, Guatemala,

[136] 3B Witness to Truth: Report of the Sierra Leone Truth and Reconciliation Commission ch. 6, pp. 5–6 (2004).

Timor-Leste and Sierra Leone have seen significant United Nations involvement and support and United Nations missions in Liberia and the Democratic Republic of the Congo are now engaged in supporting consultative processes for truth commissions in those countries. Truth commissions have the potential to be of great benefit in helping post-conflict societies establish the facts about past human rights violations, foster accountability, preserve evidence, identify perpetrators and recommend reparations and institutional reforms. They can also provide a public platform for victims to address the nation directly with their personal stories and can facilitate public debate about how to come to terms with the past.[137]

The entire thrust of the Secretary-General's approach is one of complementary institutions, with courts and truth commissions operating side-by-side. In his remarks to the Security Council while presenting the report, on 6 October 2004, the Secretary-General said that 'where transitional justice is concerned, the best approach is usually not an "either/or" choice between prosecutions and truth commissions. Instead, a nationally determined combination of mechanisms will generally work better – including, where appropriate, traditional justice mechanisms'.[138] This general philosophy of post-conflict justice was largely endorsed during the debate on the report in the Security Council.[139] At its conclusion, the President of the Security Council issued a statement that included the following: 'The Council draws attention to the full range of transitional justice mechanisms that should be considered, including national, international and 'mixed' criminal tribunals and truth and reconciliation commissions, and underlines that those mechanisms should concentrate not only on individual responsibility for serious crimes, but also on the need to seek peace, truth and national reconciliation.'[140]

Increasingly, then, given the presence of the ICC, the coexistence of the two bodies will no longer be an option, but simply a fact. The lessons of the Sierra Leone experience suggest that it is not unreasonable for the two bodies to operate in parallel. Fears that the threat of prosecution may discourage perpetrators from testifying are simply a fact with which we shall have to live. But experience in Sierra Leone suggests that such fears are more imaginary than real.

[137] 'The Rule of law and transitional justice in post-conflict societies', UN Doc. S/2004/616, para. 50.

[138] UN Doc. S/PV.5052 (2004), p. 3.

[139] *Ibid.*, pp. 7 (Russian Federation), 14 (Brazil), p. 15 (Romania), p. 22 (Angola); UN Doc. S/PV.5052 (Resumption 1) (2004), pp. 19 (Argentina), 22 (Burundi), 27 (Japan), 28–29 (Peru), 31 (Sierra Leone), 37 (Indonesia).

[140] UN Doc. S/PV.5052 (Resumption 1) (2004), p. 38.

Willingness or unwillingness to testify seems to have more to do with the mysteries of the human soul than it does with issues of amnesty, use immunity and compulsion to testify. The issue of testimony by detainees has been explored, and a reasonable solution proposed, though there is nothing to prevent the International Criminal Court from reaching a different conclusion on the matter. The Commission was unhappy with Judge Robertson's disposition of the case. But to be fair, he did not prevent Norman from meeting with it and providing information, and ultimately it was Norman who obstructed the work of the Commission by refusing to testify in private after agreeing to testify in public.

International justice continues to evolve in unexpected ways. The investigations in Uganda and Congo now being undertaken by the Prosecutor of the ICC reveal an original construction of article 17 of the Rome Statute. Rather than treat governments as adversaries of the Court, the Prosecutor seems to view them as partners, seeking referrals of situations by States against themselves, so to speak. This cooperative approach would also seem to point the Court towards a friendly attitude with respect to alternative accountability mechanisms, like truth commissions. Certainly, the issues and problems encountered in Sierra Leone are not going to go away.

There have been frequent expressions of frustration that ordinary people in Sierra Leone did not appreciate the distinction between the two institutions, Special Court and Truth Commission. They often seemed confused about the respective roles of the two bodies. There was no shortage of proposals to develop 'sensitisation projects' in order to help improve the situation. But is this really such a problem? Most law students would be challenged to explain the difference between the European Court of Justice and the European Court of Human Rights, so is it reasonable to expect a sophisticated grasp of the distinctions between post-conflict transitional justice institutions from ordinary people in a country with a high illiteracy rate? The fact is, if average Sierra Leoneans now understand that there are two institutions working towards accountability for the atrocities and victimisation that they suffered, this is mission accomplished. In the end, it may be that the term 'complementary' as a description of the relationship between the Court and the Commission is too conservative. 'Synergy' may well be the better term. While the coexistence of the two bodies inevitably raises issues and complications, as the Sierra Leone experience shows, ultimately they probably have an additive effect.

EDUARDO GONZÁLEZ CUEVA*

THE CONTRIBUTION OF THE PERUVIAN TRUTH AND RECONCILIATION COMMISSION TO PROSECUTIONS**

The experience of the Peruvian Truth and Reconciliation Commission (TRC) may stimulate useful comparisons, help to set the agenda for future research and provide an example of candid self-assessment. I will first introduce a general picture of the political context where the TRC emerged in order to understand the choices it made. Then, I intend to present the general scope of the mandate, and discuss the different ways in which the notion of cooperation between a TRC and judiciary bodies can be understood. Finally, I will present the strategies chosen by the TRC to cooperate with the Attorney General's Office and the experience of our Special Investigations Unit.

I. THE PERUVIAN CONTEXT

During the last two decades of the past century, Peru suffered under the twin evils of a politically motivated internal armed conflict and the steady erosion of democratic liberties. On the one hand, guerrilla actions were unleashed in May 1980 by the extremist Communist Party of Peru, also known as "Shining Path". Those actions escalated progressively until it engulfed most of the country's territory in an orgy of blood that produced close to 30,000 deaths, among which a significant number, at least 6000 cases, are believed to be enforced disappearances of persons.

On the other hand, the pressure to respond to the challenge posed by the "Shining Path" and – at the same time – contain popular discontent with neo-liberal economic policies, moved successive

* Coordinator of the Reconciliation, Public Hearings and Educational Initiatives Unit of the Peruvian Truth and Reconciliation Commission.

** This paper was written in 2002, during the mandate of the Peruvian Truth and Reconciliation Commission (TRC). It does not take into consideration the findings made in the Final Report of the TRC, published on August 28, 2003. The report can be consulted at http://www.cverdad.org.pe.

Criminal Law Forum **15:** 55–66, 2004.
© 2004 *Kluwer Academic Publishers. Printed in the Netherlands.*

civilian governments to trample on civic liberties and to tolerate massive abuses by the security forces. Eventually, this process led to a *coup d'etat* in 1992 and the creation of a *sui generis* corrupt autocracy led by Alberto Fujimori, president of the country between 1990 and 2000.

The capture of the "Shining Path" leader, Abimael Guzmán, by police detectives in 1992, his subsequent frustrated attempt to negotiate a peace agreement with the Fujimori regime, and the passage of draconian emergency laws, determined a dramatic decrease of actions by the "Shining Path", due in part to a mass desertion and incarceration of hundreds of alleged terrorist leaders and militants.

Thus, from 1992 onwards, the pattern of violations of civil and political human rights in Peru changed: from the massive violations against life typical of an internal conflict, to selective crimes against civil liberties perpetrated against peaceful dissenters, as is typical of authoritarian governments.

The Fujimori regime collapsed in 2000 after the disclosure of fantastic levels of corruption involving the president and his main advisor, the shadowy intelligence advisor Vladimiro Montesinos. These revelations occurred in the unstable context created by Fujimori's attempt to be elected for a third five-year term. Fujimori was brought down by the pressure of a wide opposition alliance ranging from the main political parties to the academic elites, including the labour movement, sections of the military and human rights organisations.

The issue of human rights violations was fundamental to discredit Fujimori's regime. In spite of his self-proclaimed achievements in the field of economic stabilisation and internal order, the stain of human rights abuses and his refusal to comply with judgments by the Inter-American Court of Human Rights (IACHR) were a permanent source of questioning of his authority.

Human rights demands, including the clarification of the grossest deeds of the internal conflict, were of chief importance in the platform of the opposition groups at the moment of Fujimori's fall and of the formation of a provisional government in November 2000, headed by the opposition leader, the former president of Congress, Valentin Paniagua.

Two unique factors need to be highlighted in the general picture of Peru's transition in order to understand the political context that led to the creation of the Truth and Reconciliation Commission. The first factor is the consolidation, over the years, of a nationwide coordinating board for all human rights organisations in the country (*Coordinadora Nacional de Derechos Humanos* or CNDH). The existence of a united organisation capable of acting with one voice on human rights issues was certainly an asset for the nation's political transition and a safeguard against transitional pacts that would exchange stability for impunity. The second factor is external. The IACHR proved to be a permanent obstacle to the regime's attempts to shield state criminals with legal obstacles to prosecution, such as through amnesties.

The combination of these two factors had a concrete result in April 2001, when a ruling by the IACHR determined that Peru should repeal a blanket amnesty law that was enacted in 1995 to prevent the investigation and prosecution of all human rights abuses committed by the security forces during the internal conflict since 1980. The *Barrios Altos* ruling, a case involving a massacre committed by a death squad linked to the Army, held that the State had the duty to investigate and prosecute the criminal suspects and that amnesty laws that had the effect of impeding investigation of crimes against humanity were void and contrary to the American Convention on Human Rights.

The ruling was the result of a well argued complaint submitted by the CNDH and came in perfect timing, as the provisional government of Paniagua made efforts to put Peru back in line with its international obligations, departing from past decisions of the former dictatorship that had resulted in a *de facto* renunciation of the inter-American system of human rights.

Indeed, during the transitional government (November 2000– July 2001) several substantive human rights initiatives were undertaken. Peru reinstated the jurisdiction of the IACHR and agreed to negotiate friendly settlements with claimants in almost 200 cases brought to the Court. In addition, Peru signed the Rome Statute of the International Criminal Court and opened the process of its ratification, while at the same time creating a special inter-institutional group with members from State and Civil Society groups in order to draft the mandate of a Truth Commission. The scope of these initiatives clearly reflects the influence achieved by human rights groups in the transitional agenda.

II. THE MANDATE OF THE COMMISSION

The inter-institutional working group was formed in December 2000 with representatives from the Ministries of Defence, Justice, Home Affairs, Women's Advancement, the Ombudsman Office, the CNDH and the Catholic and protestant churches. In little over three months, the group drafted a decree that was submitted to President Paniagua that – with little change – was enacted in June 2001.

Supreme Decree 065-2001-PCM created a Truth Commission charged with the task of "clarifying the process, facts and responsibilities of the terrorist violence and human rights violations produced from May 1980 to November 2000, whether imputable to terrorist organisations or State agents, as well as proposing initiatives destined to affirm peace and harmony among Peruvians". The mandate of the TRC defines its roles regarding the rights of victims to know the truth, attain justice and obtain reparations, as well as regarding the obligations of the State to ensure guarantees of non repetition of the past crimes.

The clarification, or right-to-truth, component of the mandate is very ambitious. It encompasses the need to "analyse the societal conditions and institutional behaviours" that formed the breeding ground for political violence, which includes uncovering related facts and clarifying responsibilities. It leaves to the discretion of the Commission, whether or not to clarify moral, political and/or criminal responsibilities, at both the institutional and personal level, as well as the way in which to make these determinations.

The justice component of the mandate, though, made important qualifications. Specifically, the Commission is to identify, "when appropriate", "presumptive" responsibilities "to the extent possible" within the framework of contributing to the task of courts to investigate and prosecute. The mandate made explicit, however, that the Commission had "no jurisdictional powers" and that it did not "substitute" the functions of the judiciary.

The subject matter of investigation was a hotly debated issue during the drafting of the Decree. While human rights groups favoured encompassing formulas with clear links to applicable international human rights and international humanitarian law, the representatives of the security forces fiercely opposed any mention of anything that – in their opinion – would amount to the recognition of a state of armed conflict covered by the Geneva Conventions, since this would supposedly grant a belligerent status to terrorist groups.

The latter position was adopted and no explicit reference to international humanitarian law was made. In the place of listing heinous crimes committed by anti-state armed organisations as war crimes, generic language was adopted, such as "incidents of terrorist violence" or merely "crimes". However, this setback in doctrine was balanced by a list of "crimes and serious violations of human rights" that specified murder, kidnappings, enforced disappearances, torture, violations of collective indigenous rights, but also left open a clause on "other" violations, permitting the extension of the list by analogy.

The Commission was designed in the context of the repeal of the 1995 amnesty law. The creation of the Commission occurred in a country, where the most important guerrilla group had collapsed years earlier due to the capture and surrender of its leader; where an authoritarian ruler had ignominiously escaped without the chance of serious negotiation; and where hundreds of generals, businessmen and politicians involved in acts of corruption were shamed by the public exhibition of videos in which they are seen accepting huge sums of illegal money. Many of these formerly important potentates were to be locked away in prison, facing charges before the recently created special anti-corruption prosecutors and judges.

These extremely positive political conditions need to be recognised. Every truth commission is created in a given political environment, which determines its mandate, both in terms of its scope and in the way in which the mandate is to be interpreted and applied. In the case of Peru, the Truth Commission was created under specific conditions that determine its place in relation to the judiciary, and these conditions have not changed substantially since the TRC's inception. Moreover, since the founding of Peru's TRC, amnesty laws have been voided, human rights cases have been taken to court and the judiciary has reasserted its role through the creation of a special prosecutor's office charged with investigating human rights violations. These developments create a context in which to interpret the TRC's mandate as contributing to jurisdictional tasks, while at the same time pursuing additional objectives that are not naturally covered by courts such as analysing historical contexts, providing a platform for victims to speak their truth, drawing up proposals for reparations and advancing reconciliation initiatives.

III. SCOPE OF COOPERATION BETWEEN THE COMMISSION AND THE JUDICIARY

The contribution of the Truth Commission to the work of the judiciary tends to adopt two different forms of cooperation, one is generic; the second, specific.

In a generic fashion, the Truth Commission, recognising that its task is not to establish truth in the way a court of justice does, serves a legitimating function by helping to strengthen the judiciary. Truth Commissions emerge in countries where the plea of victims has been systematically ignored because they often belong to disenfranchised sectors of society, traditionally segregated from the public sphere. In such a society, the demand for justice tends to occupy a low place on the national agenda, and efforts by the judiciary to prosecute may be regarded with little interest if not with suspicion.

In that context, the role of a truth commission as a player in the political arena is undeniable, and it becomes important to design mechanisms to engage societal expectations and arguments. The Peruvian TRC, for example, has had, from its inception, a built-in mechanism to impact the public sphere well before the anticipated publication of its final report. Indeed, different from all other commissions created in Latin America, the Peruvian Commission decided to carry out a wide range of public activities such as public hearings and open dialogue sessions with civic leaders.

A second form of cooperation between truth commissions and courts is through the sharing of information. In the case of the Peruvian TRC, the judiciary shall obviously have access to the findings in the TRC's Final Report, which will include, "when appropriate" and "to the extent possible", the identification of those presumptively responsible for criminal acts. Moreover, nothing in the mandate precludes the TRC from making information available prior to the issuing of its final report, if the Commission deems such action as necessary to initiate investigative procedures.

This discretion is especially clear in the case of the exhumation of mass graves. While the exhumation of illegal graves is an exclusive privilege of the Office of the Attorney General, the TRC is in the position – due to its contact with the witnesses – to propose the sites that hold the promise of unearthing more evidence.

This information-sharing capacity obviously begs the question of what to do regarding those investigative steps that are carried out confidentially, which is the case of the vast majority of the Commission research. However, given the fact that the Peruvian amnesty laws are void, the Commission should be aware not to interpret confidentiality in any way that would amount to hiding information from the Attorney General's Office. Confidentiality is supposed to work to protect victims and witnesses, including perpetrators, who agree to cooperate with investigators in order to reveal evidence of what happened.

Field investigators have to clearly explain the tasks of the Commission to every person interviewed. It is up to possible perpetrators approaching the TRC to opt for two possible options: either give anonymous testimony, so that the TRC will learn about the facts without being able to identify the source should the

Attorney General request the identity of the person who gave such information; or they can give confidential testimony that will be passed on to the judicial authorities for them to process under the condition that perpetrators may utilise traditional judicial mechanisms that permit the exchange of information for substantially reduced penalties.

IV. THE MANDATE'S INTERPRETATION

The Commission analysed its mandate in order to ascertain, whether it should emphasise one form of contribution above the other. This is related to another discussion concerning the Commission's interpretation of its mandate to establish "truth". From the earliest moments, the Commission initiated a theoretical discussion on whether it should establish "historical truth" or "judicial truth", that is, whether it would best serve its objectives by creating a new narrative of the years of violence or by assigning responsibility to people who could be taken to Court. An emphasis on "historical truth" as opposed to "judicial truth" could prioritise a generic form of cooperation with the courts. Thus, it was important to overcome a false division that would polarise sociological and juridical perspectives in the Commission.

Those convinced that the TRC's main task was to establish historical truth should admit that hard evidence forwarded to courts and transformed into verdicts makes it more difficult for perpetrators to deny what happened and would help to deconstruct the narratives advanced by authoritarian rulers interested in denying the crimes. In turn, those convinced that the first and foremost role of the TRC was to conduct pre-judicial investigation to support the Attorney General's office would have to conclude that a wide mandate of historical clarification allows the TRC to challenge, in a moral sense, cases that had been already tried and sentenced by the judiciary and were therefore protected by the principle of *ne bis in idem*.

Indeed, before the 1995 amnesty laws, the judiciary had tried very few human rights cases but, when it did, it summarily disposed of them by punishing lower ranking perpetrators and declaring the higher echelons innocent, or by closing cases for lack of evidence, procedural mistakes or intimidation of witnesses. Those cases remain in our collective memory as fundamentally flawed and unfair, however, many of them present very little possibility of being re-opened at the national level. Thus, putting then into a larger historical context could do some measure of justice to the victims.

It is important to notice, however, that this discussion was not solved necessarily by means of formal decision-making by the different bodies of the Commission, but rather under the conditions of its evolving engagement with Peruvian society. It was the exposure of the commissioners to the victims' expectations through public hearings, and the impact that those hearings had on public opinion, that cut the Gordian knot. At the hearings, victim after victim demanded that the criminals be punished. In the victims' view, only after criminal justice was achieved, would other forms of reparation be asked for and reconciliation attained.

The impact of the public hearings, that were nationally broadcasted and debated can be measured in a recent public opinion poll in the capital, Lima.[1] When asked about the four main policies that would contribute to national reconciliation, the public answered in this order: punishing the criminals, 60.1%; anti-poverty programmes, 44.6%; reparations for victims, 41.5%; human rights education, 38.6%.

Before the public hearings, the discussion about "historical" or "juridical" truth had resulted in a thorough investigation about the law applicable to the mandate of the TRC and to the indirect revival of the inter-institutional group debate about international humanitarian law. It also resulted in the identification of about one hundred "cases that must not be forgotten" with a possible view to justice. However, no specific investigative steps were taken, in the sense of pre-judicial investigation consistent with creating a wealth of information that could be shared with the courts.

It was only after the first public hearings in April of 2002 that the TRC formally decided that it was imperative to attend to the demand for justice made by the victims and set up a Special Investigations Unit, charged with the task of organising legal cases against specific individual perpetrators so that those cases could be presented to the Attorney General's Office for prosecution.

At the same time, the hearings proved instrumental to boost the negotiation of a cooperation agreement between the TRC and the Attorney General's Office, which was finally signed in August of this year. This agreement set up forms of cooperation in four areas: information sharing in order to proceed with the exhumation of clandestine graves; information sharing on cases of enforced disappearances and extra-judiciary executions; the conduction of exhumations; and the protection of victims and witness.

---

[1] Grupo de opinión pública de la Universidad de Lima. Estudio 165, barómetro septiembre 2002. Lima Metropolitana y Callao, sábado 21 y domingo 22.

It seems, then, that it was reality that imposed a solution to many theoretical conundrums. In fact, the discussion on "historical" versus "judicial" truth was never formally closed, but the specific political, institutional and public opinion conditions made it possible to take decisive steps regarding specific cooperation with the Attorney General's office. Given the exceptional nature of its mandate, the TRC has – to put it bluntly – the advantage of initiative. As the TRC is not subject to cumbersome procedures and is permanently under the public light it enjoys ample political autonomy and legitimacy.

In contrast, the Attorney General's Office tends to be slower and opaque to the public. In such a situation, even though the Attorney General has the unchallenged prerogative to conduct all criminal investigations, it tends to coordinate with the TRC about the most promising investigations to open. Given the fact that Peru has suffered massive crimes and that no legal body will ever be able to investigate fully all of them, it is self-evident that a decision on priorities has to be made and it is there, where the TRC has proven to be of great help to the Attorney General.

V. THE SPECIAL INVESTIGATIONS UNIT

The Special Investigations Unit (SIU) receives material from the processed testimonies taken by the many field offices of the TRC, non-governmental organisation (NGO) depositions, past legal files, transcripts of the public hearings and the TRC database. The SIU expects to identify a group of cases where solid evidence could convince the Commissioners that presumptive individual responsibilities can be ascertained and, therefore, information should be forwarded to the Attorney General.

Technical criteria regarding the corroboration of testimony, availability of evidence and opportunities to obtain the custody of alleged perpetrators are objectives chiefly important to the Unit. However, a qualifier must be made: technical criteria are never purely objective, since they have a normative presupposition. It is more responsible to prefer cases with better conditions of successful prosecutions, since doing otherwise would expose the victims to the risk of going through cases based on flimsy evidence that could result in sentences favourable to shrewd, powerful perpetrators.

It must also be noted that the Unit reports directly to the Commissioners through a special group delegated by the Plenary Assembly of Commissioners. This special group supplements technical criteria with other information that point towards constructing a *corpus* of cases that is representative of the violence experimented in Peru. This means that the crimes investigated by the Unit attempt to cover a wide range of descriptors regarding the time and place of their commission, the kind of conducts involved, the kind of agents of the crime and its victims.

Using those criteria, the Unit expects to identify a handful of very strong cases that will be ready for submission at different moments during the mandate of the Commission. Naturally, its work will also serve the purpose of identifying a second stratum of several cases, where insufficient evidence or other technical problems do not allow the Commission to reach the level of certainty previous to submission to the courts. Many of those cases nonetheless will be robust enough to convince the Commissioners that at least they can identify political responsibilities though not through the stringent methods used by a court of law.

Obviously, too, the largest proportion of cases will never be in the position of being thoroughly investigated. The TRC set itself the goal of processing 12,000 individual testimonies, a number that was both feasible to achieve and capable of being processed into a comprehensive database. The major bulk of cases that will not reach a reasonable degree of corroboration and exhaustive investigation to be transferred to the courts will nevertheless have indicative value and will serve to identify general patterns of violations. Those patterns could confirm the generalised or systematic character of the types of conduct under investigation by the Commission and thus be instrumental to arrive at conclusions regarding the category of crimes against humanity committed in our country.

It is still too early to say how many crimes will fall within the three above mentioned categories of cases. The first stratum, however, will surely be exceedingly small. The question is how to ensure that they will nonetheless have a decisive impact in the struggle against impunity, on the moral convictions of the public and the success of the democratic transition. To answer this question it is important to notice that nothing in the Commission's mandate forces it to wait until the end of its work to make its recommendations of prosecution.

The Commissioners' evaluation of the general situation of the country is essential to determine, when to present cases for prosecution. They may think that the day after the presentation of the Final Report the legitimacy and political strength of an active TRC will not be there to support diligent action by the courts. In addition, the TRC is interested in "aiming high", that is, to ensure that justice is done in cases involving the higher echelons of the criminal chains of command and not only against the small fry. If that is the objective, the Commissioners may consider that it is politically unlikely that high-profile cases against powerful perpetrators will be immediately feasible. It is probable that the early initiation of prosecutions against the most heinous immediate perpetrators, such as military officers or terrorist cadres, will have the social result of stimulating the demand for justice to go higher.

The TRC is extremely conscious of the value of public impact and civic dialogue. The empowerment of the victims' voices through the public hearings was instrumental to gain public acceptance of its mission and its place in the national agenda. That communicative setting may be again valuable to eventually legitimise trials.

There is the precedent of a human rights case brought post-Fujimori that ought to be carefully examined, when designing a litigation strategy: specifically, the prosecution of about 40 military commandos and their leading officers, following accusation that they executed terrorist hostage takers that had been put *hors de combat* during a daring rescue operation at the Japanese ambassador's residence in Lima in April of 1996.

Since that action was not covered by the 1995 amnesty law, in 2000 a human rights NGO asked the Attorney General's Office to initiate investigations. Forensic evidence obtained in the exhumation of the bodies of the 14 dead members of the terrorist group suggested a clear pattern of execution of badly wounded or surrendered hostage takers. Moreover, the special prosecutor in charge of the case had been able to secure key testimony regarding executions, and the military leaders in charge of the operations had publicly boasted about dubious tactics for situations involving hostages.

In the Japanese Ambassador's residence case, even though the majority of the public supported the hypothesis of executions and held them to be morally contemptible, it also supported nothing less than a new amnesty law for the military commandos, widely regarded as heroes for their operation in a successful raid against a terrorist group. Political tensions ran high but came to an end after a ruling by the Supreme Court divided the accused in two groups, sending the rank and file and a few leaders to military courts and a few of their superiors and members of the intelligence units linked to Montesinos to civilian courts.

Military courts have been traditionally lenient on members of the security forces accused of human rights violations, so the Supreme Court ruling amounted to nothing less than salvation for most of the commandos and a real risk only for the Fujimorista leaders sent to civilian courts for the same conduct. Such a biased result would be hardly defensible for cases brought forward by the TRC. Thus in assessing the kind of case to recommend for prosecution, the TRC needs to carefully assess the kind of case that would obtain the widest moral empathy from the nation.

Additionally, the TRC is conscious that it needs to utilise its political capital in the still existing window of opportunity created by the transition. In a context of economic incertitude and political instability it is hard to predict, whether favourable conditions will exist tomorrow for the struggle against impunity.

VI. CONCLUSIONS

The Peruvian experience has several particularities that make it unique, among them several very favourable political and institutional variables. These variables had a direct impact in the way in which the TRC interpreted its mandate regarding justice.

The fact that the Commission sees its task as having a public component has been essential to create a space for dialogue with victims, and to stimulate civic reflection that also deeply impacted upon the commissioners themselves, and led them to resolve many problems in the interpretation of the TRC's mandate. At the same time, the public's engagement with the task of the Commission has helped it gain wider legitimacy that makes it a desirable ally for the Attorney General's Office.

It may be reasonably said that a harmonious adjustment between a TRC and the judiciary depends not only on characteristics built into the TRC mandate, but above all else, in its ability to interpret that mandate according to its spirit and under the moral sense of urgency provided by the empowerment of victims' voices.

SUSAN KEMP*

THE INTER-RELATIONSHIP BETWEEN THE GUATEMALAN COMMISSION FOR HISTORICAL CLARIFICATION AND THE SEARCH FOR JUSTICE IN NATIONAL COURTS

In exploring how truth commissions and criminal justice can and should complement one another, we should investigate not only the technical problems arising from the simultaneous operation of truth seeking programs and prosecutions but also what this complementarity implies for the wider debate surrounding truth and justice as responses to massive human rights abuse. The automatic assumption that truth-seeking and/or criminal prosecutions are necessary in every transition to democracy is to be avoided. In situations where they are likely to bring benefits, it is essential that their distinct roles be preserved and their limitations appreciated. Analysing how truth-seeking and criminal trials can complement one another should also spark more discussion about their relationship to other equally important post-conflict responses.

Truth-seeking can work to address a variety of important needs – of victims, their family members, communities, wider society, politicians and state institutions. It may even provoke catharsis for victims, perpetrators and some sectors of society.[1] But what should we really expect from it? It is difficult if not impossible to evaluate whether a truth commission has achieved the objective of telling the truth about a certain historical period. Even if one sets more modest criteria for evaluating truth-seeking initiatives, say, contributing to the historical study of a country's past, expectations may be met but the point is often missed that truth commissions and traditional historical study

* Solicitor and Independent Legal Consultant. Formerly Legal Director, Centro para Acción Legal en Derechos Humanos, Guatemala City.

[1] I am somewhat sceptical of the claim that a *national* catharsis can be provoked by truth-seeking initiatives, especially following non-international armed conflicts and situations of selective state repression.

Criminal Law Forum **15:** 67–103, 2004.
© 2004 *Kluwer Academic Publishers. Printed in the Netherlands.*

are very different in nature.[2] The work of truth commissions will generally take place in the public spotlight and the results will be more widely publicised at national and international level than most historical publications.[3] Added to this is the high level of resources which have been dedicated to truth-seeking in many countries as compared to academic historical study. Among the many possible outcomes of truth-seeking, future governmental and international policy decisions may be based in part on the facts uncovered and conclusions reached. The unintended result may be that the report of a truth seeking body comes to be considered by many as *the* definitive version of a stage in the nation's history.[4]

I therefore think we should ask more of truth-seeking exercises than simply that they contribute to our understanding of history, but without going so far as to claim that they can in themselves provide accountability. The success of truth-seeking (which one can only assess by ongoing and thorough study) may perhaps be better measured by looking at the extent to which it has increased public knowledge[5] about the past, informed national debate at a political level and increased the likelihood of victims' demands being met. In most post-conflict situations the choices, design and potential impact of activities such as truth-seeking, criminal trials and institutional reform should be linked to the possibility of implementing political, social, economic or other measures, which address the root

---

[2] For a detailed critical analysis of truth-seeking in a historical context see Tristram Hunt, *Whose Truth? Objective Truth and a Challenge for History*, in this issue.

[3] The book Nunca Más, the result of Argentina's truth seeking initiative, spent many months at the top of the national Bestseller list.

[4] A recent example serves to illustrate the danger of treating truth commission reports as definitive versions of "the truth". Towards the end of 2002, a person justifiably admired as a national leader who defends Guatemalan victims and indigenous rights, suggested to representatives of the state, victims and civil society groups who were then negotiating a National Reparations Plan, that the victims from four geographical districts of the country must have priority in receiving compensation since the Guatemala Commission for Historical Clarification had concluded that acts of genocide had occurred in these regions. The Commission's report clearly states that these four regions were in fact simply selected for in-depth study as examples indicative of the kind of violence which had been committed across the entire highland area of Guatemala.

[5] It cannot be overemphasised that any post-conflict initiative to deal with past abuses must aim first and foremost at the domestic population (as opposed to the international community), for example see Neil Kritz, *Progress and Humility: The Ongoing Search for Post Conflict Justice*, in POST-CONFLICT JUSTICE 777 (M. Cherif Bassiouni, ed., 2002).

causes of civic unrest or armed conflict and not only their consequences. Within these wider objectives, increased knowledge and dissemination of the information gathered by a truth commission can be a precursor to achieving some form of justice for international crimes or serious violations of human rights.

By "some form of justice" I do not mean simply criminal convictions. It should be borne in mind that not all victims desire criminal justice, for various reasons, and it is their right not to do so. Depending on the circumstances there may also be risks involved in carrying out criminal trials.[6] A wider concept of justice should encompass an adequate response by state or non-state actors responsible for human rights abuses or crimes, which creates positive effects both for victims and for the transition to democracy. As such, justice must include a component of accountability. Accountability is most commonly described in legal or moral terms: the fulfilment of state obligations to prosecute crime, or the necessity of providing a satisfactory response to victims and their families.[7] State obligations to prosecute clearly exist in relation to certain crimes and would preclude the granting of amnesty. Nonetheless, some would regard a purely legal analysis as unrealistic because it does not offer much room for political manoeuvre, for example during a negotiated peace settlement. Nor does it make allowance for a meaningful assessment of a legal system's capability, particularly if the legal obligation to prosecute is interpreted widely

[6] These have been widely debated elsewhere; for example, see CARLOS SANTIAGO NINO, RADICAL EVIL ON TRIAL (1996), who discusses the obstacles and risks related to prosecutions in certain circumstances as well as the benefits they can bring to transitions to democracy. He considers that Argentina benefited from the conviction of members of the military junta notwithstanding the subsequent pardons by President Menem, a view shared by at least one former Argentine General. Cf. JAIME MALAMUD, GAME WITHOUT END: STATE TERROR AND THE POLITICS OF JUSTICE (1996).

[7] On which, see Diane F. Orentlicher, *Settling Accounts: The Duty to Prosecute Human Rights Violations of a Prior Regime*, 100 YALE L.J. 2537 (1991). Even on a strictly legal view of things, the truth can form part of the state's obligations under human rights instruments to investigate but the serious nature of the violations which are examined by truth commissions, would demand criminal investigation as part of an effective remedy. See *X and Y* v. *The Netherlands* (App No. 16/1983/72/110, 25 arch 1985, the case of the massacre of fifteen people at Barrios Altos in Peru, Inter-American Court of Human Rights Series C, Case No. 75, 14 March 2001, and Paul Seils, *The Limits of Truth Commissions in the Search for Justice: An Analysis of the Truth Commissions of El Salvador and Guatemala and Their Effect in Achieving Post-Conflict Justice*, in POST-CONFLICT JUSTICE, *supra* note 5 at 775.

to cover a vast range of crimes or to demand prosecution of tens of thousands of perpetrators. As to the moral element, without venturing to discuss the content of such a norm, one can say that if we accept that a satisfactory response to massive human rights abuse or acts of violence may take a variety of forms,[8] then it is of extreme importance that victims (or family members in the case of the deceased) are consulted on the issue prior to setting up any transitional justice mechanism. This not only recognises the dignity of the victims and their moral and legal claims to recourse but is also an exemplary democratic exercise in itself. Consultation can if carried out properly, help to avoid the imposition of policies which turn out to be unpopular or misconceived, even if they have ostensibly been designed to satisfy victims' wishes. Conversely, a lack of participation by victims in the formulation of those policies can ultimately militate against their success.

This leads on to another justification of the need for accountability asides from legal and moral arguments. The benefits of accountability – including the application of criminal law – ought to be understood from the point of view of benefiting the transition to democracy. This view is premised on a concept of democracy which goes far beyond mere formalism. It requires a participatory model and aims for strong citizen–state relationships based on transparency, accountability and efficacy. The creation or reconstruction of public confidence in the political, military and legal institutions of an emerging democracy will be problematic if those same institutions are seen to be incapable or unwilling to function when faced with the most serious situations of lawlessness they will probably ever have to tackle. In those situations in which the state itself has failed to protect or has even attacked its own citizens, that task will be much more difficult to carry out but all the more important to the transition. Accountability is acutely necessary when the persons, institutions or sectors of society responsible for past crimes retain, or have consolidated, their power despite an end to armed conflict or repressive rule. They can continue to impose serious obstacles to consolidating the democracy, since they are likely to obstruct any efforts to hold them accountable for their actions or to otherwise reduce their power and influence.

---

[8] A state response could for example be acceptable to victims by including full state acceptance of responsibility, apology, adequate reparations and vetting of personnel linked to the offending institutions.

By accepting that criminal sanction may not be necessary or appropriate in all transitions to democracy, or in relation to all crimes, is not to say that the criminal law has no place in responding to mass atrocities unless all attempts to achieve accountability by other means have failed. The criminal law should be applied if crimes have been committed and if the possibility to apply it exists. Bypassing the application of criminal law should be considered a last resort, given that it not only subverts the rule of law but violates the individual rights of hundreds if not thousands of victims to seek protection and recourse through their legal institutions. If one sees the application of criminal law as the reassertion of accepted social norms of behaviour, it is difficult to argue that this is any less necessary when a society is confronted with violence of the utmost magnitude and gravity simply because it occurred during armed conflict or authoritarian rule.

The practical problem however lies more with who decides whether criminal justice is possible or desirable, when, and on the basis of which criteria or advice. The perceived negative effects of criminal justice on stability are often exaggerated, in many cases by mistaken analogy to other countries' experiences or even on the basis of mere presumption. This can justify hasty wide ranging amnesty legislation or other measures of direct benefit only to the parties brokering power following the collapse of a regime or the end of armed conflict. Avoiding criminal trials, particularly against leading military and political figures, may give the impression of offering a fast-track to stability and hence speedier participation in the global economy. However, whatever the motivation, avoiding any prosecutions when they may in fact be possible can simply store up problems for the future. Decision-makers should instead analyse carefully whether longer term benefits could be gained by recognizing a potential convergence between victims' desire for accountability (whether through criminal sanction or other measures) and the promotion of democratic behaviour among state institutions and citizens alike.[9] If criminal trials are considered to be impossible in the short term, attempts should be made to create the conditions for their future feasibility, rather than formalising a current impossibility into a

---

[9] For a fuller discussion see Steven Ratner, *Democracy and Accountability: the Criss-crossing Paths of Two Emerging Norms*, in DEMOCRATIC GOVERNANCE AND INTERNATIONAL LAW 449 (GREGORY H. FOX & Brad H. Roth, eds., 2000).

permanent one.[10] Even if prosecutions are denied in the short term, that does not mean their utility for victims and for democratic consolidation diminishes over time.[11]

If tangible and serious obstacles to the possibility of obtaining criminal convictions do exist and cannot foreseeably be overcome in the short term, it is incumbent on the parties involved and the international community not to attempt to portray other measures such as truth-seeking as capable of filling that gap. To present truth-seeking itself as a challenge to impunity or as a form of accountability is not only to misunderstand its functions but is also to short-change victims. Even if a truth-seeking exercise results in the publication of clear allegations against named individuals, whether accountability follows will depend on the response to those allegations. Claiming that information about the past is itself a form of accountability can also easily strengthen the hand of those who oppose criminal sanctions, providing them with ammunition to justify their own impunity and to marginalize those victims who seek criminal accountability as out for revenge or as obstacles to "national reconciliation."

I. THE GOAL OF RECONCILIATION

Reconciliation is talked of as an objective of truth-seeking initiatives often in the absence of any clarity as to the definition of the concept and without a realistic view of whether and when it can be achieved. Some time after the publication of the report of the Guatemalan Commission for Historical Clarification (CHC), which recommended measures to promote reconciliation, the United Nations organised a series of meetings between Guatemalan governmental and non-governmental bodies to explore the meaning of reconciliation in the national context. The various concepts put forward ranged from the micro to the macro and of course did not by any means pretend to

[10] For example, in the situation of cease-fire or global peace negotiations, amnesty will generally be an unavoidable part of discussions as a condition imposed by a party or parties. While in many cases the imminent priority generally will and should be to prevent further loss of civilian life, efforts can be made to mitigate the "blanket" nature of amnesty laws. One important factor is to preserve the role of the judiciary in determining the authorisation of amnesty on a case by case basis; others often include limiting the protection by excluding certain crimes or by targetting commanders rather than enlisted troops.

[11] I agree wholeheartedly here with the comments of Neil Kritz on the need for domestic capacity building in the criminal justice sphere; see Kritz, *supra* note 5.

offer a definitive explanation. At the micro level (and in particular focussing on perpetrators and those who were complicit or were bystanders during the armed conflict) is reconciliation with oneself, with one's conscience and past actions or inactions *vis-à-vis* the mass atrocities which were going on. Moving outwards to victims, it can refer to reconciliation directly with the perpetrator if his or her identity is known, or with the group or institution responsible. For direct victims and others, reconciliation can also refer to the relationship with one's family, social group, professional group, church, political party and suchlike. Thereafter the matter widens further to a reconciliation of society with the state itself: the guarantor of rights and source of citizen protection, and it is this idea of reconciliation which is most directly linked to successful democratic transition. If the above scenarios are examples of reconciliation then one should, in the national context, analyse whether and how knowing the truth and acting upon it can contribute to achieving these goals. This analysis will be as different for each individual as for each transitional society, which leads me to another important factor.

The difficulties springing from identifying reconciliation as one of the goals of truth-seeking "and of post-conflict policies in general" not only have to do with the lack of prior debate as to what it means for each society (and the resultant difficulty in assessing its progress) but with the unfair demands which the discourse often makes on victims of the gravest of crimes to forgive those responsible, in the name of national reconciliation. There is insufficient space here to discuss the conditions which may be thought necessary to promote forgiveness but revealing information about the past is probably only the first step. Consultation and an imaginative approach towards accountability can be further steps.[12] As well as being an abuse of victims' dignity, it is an absurdity to expect them to forgive or to reconcile with the persons or institutions responsible for their suffering, if the latter have denied outright that the abuses occurred, failed to accept responsibility for their actions or have even blamed the victims themselves for their fate. To thereafter label victims as somehow inadequate because they cannot forgive is particularly cruel. We should therefore be wary of making exaggerated claims in relation to reconciliation, particularly in terms of the speed at which it can progress and what can reasonably be expected of victims.

---

[12] The Timorese and Rwandan attempts to use local approaches to atonement and reinsertion of perpetrators into society and community are noteworthy in this respect.

II. RELATIONSHIPS BETWEEN TRUTH-SEEKING AND CRIMINAL PROSECUTIONS

The inquiry into the fate of the disappeared in Argentina and similar efforts in Chile took place in a context in which prosecutions were already on the agenda, notwithstanding the existing obstacles to criminal accountability. In the years since those efforts occurred, truth commissions have varied vastly from these two models, both in the scale and nature of the violence to be investigated and the scope and depth of study required of them.[13] Mandates have widened, expectations increased and the relationship to prosecutions has taken many forms. Perceptions of what that relationship should be now range from treating truth-seeking as a replacement for prosecutions at one extreme, to truth-seeking with an explicit goal of promoting prosecutions at the other. It is, as one would expect, in the grey area between these two positions where one finds most difficulties.

If a truth commission wishes to provide complex social and historical analyses and maintain a direct link to criminal justice, then it must make compromises. The wider but in-depth study of history does not easily coexist either conceptually or operationally with the role of identifying alleged individual perpetrators of crime. Taking on these dual roles can also tend to promote a perception of truth seeking as an alternative to criminal and other forms of accountability. The attendant risk is that once the truth commission has produced its report, a "move on" mentality will emerge, prioritising national reconciliation over demands for the very accountability which is crucial to achieving a prerequisite of that goal: democratic consolidation.

Some truth-seeking bodies do attempt to retain their discreet non-legal functions and operational autonomy from criminal justice bodies, while at the same time taking on a quasi legal function of investigating alleged individual criminal responsibility. The Peruvian Truth and Reconciliation Commission, PTRC, sought to marry the two roles by attempting a wide ranging historical investigation but also having an in-house "judicialización" team, which investigated certain individual crimes and named alleged perpetrators. The information was thereafter passed to state prosecutors. In this way, by

[13] For excellent analysis of the Argentine, Chilean and other experiences in Latin America see TRANSITIONS FROM AUTHORITARIAN RULE (Guillermo O'Donnell, et al., eds., 1986), volumes two and three on Latin America as well as the comparative perspectives volume.

effectively exercising discretion as to those cases which most urgently required prosecution, the PTRC had a direct effect in shaping criminal justice policy on these matters. It should therefore be noted that, if selecting key cases to promote criminal investigations, a truth commission has a historical responsibility to accurately reflect the various kinds and levels of violence suffered by many sectors of society.

The Peruvian experience illustrates the need to define the interrelationship between truth-seeking and criminal justice from the outset, with reference to the capabilities of state institutions and recognising the importance which investment and training for those institutions can have for a democratic transition. The PTRC was instructed to perform quasi legal functions notwithstanding the apparent willingness of the prosecutorial authorities to investigate past crimes. Many would consider that the naming of alleged individual perpetrators by a truth commission is more apt in those situations in which there is little short term prospect of the justice system investigating these crimes and prosecuting those responsible. In such situations, naming names can function as a catalyst for progress towards accountability in the future, including criminal accountability if possible. If, however, conditions exist in which a legal system is willing and able to act, then it is surely more logical that it should be that system, and not a truth commission, which carries out the investigation of individual criminal participation. National and international bodies which fund truth-seeking initiatives should support cooperative national prosecuting authorities with the funding and training needed to investigate the crimes in question, since these authorities will play a key role throughout the democratic transition and beyond, long after the truth seeking body has disappeared.

In determining the relationship between truth seeking and prosecutions, decisions will also have to be taken on whether to exclude or limit information-sharing with prosecutors.[14] I would argue that if promoting prosecutions is one of the mandated aims of a truth-seeking body then the general rule should be that the body provide such information to prosecutors as its mandate allows, rather than itself weighing the evidence and coming to conclusions about alleged individual guilt. It is true that valuable information can be obtained

[14] I have directed my comments on information-sharing to the provision of information by a truth commission to prosecutors and judges, although of course this sharing is a two-way street. The legal system can inform a truth commission about the progress in investigating and prosecuting abuses.

by a truth commission from perpetrators and informants if complete confidentiality is guaranteed. In practice however, confidentiality is rarely *the* overriding factor which motivates those persons or their institutions to cooperate with the truth-seeking exercise.[15] One should be wary of presuming that all informants will be opposed to cooperating with the legal system and consider consulting them as to the ultimate fate of the information they provide.

Truth-seeking can assist efforts to prosecute not merely in terms of information-sharing but also in shaping a social and political climate in which a range of responses to past violence, including prosecutions, have more chance of taking place. In any event, it must be defined at an early stage how best to structure the inter-relationship between truth-seeking and criminal justice. Among the many factors influencing the inter-relationship is the nature of the regime-change, the motivations of all interested parties to cooperate with both mechanisms, whether criminal justice programmes will coexist with truth seeking initiatives and whether those programmes will be in the form of international, hybrid or national tribunals.

In summary, while there may be good reasons why a truth-seeking body should be charged with investigating alleged criminal activity, it should avoid overshadowing existing national institutions.[16] This is

[15] Clearly a complex combination of reasons may exist such as the perpetrator's emotional response to what he has done, family, peer or institutional pressures, his political views, his opinion on the impartiality, legitimacy and potential outcome of the truth-seeking exercise, whether he already been granted amnesty, among others.

[16] While it is true to say that international bodies will generally have greater access to expertise and resources, trials conducted in national courts have their own specific advantages as regards the needs and wishes of the population which, in certain circumstances, international bodies or universal jurisdiction based trials would not be best placed to address. There is insufficient space to discuss this point in detail but it is worth mentioning that national trials can create a different kind of pressure on national political and military institutions than would a decision from an international forum or foreign court, particularly if there is a history of scepticism or outright rejection of perceived international "intervention" and a strong if misguided, sense of sovereignty at play. Having civilian legal institutions investigating past abuses by the military is one example of how national prosecutions can contribute to transition by fostering democratic civil–military relations. There are also benefits to be gained from citizens who were victims using their own national institutions and demanding that those institutions recognise their equality and their suffering. Finally, the international community should be aware of what could be achieved in the local system if even some of the massive resources used to create and operate international or foreign legal processes were invested nationally.

all the more necessary if the truth-seeking body is an international one which will cease to exist and whose staff will depart once its work is done. Domestic legal systems need to be encouraged and supported as much as possible by the international community to take an active role in the post conflict period given that, over and above the need to respond to past abuses, an effective criminal justice system is essential to any new democracy.

III. THE GUATEMALAN EXPERIENCE

The Guatemalan, Commission for Historical Clarification, CHC demonstrated the benefits of truth-seeking under a wide mandate with less focus on individual responsibility. It did not seek to provide accountability but instead to make a vital step towards eventual accountability, national reflection and the implementation of measures designed to ensure non repetition.[17] The CHC did not consider itself an evidence-gathering exercise for prosecutors or an alternative to criminal prosecutions, nor was it perceived as such by the public. This allowed the CHC to take advantage of its many strengths, which are discussed in more detail below. Its weaknesses, in my view, lay in the lack of forward planning as to how to maximise the impact of the CHC report, and on how the report and the information gathered could later be of assistance in criminal prosecutions.

In 1945, a revolutionary liberal government came to power in Guatemala as a result of efforts by both the national armed forces and a population which was at breaking point after a series of undemocratic and repressive regimes. It was an attempt to set the country on a path of social and economic reform, countering a long history of dictatorship and political clientelism which had perpetuated massive economic inequality in the country. In 1954 however, with the armed assistance of the United States government, Guatemala's second revolutionary President was forcibly removed from office.

The coup was intimately linked to United States' economic interests in the country and fuelled by larger worries that the President had developed communist leanings. (Not long before, he had sanctioned a large scale land reform programme to benefit rural peasants living in poverty.) A series of military regimes was to follow,

[17] The peace agreement creating the CHC describes the purpose of truth-seeking exercise as "a contribution towards the aim of ensuring non-repetition".

prompting dissident soldiers and civilian Marxist groups to join in taking up arms against the state. The ensuing conflict, which would continue for more than three decades, began in 1962. The armed forces however began to shift towards a "democratic" form of governance in 1982, albeit by way of a project which began with a military coup and which would require a preliminary stage of "pacification." This would be achieved through mass violence and terror in order to annihilate the insurgents along with those civilians (particularly indigenous Mayan civilians) deemed to be communist sympathisers. I will mention later the current impact of the military-controlled democracy which was the ultimate aim of the armed forces.[18]

Due to an array of factors occurring nationally and internationally,[19] the Presidents of El Salvador, Guatemala and Nicaragua met in 1987 to sign the Esquipulas II agreement and thereby assume the task of securing peace in the region. This agreement was to be the key impetus towards ending Guatemala's armed conflict through negotiation. The negotiations took place between April 1991 and December 1996[20] and finally brought the conflict, which had left some 200,000 civilians dead or disappeared, to a close.

A truth commission for Guatemala was conceived of during the ensuing talks between the government and the leadership of the armed insurgent forces (which had by then formed a coalition called the URNG or Guatemalan National Revolutionary Unity). It is worth mentioning three important points relating to the peace negotiations which inform a current analysis of the search for truth and justice in post-conflict Guatemala.

First, the country had in theory experienced electoral democracy since 1986, long before the signing of the peace accords, but fraud was rife, participation low and the military clearly in control of the

---

[18] For more detail see JENNIFER SCHIRMER, THE GUATEMALAN MILITARY PROJECT (1998).

[19] It is said that these included intense international pressure on the regions leaders and that in Guatemala the military was swayed by the prospect of the continuing human, financial and political costs in a conflict which, although the state had by far the more powerful military position, it had little prospect of an outright and conclusive victory.

[20] For an overview of the negotiations and positions of the parties see HÉCTOR ROSADA-GRANADOS, EL LADO OCULTO DE LAS NEGOCIACIONES DE PAZ, (THE HIDDEN SIDE OF THE PEACE NEGOTIATIONS) (1998). Mr. Rosada was a member of the government negotiating team and is currently a respected military and political analyst.

civilian administrations. Notwithstanding, the armed forces entered the peace negotiations in 1991 firm in the view that Guatemala's democratic transition had fact begun back in March 1982 with the military coup which brought General Efraín Ríos Montt to power. The army still considers itself responsible for creating the Guatemalan democracy and this view shapes its current actions and attitudes towards that democracy. As guardian of democracy, the military's old definition of "internal enemy" has now been modified to "enemy of democracy." In the latter category, one will now find not only drug traffickers, mafia members and delinquents, but also human rights and popular organisations which, in the army's view, present a threat to public order. This is an obvious hang-over from the army's anti-communist doctrine of the cold war era.[21] The insurgency, the bulk of the population and international observers take a very different view of the emerging democracy. Even today, Guatemala is at best an electoral democracy and even then in name only; intimidation and bribery of many voters in the last two elections was commonplace, particularly in rural areas. For those who do not share the military outlook on democracy, the importance of truth-seeking and criminal justice in the Guatemalan transition is inextricably linked to the extent to which they can help break the cycle of military power over civilian government and state institutions.

Second, it is extremely important to see Guatemala's truth commission in the context of the global peace agreements. These agreements were designed not only to achieve a definitive ceasefire and address the effects of thirty-four years of armed conflict but also to deal with the original causes of that conflict. As a result, the agreements attempt to address such issues as land distribution, socio-economic provisions, the protection of human rights, equality of the indigenous peoples and fighting endemic racism, and, vitally, the reduction, reform and modernization of the armed forces. The work of the truth commission was therefore not seen as a gateway to the solution of a variety of social ills, or as a short cut to democracy and national reconciliation. This context is important because the public's expectations of the CHC were not unrealistic or exaggerated but necessarily bound up with its expectations of the peace agreements as a whole.

Third, during the peace negotiations the attitude of the state and guerrilla forces to truth-seeking was driven by their fear of future

[21] See Schirmer, *supra* note 18, chapter 11

criminal trials.[22] Both stressed that the only institution competent to ascribe individual criminal responsibility would be the national judiciary. The creation of a truth-seeking body was not proposed by either party to the negotiations. (Accounts given by two former peace negotiators differ as to who suggested it: one emphasises the role of civil society organisations joined together in the Civil Society Assembly, which made a range of direct proposals to the negotiating parties during the Oslo talks, while the other attributes the initiative to the intervention of international actors, in particular Norway and the United Nations, who were keen to repeat the earlier El Salvador peace package.) The United Nations offered to sponsor the initiative, giving the proposal international support. The army had instructed government negotiators that its initial position should demand that any truth commission would not publish its findings until fifty years hence, a position which, during the talks, was later lowered to five years. The five years would, in effect, be ten since the period would run from the date on which the report would be presented to the United Nations following a five-year investigation. Despite the final terms of the mandate, discussed below, current attitudes among military veterans, in whose ranks one finds most of those persons implicated in war crimes, revert to the same logic of the original army bargaining position: in the absence of any internal dialogue or policy on the matter, obstruction tactics are the norm in order to delay criminal prosecutions until such time as there are neither witnesses nor accused still living, and the evidence has deteriorated or been lost.[23]

The guerrilla groups meanwhile wanted the truth-seeking exercise to focus on state atrocities, including genocide. The massive level of state violence, as compared to the more sporadic but nonetheless serious abuses committed by the guerrillas, did give the insurgents

[22] This despite the fact that the military clearly had a greater capacity to delay or obstruct justice by non legal means than did the guerrilla groups.

[23] Recently, information has been obtained which shows political back-up for such a strategy. Rural peasants reported that the Guatemalan Peace Secretariat (Secretaría de la Paz, or SEPAZ) had approached indigenous villages where military personnel are said to have massacred hundreds of civilians. It is alleged that SEPAZ promised survivors financial reparation on the condition that they themselves performed the exhumation of mass graves and that they immediately inter any human remains they discover. This obviously contaminated any forensic evidence which could be used in trials. In another example, corroborated information which the author has received implicates a local prosecutor in illegally obstructing exhumations.

something of an advantage here but to this day there remains a profound polarization of Guatemalan society as to what the "real truth" of the armed conflict is. Against a backdrop of state propaganda geared towards equivalence of blame, this polarisation revolves around the allegation that the guerrillas, having lost the war militarily and politically, are now seeking to vindicate themselves by using the "truth" as a propaganda weapon and criminal trials of former military personnel as revenge. In familiarly racist rhetoric, military veterans and their sympathisers accuse the guerrillas (and human rights organisations) of having "duped" rural indigenous victims into exhuming mass graves and bringing criminal law suits. But the polarisation does not exclude marriages of convenience. Some former fighters on both sides now appear to have more in common with each other than the needs of the population. Former guerrilla fighters and leaders, who have since moved into politics, some even joining the political parties of their old military enemies, remain all too aware that pushing for trials of military personnel is a double-edged sword.[24] Most commentators would safely say that the current political left cannot be relied upon to actively support victims seeking prosecutions for atrocities committed by the state, or to oppose a blanket amnesty if one was to be proposed.

3.1. *The Mandate of the Guatemalan Commission for Historical Clarification*

The peace agreement creating what was to be the CHC[25] was finally signed in Oslo on 23 June 1994. In the end, the state accepted immediate publication of the CHC report on the basis that it would not pronounce on individual responsibility[26] for any crime (that being the function of the courts), although it could make findings of institutional responsibility for human rights abuses and international crimes. The report was not to have judicial effect, that is to say, it is not a legal finding of guilt. The Commission was to collect and

---

[24] There have already been several attempts to prosecute former insurgent commanders although none have so far reached trial.

[25] The full title is The Commission for Historical Clarification of the Violations of the Human Rights and Acts of Violence which have Caused Suffering to the Guatemalan Population.

[26] The military were taking something of a belt and braces approach by demanding amnesty and anonymity in the truth commission report, their ultimate fear being prosecution.

analyse all available evidence within a period of six months, which could be extended to twelve. Its task was to investigate human rights abuses, acts of violence and violations of international humanitarian law[27] during the entire conflict, a very tall order in such a short time. Government negotiators were adamant however that fulfilment of the peace agreement establishing the CHC would be dependent upon a new amnesty law being passed before investigations began.

3.2. *Amnesty*

The Law of National Reconciliation was approved by the Congress in May 1996.[28] It repealed previous amnesty legislation and permitted the granting of amnesty to all those involved in "political crimes and connected common crimes." At the insistence of the mediators, however, it excluded the grant of amnesty to anyone accused of genocide, torture, forced disappearance or crimes considered not to be subject to statutory limitation.[29] The 1996 law is considered, even by many of those strongly opposed to such measures, as an acceptable example of legal and political compromise in the circumstances which preserves criminal accountability for the most serious of crimes.[30] Nevertheless, it could be strongly argued that the principal reason behind the state accepting the exclusions of the above crimes was because the military permitted it to do so, convinced as it was of

[27] This focused mainly on common article 3 to the Geneva Conventions of 1949, as Guatemala did not ratify Additional Protocol II until 1987, after the most intense period of armed conflict.

[28] At the time of the Esquipulas Agreement, interested foreign states encouraged the passing of amnesty laws to benefit armed insurgents in Central America. (In Guatemala, crimes perpetrated by the military were already amnestied under a 1986 law.)

[29] This is a somewhat problematic use of legal terminology since Guatemala is not party to the Convention on the Non-Applicability of Statutory Limitations to War Crimes and Crimes Against Humanity. Even if a cast-iron case were made for the existence of the norm in international customary law, it is by no means certain that domestic courts in Guatemala would be willing to apply it. Victims presenting cases for prosecutions have therefore erred on the side of caution and lodged them prior to the twenty-year statutory limit.

[30] This runs counter to the argument that the more serious the atrocity and more widespread the responsibility among the populace, the less adequate or appropriate the criminal law is as a forum to deal with it. Though some expected a flood of applications for amnesty, it did not happen and judges have on the whole acted fairly and reasonably in applying the legislation. One should add that however that those applying have thus far not included former heads of state or other high profile personalities.

its ability to manipulate the legal system.[31] That confidence may yet turn out to have been serious miscalculation.

3.3. *The Work and Report of the Commission*

The CHC began its work in September 1997. It was in fact the second national effort to investigate the Guatemalan conflict, the first having been an initiative of the Catholic Church (Recuperación de la Memoria Histórica or REMHI). The head of the church project, Bishop Juan Gerardi, was murdered in front of his home on 26 April 1998, days after he publicly presented the report which implicated the military institution in the large-scale massacre of civilians. Although an important and excellent resource which the church has made great efforts to publicise among the population, to date the REMHI report has unfortunately not had a significant effect on state policy regarding the prosecution of individuals for atrocities committed during the conflict.[32]

To head up the CHC, three Commissioners were appointed – two Guatemalans and one German.[33] The professional[34] staff was largely made up of non-Guatemalans. Funding was provided by foreign governments and the European Union and, as sponsor of the commission, the United Nations system provided experts, materials and logistics. The CHC used teams of investigators based in the capital city and in many regional offices to collect testimonies and documentary information during an eight-month period. It submitted its final report in February 1999, concluding that some 160,000 civilians had been killed and 40,000 disappeared.

As well as the scale of the atrocities, the impact of ethnicity distinguishes the conflict from many of its continental counterparts. Indigenous Mayans make up around 60% of the population but the

[31] It may have been the case that the higher ranks who, due to their level of knowledge and involvement in planning or ordering the atrocities, would be more likely be accused of the international crimes excluded from the amnesty law nevertheless knew they had the power and influence to protect their impunity regardless of the terms of the 1996 Amnesty Law. During the peace negotiations, they may have been concerned as to the possible reaction from the rank and file if hundreds of names were to appear in a truth commission report – even if the amnesty law was perhaps more likely to benefit lower ranking servicemen.

[32] It also stopped short of accusing the military of having committed genocide.

[33] Respectively, Otilia Lux Cotí, Alfredo Balsells Tojo – a longstanding proponent of human rights protection in Guatemala – and Prof. Christian Tomuschat.

[34] As opposed to administrative and back-up personnel such as interpreters, drivers and caretakers.

CHC estimated that 83% of all victims during the 34 years were indigenous. The majority of these people perished in the two-year "pacification", a genocidal campaign of massacres between 1981 and 1983, on which the conclusions of the CHC were more forthright than the REMHI report.[35] Finally, 93% of all atrocities recorded by the CHC were attributed to the state military and paramilitary forces. The minimal level of military cooperation with the CHC doubtless affected this percentage and it is thought by some analysts that the guerrilla committed a slightly greater number of acts of violence against civilians.

Despite the terrible track record of Guatemala's justice system, which was heavily criticised in the report for its complicity in human rights abuses, the CHC encouraged prosecution of those responsible for the most serious crimes. In accordance with the exceptions to the amnesty law, and unlike its Salvadoran counterpart, the CHC Report recommended that criminal trials take place in Guatemalan courts and that they focus on those who planned and instigated crimes against humanity and serious violations of international humanitarian law. This was a clear nod towards prosecuting those in positions of military command or political power, no doubt mindful of the scarce resources and limited capacity of the legal system, as well as the massive numbers of perpetrators spread throughout the population.

3.4. *The Commission and Prosecutions*

In assessing the impact of the CHC on criminal prosecutions in legal terms, there are several key characteristics of the Guatemalan truth commission which are relevant:

1. it could not name alleged individual perpetrators in its report,
2. the report would not have judicial effect,
3. witnesses and those who provided documents were given complete confidentiality,
4. none of the information gathered was shared with prosecutors or the public either during or after the Commission's investigation.

In order to analyse the impact of each of these factors on subsequent criminal justice initiatives it is necessary to take into account the legal framework relative to the CHC's creation, its mandate, operations, report and the evidence it gathered. One should

---

[35] It concluded that "acts of" genocide had been committed against the indigenous population of certain geographical areas studied.

also be aware of the national laws which applied to the criminal prosecutions which were already under way during the Commission's investigation and those which have since commenced. As Guatemala did not have an international or hybrid criminal tribunal, any criminal trials relating to crimes committed during the conflict would be carried out by national courts. During the last half of the 1990s the task of investigating the atrocities and bringing criminal complaints therefore fell largely on victims and human rights organizations, given the lack of action on the part of the state prosecution service (Ministerio Público).

International or hybrid tribunals may have the capacity to create their own rules regarding admissibility and compellability of evidence gathered by a truth commission, and these can be agreed upon prior to the commencement of operations. Amendments to the national law may however be necessary to ensure there is no contradiction between the agreed framework of interrelations between truth seeking and prosecutorial bodies and the national law, for example on matters such as information sharing between the truth commission and the courts or issues of confidentiality *vis-à-vis* the public disclosure of testimonies or documents. If an international or hybrid tribunal does not have exclusive jurisdiction over the crimes to be investigated by a truth commission, and if national laws are not appropriately amended, then the potential exists for national tribunals to apply rules of disclosure of evidence which the truth commission may oppose but will be legally obligated to respect. In Guatemala's case, it was in the peace agreement between the government and the guerrilla forces that the CHC mandate was created, which specified that the report of the Commission would not name names, would not have judicial objectives or effects, and that the identity of witnesses and informants would be confidential. The legal effects of an agreement between a government and groups of citizens (in this case insurgent leaders) cannot however override the Constitution or the relevant national legislation.[36]

In addition to the peace agreement creating the CHC, one other document is particularly relevant – an Act of Congress[37] giving effect

[36] This has thus far been the prevailing legal interpretation in respect of all the peace agreements.

[37] This legislation was precipitated by a letter from the United Nations to the Guatemalan government in which it was proposed that the Convention on the Privileges and Immunities of the United Nations apply to the CHC commissioners and staff.

to an agreement between the United Nations and the Government to extend certain protections to the CHC. The CHC personnel would thereby enjoy immunity from arrest, detention, seizure of their equipment, legal actions resulting from their public statements and protection of documents. These safeguards were intended to ensure that the Commission could efficiently and safely carry out its work. The legislation also stated that the Secretary General of the United Nations has the duty to remove the immunity if it would obstruct justice. Notwithstanding this last possibility, it is important to note that the immunities did not in any event extend to protecting a person from prosecution in Guatemala if he or she fails to comply with a judicial order to disclose information. Such a scenario has not yet occurred but remains a real possibility. Under national law, Guatemalan judges have complete discretion to order the production of evidence of any nature and from any source[38] that is offered by the prosecution, the *querellante*[39] or the defence. The CHC's report and the information it gathered are therefore subject to the same rules as any other proof offered at trial.

3.4.1. *Naming Names*

That the CHC did not have the power to name names was not a significant disadvantage, for various reasons. On a purely practical level, given the positions of the negotiating parties it would have been practically impossible to reach agreement on the creation of a truth commission with such powers, and which could publish its findings in the short term.[40] Also, given that it is much easier to obtain positive identification and evidence against lower ranking members of the military and paramilitary groups, naming individuals could easily have directed attention away from the highest level planners and organisers of the atrocities. Despite keeping witness' details confidential, naming individual perpetrators could also increase the risk of

---

[38] Provided it has been not been obtained illegally and its disclosure would not violate Constitutional guarantees.

[39] A victim of a criminal act, together with various others individuals or groups, who may have *locus standi* such as a family member, or in certain cases a human rights organisation can petition the court to be a party to prosecutions proceedings. The *querellante* has wide powers, including petitioning judges to order investigative measures and lodging an alternative indictment if not satisfied with that offered by the state prosecutor.

[40] See comments, *supra* note 31.

reprisals against those people who are known locally as being the only eye-witnesses to the events, as well as against family members who have spoken out, for example by seeking exhumations of mass graves. The latter is one of the possible consequences which should be fully discussed between truth commission investigators and witnesses before testimony is taken.

On a legal level, the CHC report, even it had named individual perpetrators, could not be used as direct evidence of guilt because it would not constitute sufficient evidence under normal criminal standards. Although the report can suggest lines of inquiry, a full investigation of the crimes by prosecutors would always be necessary.[41] If a truth commission does not have the power to compel witnesses or evidence, and lacks mechanisms to provide the right of reply and rigorous forms of assessing the veracity of evidence received, it can run into variety of legal problems if it names alleged criminals, not least injunctions and defamation actions.[42] More seriously, it could prejudice victims who seek justice in future criminal cases if the accused successfully argues that he cannot have a fair trial due to negative pretrial publicity caused by a truth commission report.[43] These issues can understandably create frustration for a truth-seeking body which intends to name alleged perpetrators. Nevertheless, to regard due process guarantees as "obstacles" to the truth is to run a real risk of damaging the legitimacy and credibility of the body itself, thereby undermining the impact of its conclusions.

The absence of named perpetrators in the CHC report has not adversely affected those criminal prosecutions underway during the CHC investigations or those which have started since the report's publication. Naming accused in the CHC report may have led to more criminal complaints being lodged but the difficulties of finding witnesses to come forward and the lack of resources affecting human rights groups and the prosecution service would probably have mitigated against a massive increase in the number of prosecutions

[41] Particularly where the standard of corroboration accepted by truth seeking staff is not a criminal one.

[42] This type of legal action was often used by alleged perpetrators in South Africa and obstructed the work schedule of the Truth and Reconciliation Commission.

[43] This risk increases if, as in many transitions, judges are under pressure not to convict, are open to bribery or are partial due to political bias.

which could have resulted.[44] The outcome was that, instead of focusing on how many individual crimes could be linked to identifiable perpetrators, the CHC took full advantage of the function which in my view a truth-seeking body is much better placed than the criminal law to fulfil, that is gathering complex and wide-ranging information about historical patterns of conduct and the nature of the violence. The CHC report exposed massive levels of institutional responsibility or complicity in crimes against civilians. It analysed the destabilising impact of socio-economic marginalisation, racism and foreign interests before and during the armed conflict. It put into context the work of the popular peasant movement, student bodies, journalists, churches and trades unions. The CHC report provides a very rich and important source not only on these issues but also on the objectives, tactics and lines of command of the state and guerrilla forces. The report is therefore not only an excellent and important contribution to historical study but will also hopefully provoke reflection and re-assessment of institutions and social values far beyond the phenomenon of individual criminal conduct.

3.4.2. *Lack of Judicial Effect*

To date, extracts of the CHC report have been presented as evidence in two trials relating to the murder of Archbishop Gerardi in 1998[45] and the murder of anthropologist Myrna Mack in 1990. The extracts were lodged as indirect evidence and in both cases the most useful element of the report related to information on the chain of operational command and information flow within the Presidential Guard,[46] of which the majority of the accused were former members. The report also assisted the prosecution in outlining the policy followed by the Presidential Guard towards perceived opponents of the state. In their decisions, convicting some accused and acquitting

---

[44] At this stage of the transition, a flood of cases against former paramilitaries or low to middle ranking military or a serious possibility thereof, is not without risks. Although a military coup is very unlikely, the potential exists to ignite increased intimidation of survivors, forensic anthropologists, who exhume mass graves and human rights groups. Some fear that a flood of cases relating to widespread atrocities could provoke a new blanket amnesty although to desist from seeking any criminal accountability on this basis would achieve the same objective as such an amnesty.

[45] Which occurred after the peace agreements were signed and therefore fell outside the remit of the CHC investigation.

[46] Estado Mayor Presidencial.

others, judges did not exclude the CHC report as admissible evidence. Although one cannot argue legal precedent before a Guatemalan tribunal,[47] this acceptance of the report as a legitimate source of information was warmly welcomed by victims' groups and human rights organizations.[48]

The CHC report cannot be a direct evidentiary basis for a finding of guilt. Nor would a prudent prosecutor use any truth commission report as such. The strength of the report lies in its breadth, not in its findings on individual criminal acts.[49] It brings together and analyses information from many public sources of the era which, along with other evidence, can help to demonstrate the state of knowledge of accused who held positions of command at the time. Its analysis of the political, economic and military context can also point towards possible motives for the crimes. In addition, by bringing together information on thousands of atrocities, if crimes against humanity are charged the report could help demonstrate a context of widespread or systematic attack on the civilian population, thereby assisting the prosecutor in establishing the material elements of the crime.[50] In both the abovementioned cases however, sufficient testimonial and documentary evidence to justify conviction was produced by the prosecutor. As such, there was no need for the judiciary to use the report as its primary source of evidence, rendering the judgments

[47] Except in constitutional matters where three rulings of the Constitutional Court on the same point will generally be regarded as having crystallised a rule on the matter.

[48] The defense lawyers in the Gerardi and Mack cases objected to the CHC report being lodged but their argument was confused. After correctly stating that the peace agreement delimiting the CHC mandate could not override national criminal procedure rules, they then attempted to rely on the very provisions in that agreement as to the report's lack of judicial effect. Questions regarding the scope and effect of truth commission mandates and rules, insofar as they can affect criminal trials in national courts, are matters which will ultimately be decided by judges.

[49] Dates and locations of some massacres and details of the number and identity of victims do not always correspond in different sections of the CHC report. In certain cases, the narration of events contradicts eye witnesses and other evidence subsequently obtained by way of more detailed and long term investigation with communities.

[50] Using a truth commission report in these ways is likely to be significantly easier in civil jurisdictions in which the judge is not bound by such strict admissibility rules as are generated in most common law jurisdictions.

rather less controversial than they otherwise might have been as regards the CHC.[51] The cases currently pending prosecution will similarly not rely on the CHC report but on the results of criminal investigations.

Reference to the report can also link a trial to the plight of other victims given that each case which goes to trial is often emblematic of thousands of other similar atrocities. Using the report in trials (held in packed courtrooms in the presence of the national and international media) can also link the prosecutions to the wider armed conflict and therefore to everyone in society. In this way the trial is not just a formal matter between a judge, a victim and a perpetrator but an opportunity for public reflection, a high profile test for civilian institutions and a measure of the rule of law. Being internationally sponsored report, reference to the CHC also emphasises international concern regarding the Guatemalan justice system and the legitimacy of recourse to criminal justice. As such it can raise the awareness of the international community and increase the political pressure on the justice system to act impartially.

3.4.3. *Confidentiality of Sources*

The above comments relate to the use of the CHC report itself in criminal proceedings. There is however no way of knowing whether the CHC obtained information that could have been of great use to prosecutors or defence lawyers in the Gerardi and Mack murder trials, or which could help demonstrate guilt or innocence in future prosecutions of persons accused of committing atrocities against Guatemalan civilians. The confidentiality afforded to persons who gave testimony or documents to the CHC and whose personal safety was at risk was of course entirely justified,[52] but there is an important distinction to be drawn between revealing the names of witnesses or informants who have testified or provided documentary information,

[51] It will be interesting to see how Spanish judges deal with the CHC Report in processing the criminal complaint lodged in Spain by Nobel Peace Prize winner Rigoberta Menchú which relies strongly on the findings of the CHC.

[52] As regards many victims who gave information, confidentiality was clearly necessary given the level of intimidation suffered by those who had previously publicly denounced military violence. The decision to make public declarations or initiate criminal prosecutions must always be an informed one. In the experience of the Centro para Acción Legal en Derechos Humanos (CALDH), a Guatemalan human rights groups working with massacre survivors, fear of reprisal has been the major reason cited by those who do not wish to participate in criminal justice initiatives.

and revealing those statements or documents whether wholly or partially. If disclosure would implicate the source and put his or her safety at risk, then confidentiality is obviously crucial. (In Guatemala, existing law would generally protect against such disclosure.[53]) However it is important to appreciate that there may be circumstances in which certain documents can be made public without revealing or implying the identity of the person who provided them.

Truth commissions can be given the power to ask each person who offers testimony or documents whether or not they would agree to its future complete or partial publication. This could allow important information, which could not be linked to an individual source, to enter the public domain. It will depend as much on individual motive as on the national circumstances whether confidentiality will elicit cooperation and accurate information. In Guatemala, the blanket guarantee of confidentiality to all interviewees did not alter the position of the overwhelming majority of military personnel and veterans who had decided not to cooperate with the CHC. Finally, the risk attached to revealing certain information may lessen with time. Decisions to prohibit access to information on the basis of confidentiality should therefore be reviewed in order to promote knowledge and empowerment of the population as regards its own past.

3.4.4. *No Information Sharing*

The ultimate fate of the information gathered by the CHC was left up to the parties to the peace agreement and as a result is apparently now held in secure storage in the United States. A vast amount of open-source information gathered by the CHC and referred to in its report was and is unavailable to the public – meaning that prosecutors, victims and human rights groups must

[53] In addition to professional privilege, if the information is in the hands of the state, the Constitution includes certain guarantees based on confidentiality; a forthcoming Freedom of Information Act will attempt to balance public interest with non disclosure rules. It remains to be seen however what the outcome would be if a Guatemalan prosecutor or defence lawyer were to successfully request that a judge order the production of documents gathered by the CHC. What one can say with relative certainty is that the legal framework within which the judicial decision would be taken, would not be the peace agreement defining the CHC mandate (due to its legal status) nor the Act of Congress allowing immunities (as it does not extend to such situations), but the Constitution, Criminal Procedure Act and the relevant legislation of each profession governing professional privilege.

repeat the same time consuming and often expensive research. There were plans to permit access to parts of the information for academic research but these appear to have been shelved. Since this article went to press, the United Nations decided to donate the public documents gathered by the Commission for Historical Clarification to the newly inaugurated Peace Library at University of San Carlos in Guatemala City. The Head of Mission for Guatemala, Tom Koenigs, explained that the 5 year delay in granting public access to this information was due to the failure of the Congress to comply with the CEH recommendation to create a Foundation for Peace and Harmony, to which Mr Koenigs said the UN intended to donate the documents. The details of the arrangement said to exist between the Guatemalan government and the United Nations as to how long the information it gathered will be kept secret are unclear and the issue does not seem to be addressed in any of the relevant formal and publicly known agreements. Aside from the risk of break-ins if the documentation were held in Guatemala, it is possible that the physical removal of the information from the country was also an attempt to avoid it falling prey to petitions for discovery in national courts. The matter of information sharing should have been openly debated and publicly presented before the CHC began its work. If prosecutors are not even to have access to the open source information gathered, then the consequences must be accepted. What is clear is that, without having seen the information gathered by a truth commission, no prosecutor should speculate that the information is unlikely to be of use to him in criminal proceedings.

Justifications for the secrecy of all information gathered by a truth commission must therefore be robust, transparent and have clearly defined objectives.

There is an important distinction to be drawn here on the matter of information sharing and that is between the situation, in which a truth commission provides prosecutors with some or all of the evidence it has gathered – a proactive role – and the situation, where there is already a prosecution under way and the parties request the judge to order the truth commission to hand over certain information – a reactive role. At the time the CHC was gathering evidence, only a handful of criminal prosecutions relating to the conflict were under way, all of which had been initiated and pursued by victims represented by local human rights organisations. In future trials however, if disclosure of documentation collected by the CHC were to be judicially ordered the matter would be subject only to the following rules. In the Guatemalan Constitution there are two limitations on disclosure of information: the first prohibits disclosure if it would damage national security interests; the second allows preservation of confidentiality to protect the source of the information. The latter has been interpreted to mean that the information should not be disclosed if it would lead to the person's physical integrity being threatened. The only other legislative limits of confidentiality relate to professional privilege (principally lawyers, clergy, doctors and journalists). Even in cases in which these limitations are argued, the information must in any event be handed over to the judiciary, who will then decide whether or not to disclose it.

3.5. *Recent Obstacles and Successes in the Search for Truth and Justice in Guatemala*

In recent years, the focus of the discourse in sharing lessons learned from post-conflict truth commissions has focussed largely on how to create mandates, relationships with amnesty laws and matters of operations, information management and logistics. This has had positive effects for those areas but effort is also required on the "before and after" if truth seeking is to have the desired impact; the same applies to prosecutions and other transitional initiatives. In the 'before', category are the above mentioned technical issues of the inter-relationship if both truth seeking and prosecutions are contemplated. But the question should still always be asked whether a truth seeking program, prosecutions or other initiatives are appropriate. Adequate consultation with the public and especially with victims[54] should be the ideal to be achieved – even if in practice continued hostilities and insecurity, language, poverty or funding will shape the reality of the exercise. Too often, speed is an overriding factor which serves the interests of the new authorities and the international community more than the needs of the population itself.

[54] This does not mean simply representatives of non governmental organisations or civil society groups unless one is sure that these organisations do in fact consult regularly with the population which they speak for.

As to efforts after a truth commission has published its findings, the follow-up will be central to maximising impact.[55] Since 2000, the United Nations Mission – which was distributing the CHC report – has been annually reducing its national staff by half. Dissemination and follow-up efforts by the Human Rights Ombudsman and non-governmental organisations (NGOs) have been erratic: in addition to finding suitable staff and funding to carry out this work, the already overstretched Ombudsman's office and NGOs, face vast logistical problems in reaching the rural highland population. The Catholic Church has been disseminating the REMHI report with more success through its network of local pastoral offices since 1998. This, together with the notoriety of Gerardi's murder, has had the result that the REMHI report is probably more widely known in rural areas than the CHC Report. Scores of requests for exhumations of clandestine graves from villages are pending before local prosecutors, but this has largely been the result of word of mouth from neighbouring villages or outreach by churches and concerned forensic teams.

While it is true to say that both the REMHI and CHC initiatives have had an effect in legitimising demands for exhumations, justice and reparations made by some Mayan and human rights groups, one should not assume that the same applies to the rural peasant class of Guatemala. The focus of the "popular movement", comprised of organised peasant groups with a very large rural Mayan membership nationwide, remains firmly on economic and land rights. It is in essence a continuation of their struggle of many decades if not centuries. In a country suffering extreme poverty and, in recent years, famine, it is not a surprise that these matters are the priority for thousands of Guatemalans who, while being victims of genocide or other wartime atrocities, cannot feed themselves or their families.

[55] The CHC Report was presented in the capital city and first published in Spanish. Parts of it were then translated into some indigenous Mayan languages. Although this is a laudable exercise, it is of limited utility particularly in the short term because the vast majority of speakers of those languages do not read. Efforts to have the report taught in schools and universities have so far been piecemeal and without governmental backing. Little use was made of local radio to publicise the conclusions and recommendations of the report, although this is the most effective way of reaching the Guatemalan rural population. Some civil society groups produced "popular" graphic versions. The United Nations mission to Guatemala MINUGUA, the Human Rights Ombudsman's office (Procuradoría de Derechos Humanos, or PDH), and human rights organisations undertook local workshops to disseminate the report but without central coordination, planning or sufficient funds to mount medium to longer term activities.

Some will be members of both popular organisations and Mayan groups that seek accountability for past crimes but vast numbers of rural war victims (including survivors who gave testimony to the CHC) remain unaware not only of the report but, according to national polls, of the Guatemalan Peace Accords as a whole[56] and therefore there is much work ahead in publicising these documents.

As to the political impact, in the public ceremony to hand over the report, then President Alvaro Arzú refused to receive it personally. There followed complete silence from the government on the matter for four months. The first public statement made by President Arzú regarding the CHC flatly rejected its conclusion that acts of genocide were perpetrated by the state army.[57] Since then, there has been no real demonstration of government commitment to actively take up the CHC recommendations or the content of the peace agreements as

---

[56] Following the conclusion of the CHC's work, it would have been preferable to have had regional formal presentations of the final report, especially in the rural areas which suffered the brunt of the violence and where the testimonies of victims demonstrated the immense scale and cruelty of the army's counterinsurgency methods. There was a clear necessity to implement a structured "post truth-seeking programme" assisted by the United Nations and the international community, in coordination with human rights groups across the country. This would have allowed the CHC report to be shared and debated with the victims who made it possible. Crucially, in order for the truth to empower and lead to real effects for victims, they must not only have access to the report, but also be in a position to make informed decisions regarding their options in the light of that truth. Such options could include exhumations, criminal trials, mental health provision, seeking reparations, pushing for education regarding the past, further investigations into the truth of what happened to relatives, action combating racism and social exclusion, and seeking responses from perpetrators and the state. In order to take up any of these options, victims need long term sustained support from organised civil society and the international community. One must carry out detailed research with a wide base of consultation to determine impact. As yet there has been no such research carried out in Guatemala which has canvassed the opinions of the general public, including the rural indigenous population.

[57] President Alvaro Arzú's first public comment following the presentation of the Commission's report in February 1999 was to the newspaper El Periódico on 30 June 1999. After his protracted silence, he said he did not believe genocide had occurred in Guatemala. I would regard Arzu's attitude and comment as openly critical of the CHC; cf. Rachel Seider, *War, Peace and Memory Politics in Central America*, in The Politics of Memory: Transitional Justice in Democratizing Societies 177 (Alexandra Barahona de Brit et al., eds., 2001). President of Congress Efraín Ríos Montt (leader of the Guatemalan Republican Front (FRG) party who presided over a genocidal campaign against indigenous civilians in 1982) accused the United Nations truth commission of an "emotional rather than legal" analysis of the conflict, Prensa Libre, 1 April 2000.

a whole. It is hoped that the statements in February 2004 by current President Oscar Berger to the effect that he will "re-launch" the peace agreements will be followed up by concrete actions toward their implementation. Recent efforts at cabinet level to persuade Mr. Berger to publicly accept the conclusions of the CHC report are currently stalled.

Had the state, and particularly the armed forces,[58] accepted responsibility for the atrocities attributed to it,[59] moved to implement the CHC recommendations, carried out the removal of those responsible from office, and offered reparations to victims, many victims might not have felt it necessary to seek criminal trials. Following presentation of the CHC report, in the face of outright denial and obstruction of any attempt to restore their dignity, criminal justice was a clear option. Only in 2002 did the current government begin negotiating a national reparations plan, yet to be implemented, which was in fact forced upon it by a powerful state paramilitary lobby seeking "back-pay".[60]

How did the CHC initiative affect the armed forces and veterans? The vast majority of those implicated in wartime atrocities have now retired, although the internal factionalism currently being experienced within the armed forces on a range of issues is related closely to the trafficking of influence by still powerful retired officers. The scope of this influence is not restricted to the armed forces, stretching to political parties and even delimiting government policy; as such healthy civil–military relations are still a long way off. It is likely that the political manipulation of ex paramilitaries during the 1990s will be now replaced by military manipulation for the purposes of social

[58] The URNG, now a political party but with little congressional representation, accepted responsibility for those abuses detailed in the report.

[59] In mid-2000, the state publicly accepted responsibility in some cases before the Inter-American Human Rights Commission, although many of those cases remained unresolved for years and the victims without compensation, leading to severe criticisms that it was simply window dressing for the benefit of the government's international image.

[60] Former President Alfonso Portillo thanked these paramilitary groups for their services to the fatherland despite the CHC finding that they were responsible for 11% of all human rights violations committed during the conflict: Presidential speech, Chiquimula, 10 July 2002, Diario de Centro América 11th July 2002. Current President Berger has pledged to honour the payments of "compensation" to these paramilitaries promised by Portillo. Retired General Efraín Ríos Montt, has had an agreement with these former paramilitaries since the mid nineties to financially compensate them in return for their votes and assistance in intimidating their local communities into voting for his party, the FRG.

control, putting back on track the original intention of the armed forces.

The current leadership of the institution has not pronounced on the CHC's findings but it is clear from the statements of the more vocal veterans that the content of the CHC Report is hotly disputed by those who served during the conflict. The creation, composition, financing, investigation and conclusions of the report have been variously criticised or rejected by military sympathizers in the national press. United Nations staff, truth commissioners and foreign donors have been accused of communist bias. Victims, relatives and human rights lawyers are routinely portrayed by veterans and their supporters as having leftist leanings, seeking self enrichment from foreign donors and being bent on revenge and obstructing peace and reconciliation.[61] On prime time television an army veteran attacked CHC supporters who "think they are the owners of the only truth".[62] While there are some former military officers, who have recognized that "excesses" were committed by rogue troops, this has not yet had any discernible effect on military or governmental policy regarding prosecutions. The strongest sign of military and veteran opinion regarding the truth-seeking exercise is that after the publication of the CHC Report they backed their own publications detailing what they consider to be the "real" truth of the Guatemalan armed conflict.[63] In terms of truth-seeking being a catalyst for changes in the military, be it in outlook or in concrete reforms, the current signals are not positive although longer-term analysis will permit a more thorough understanding.

Turning to criminal trials, despite entrenched views on the ideology and motives of victims and their lawyers, it has become more difficult for the military, veterans and those sectors of society

[61] In a statement typical of this phenomenon, one of the three soldiers convicted in the Gerardi case labelled the Catholic Church lawyers communist guerrillas (Siglo XXI, 9th October 2002).

[62] On the live television debate programme Libre Encuentro (similar in format to the British "Question Time") in September 2002, the Chairman of the veterans groups Asociación de Veteranos Militares de Guatemala (AVEMILGUA) accused the United Nations, foreign countries who financially assisted the CHC and Christian Tomuschat, Commissioner of the CHC, of communist leanings.

[63] See for example "Venganza y Juicio Historico" (Revenge and Historical Judgment) by former officer Mario A. Merida, a book regarded by his supporters as setting the record straight and by his detractors as revisionist polemic.

who continue to support them, to dismiss the national legal system as an illegitimate arbiter of responsibilities for past atrocities.[64] This is in part due to a combination of the Guatemalan public's reverence for the law and a strong sense of nationalism and sovereignty. This is particularly prevalent among the military which, during and after the armed conflict, continually used or abused the law as its frame of reference and justification for its actions.[65] Former military personnel accused of human rights abuses regularly invoke the Constitution in regard to the duties of the armed forces and to assert their rights to due process. The armed forces also harbour a long-standing and somewhat contradictory suspicion of what they see as international intervention in Guatemalan affairs, one expression of which is the position only national courts have the necessary authority to determine the truth of the past and the guilt or innocence of individuals.[66] Although the army usually refuses to produce documents when asked to do so by a judge, military accused have generally responded positively to court citations and participated fully with defence counsel in criminal trials. Several have been remanded in custody prior to or jailed following trial and pending appeal.[67] Recent events demonstrate that today's battle is less between two versions of the "truth" than between a legal system slowly finding its feet and a military institution seeking to retain the control it had over that system throughout the armed conflict.

[64] Whether they would consider a written judgment as the "truth" of the matter is a discussion beyond the scope of this comment.

[65] See Schirmer, *supra* note 18, chapter 6.

[66] Until early 2004, the Guatemalan Presidential human rights commission (COPREDEH) charged with representing the state before the Inter-American Commission on Human Rights (IACHR) took this view to particularly confused lengths due to misunderstanding the difference between human rights obligations and criminal law. In a case in which the author represented a victim of abduction and torture, COPREDEH advised the IACHR that it could not negotiate any friendly settlement which would involve accepting state responsibility for the conduct until such time as a national court had convicted an individual state agent. The reason given was protection of the exclusive jurisdiction and impartiality of national criminal courts.

[67] A notorious exception was the freeing of former military officer Juan Valencia Osorio pending his appeal against conviction for the murder of Myrna Mack. When his appeal was rejected, specialist police officers arrived at his home to return him to custody only to find an army unit blocking the street. After the unit had left, police gained access to the area to discover that Valencia had absconded. Prosecutors are now investigating military personnel for their role in assisting a fugitive.

Since the end of the armed conflict there have been several convictions in domestic courts of military and paramilitary personnel for wartime atrocities. The first conviction in relation to mass civilian deaths at the hands of the military was secured in the case of the massacre of Río Negro, only one of more than 600 massacres which the CHC estimates occurred during the conflict. In Río Negro in March 1982, soldiers and paramilitaries killed 177 women and children, raping many beforehand, one month after murdering their menfolk near the same village.[68] In another similar case, a conviction was obtained in 1999 and upheld on appeal, against a slightly higher-ranking paramilitary[69] for the massacre of civilians in the village of Tululche. More recently, following the conviction of a lower ranking member of the Presidential Guard, an army colonel[70] was convicted in October 2002 of the murder of Myrna Mack. Although the murder of Bishop Gerardi occurred post-conflict, the crime itself was typical of earlier extra-judicial executions. Three army officials[71] and a priest were convicted in 2001 of the murder of the Bishop. The case is currently at appeal.[72] Currently, state prosecutors are investigating eight Military High Command members accused of genocide, crimes against humanity and violations of international humanitarian law. Former military President Mejía Víctores is also under investigation in relation to mass forced disappearances.

These gains have been largely made possible by the efforts of determined victims, who have managed to secure the backing of human rights NGOs and other civil society groups. They have taken place amidst severe intimidation of judges, prosecutors, witnesses, forensic scientists and lawyers. Judges' homes have been the subject of machine gun and grenade attacks and state prosecutors forced into

[68] The first trial, which took place before the CHC report was published, also resulted in a conviction. Paramilitary members are currently serving long periods of imprisonment and the local Prosecutor is seeking to bring indictments against others involved, including the local army commander.

[69] Candido Noriega, who was in direct command of local peasants organised by the armed forces from 1981 onward into community level paramilitary groups originally named Civil Self Defence Patrols (Patrullas de Autodefensa Civil).

[70] Col. Juan Valencia Osorio, Chief of the Security Department, Presidential Guard (Estado Mayor Presidencial). He is currently a fugitive, see above.

[71] Col. Disreal Lima/Capt. Lima Oliva and José Obdulio Villanueva.

[72] The State Prosecutor is challenging the competence of the appeal court ruling on the basis that it revisited witness credibility, an issue which is outside appeal court jurisdiction.

exile. A former Attorney General was the subject of a shooting attack in which he escaped injury.[73] It is clear nonetheless that prosecutors and judges are making headway in some cases and are trying to overcome a long history of intimidation and corruption as well as the serious obstacles in their path relating to resources and training. The fact that the CHC recommended criminal trials[74] was perhaps the most important aspect of the relationship between truth and justice in Guatemala. It legitimised victims' demands, brought a degree of international pressure to bear on prosecutors and also helped NGOs persuade some donors to assist them in investigating crimes and bringing prosecutions. That said, the recommendations of the CHC and the enthusiasm with which they were initially met by the international community[75] and donor organisations have not translated into the financial and moral support necessary in the medium and long-term for the prosecutions initiatives to reach their conclusion. The truth-seeking exercise having been completed, civil society organisations are often advised that their projects should now "concentrate on reconciliation".[76]

[73] It is likely that this attack was related to former Attorney General Mr. Carlos De León's United States-backed attempts to prosecute former high ranking military intelligence figures for drug and contraband related activities, rather than his institution's investigation of crimes committed during the armed conflict, although one cannot be sure. The State Department and U.S. Embassy in Guatemala issued a number of damning statements during the week of 7 October 2002 regarding the alleged criminal activities of former army generals. The Attorney General then initiated investigations against five of them. The United States also publicly denounced the use of clandestine units linked to army intelligence to attack human rights defenders seeking justice for past military crimes, which may yet be investigated by a UN backed special commission.

[74] Recommendations 46 and 47.

[75] The European Parliament issued two Resolutions supporting prosecutions on 18 May 2000 and 14 June 2001 and a further Resolution condemning acts of intimidation against victims, witnesses and lawyers involved in prosecutions initiatives: P5_TA(2002)0189, European Parliament.

[76] How this reconciliation can occur when the state has not only refused to accept responsibility for the atrocities attributed to it by the CHC but has awarded former military personnel directly implicated in mass atrocities with high level political office is difficult to see. Perversely, the idea that prosecutions might rock the boat and lead to instability for the emerging democracy comes at a time when Guatemalan military and political analysts consider criminal accountability more vital than ever to break the cycle of military control of democratic activity.

3.6. *Conclusion*

Despite the obstacles, the Guatemalan experience follows Argentina and Chile in showing that it is important not to underestimate the capacity for long-term struggle for accountability. This is particularly notable in societies that have suffered extended periods of repression. Accountability is understood as a lengthy but necessary process, which can also bring its own benefits along the way, such as empowerment of citizens to mobilise, articulate demands and to lobby government on many other issues. Accountability has become more not less crucial in Guatemala with the passage of time. While President Berger makes efforts to prosecute corrupt officials and to improve Guatemala's image with investors and the international community, the massive underlying obstacles to democracy remain untouched. Military power and economic exclusion survived the conflict and the peace intact. In fact, one could characterise the current government as a modernised version of the traditional oligarchy–army coalition which never really loosened its grip on political and economic power in the Republic. Military power, whether official or exercised by retired officers, continues to actively delimit democratic participation and is bolstered further by impunity for past crimes.[77] The tentacles of organised crime, in particular drug trafficking, have extended to public administration, official and clandestine security forces and powerful former and current military figures. In many rural areas, the drugs trade offers many a dangerous escape from severe poverty.

Impunity in Guatemala is a tangible barrier to healthy civil–military relations and to building trust between the populace and the military. The difficulties of combating this situation are compounded by the demands made on the justice system both by victims of war crimes and victims of today's unprecedented levels of common and organised crime. As high profile politicians and civil servants are prosecuted daily for stealing public money, whether and how the state will respond to the genocide will be a true test of Guatemala's commitment to racial equality, democracy and the rule of law. If the

[77] Mr. Berger recently announced budget and personnel cuts in the armed forces. This is an important aspect of the peace agreements, however in reality, although it will infuriate hard liners, it is something of a no-cost decision for the government. Many retired military figures who support the continuance of the controlled democracy project are in fact now part of the political scene, and can therefore manage the project from their new positions rather than having to engage in factional fighting within the institution and among influential veterans.

legal system cannot respond to the worst atrocities of the past and hold state agents accountable, then it is failing and that bodes ill for any emerging democracy. The Guatemalan legal system has produced unexpected and brave convictions in a small number of cases. More than legal ability, resources or countering intimidation, experience in Guatemala shows that it will be international pressure on the government and prosecuting authorities which will determine if the legal system will rise to the occasion regarding the highest level military personnel currently under investigation for wartime atrocities.

NOTE: *About CALDH and the Prosecution of Genocide in Guatemala*

The Centro para Acción Legal en Derechos Humanos (CALDH) is a Guatemalan non-profit organisation based in the country's capital city. Since 1994, it has worked with rural indigenous victims of the armed conflict, giving free legal advice[78] and is the legal representative of The Association for Justice and Reconciliation (AJR). Founded in May 2000, the AJR is a grass-roots group of indigenous communities, where state troops carried out massacres of civilians during the Guatemalan military's counter-insurgency campaign of 1981–1983. In 1996, CALDH's legal team began an extensive criminal investigation and preparatory work for a domestic prosecutions initiative. This led to the presentation by AJR in 2000 and 2001 of the first and currently the only criminal complaints (querellas) of their kind in national courts. The accused are eight members of the Guatemalan Military High Commands of 1981 and 1982 and include former Presidents, Ministers of Defence, Army Chiefs of Staff and Junta members. The allegations relate to genocide, crimes against humanity and violations of international humanitarian law, which are proscribed by the national criminal code of 1973 and were excluded from the 1996 amnesty law. To date, over 100 eyewitnesses have given statements to Special Prosecutor Mario Leal, who is heading the state's investigation into these crimes. Three of the accused have voluntarily given extensive statements and documents

[78] The organisation also represents some 400 other victims of a range of human rights abuses before national courts and the Inter-American Commission on Human Rights. Until 1998, CALDH's forensic team carried out exhumations of mass graves. Its lawyers represented the above mentioned Rio Negro community, assisted the prosecutor in the Tuluche case and represented the village of Plan de Sánchez and Maritza Urrutia in ground-breaking cases before the Inter-American Court of Human Rights.

to Mr. Leal. CALDH continues to gather evidence to assist the official investigation, including forensic reports, expert testimony and military documents. With backing from the author provided the prosecutors: The International Centre for Transitional Justice in New York, with ongoing technical assistance. Invited specialists from the International Criminal Tribunal for the Former Yugoslavia have also carried out training with Guatemalan prosecutors and judges. The first petition for arrest warrants is expected to be issued towards the end of 2004. For more information consult www.justiceforgenocide.org

MARGARET POPKIN*

THE SALVADORAN TRUTH COMMISSION AND THE SEARCH FOR JUSTICE

From today's vantage point, the Truth Commission for El Salvador must be seen as an early model. In designing the Truth Commission for El Salvador, the peace negotiators drew on the experience of commissions previously established in Argentina and Chile. The Salvadoran commission, while *sui generis,* raises important issues about the relationship of a truth commission to the justice system that may be relevant to subsequent efforts to address impunity.

The establishment of a truth commission is now widely seen as part of an overall strategy to address massive human rights and humanitarian law violations. Often serving as an initial component of a broader effort, a truth commission can play a vital role in setting the stage for additional efforts to overcome impunity and promote reconciliation. In Argentina, the work of the National Commission on Disappearances (CONADEP) was designed to lead to prosecutions. Chile's Truth and Reconciliation (Rettig) Commission led to the formation of a successor entity, which continued the effort to find out what had happened to individual victims. With a strong victim focus, Chile's Commission designed an individualised reparations scheme for those killed. As the Chilean TRC had recommended, the National Corporation for Reparation and Reconciliation was formed to continue investigations into the fate of victims. South Africa's Truth and Reconciliation Commission, which came after El Salvador's, was explicitly designed to substitute for justice. The South African TRC held public hearings in different parts of the country and was empowered to grant amnesty to perpetrators who came forward and fully acknowledged their crimes. The willingness of perpetrators to come forward was, however, influenced by the seriousness of ongoing prosecutorial efforts.

* Executive Director, Due Process of Law Foundation, Washington, DC.

Criminal Law Forum **15:** 105–124, 2004.
© 2004 *Kluwer Academic Publishers. Printed in the Netherlands.*

A truth commission should provide a unique opportunity to develop consciousness about the violence that took place, to change the understanding and create a new discourse about what is possible and what still needs to be done. Doing so, however, is particularly challenging in a context such as El Salvador's where the regime responsible for many human rights violations remained in power and where state institutions remained weak and those primarily responsible for the violations retained significant power.

In this regard, the Salvadoran experience raises a number of important questions. When a justice system is totally compromised and actually complicit in the non-investigation of human rights and international humanitarian law, what are the options for a truth commission that seeks to contribute to overcoming impunity? In that type of context, what can a truth commission do to contribute to making justice possible – or less unlikely? How does the international composition of a truth commission affect its interaction with the national justice system, particularly when the justice system and the government have not been changed? How can a truth commission promote justice sector reform aimed at achieving an independent and impartial justice system capable of providing justice? How, if at all, can a truth commission's work (*e.g.*, documentation and findings) be used in judicial or other proceedings designed to establish responsibilities and overcome impunity?

In January 1992, the Salvadoran government and the insurgent Farabundo Martí National Liberation Front (FMLN) signed the "Chapultepec Agreement", the United Nations-brokered peace accords that ended 12 years of bitter civil war, with an estimated 75,000 civilian victims. The Salvadoran conflict was fundamentally a class war that stemmed from enormous economic inequalities and exclusion, repression, spiralling violence, and fraudulent elections that appeared to preclude peaceful change. The United States was deeply involved in supporting the Salvadoran military, and the conflict was one of the last Cold War battlefields.

The Salvadoran military and its paramilitary allies engaged in a ruthless counterinsurgency campaign that included torture, forced disappearances, assassinations, massacres, and forced displacement. The FMLN also carried out selective assassinations and at times utilised strategies that violated international humanitarian law. In the 1980s, El Salvador was notorious for egregious human rights violations including the death squad assassination of Archbishop Oscar Romero as he said mass in a hospital chapel, in March 1980, the rape and murder of four United States churchwomen by National Guardsmen, in December 1980, the abduction and murder by security forces of six leaders of the political opposition, in November 1980, the "El Mozote" massacre of hundreds of men women and children by United States-trained troops – reportedly the largest single massacre of unarmed civilians in Latin America in the last half of the twentieth century, in December 1981 (and dozens of other massacres in the countryside), and the army's murder of six Jesuit priests and two women who worked with them, in November 1989. The few human rights crimes even partially investigated by the justice system were the result of substantial international pressure, notably threats to withhold United States military assistance. During the 1980s, no officer was tried and convicted for any human rights crime.

By 1990, both parties to the conflict had realised that they had reached a stalemate in terms of the possibility of a military victory. With a drastically changed international situation heralded by the end of the Cold War, international players urged a negotiated settlement. In this context, the parties to the Salvadoran conflict sought the United Nations' mediation and undertook serious peace negotiations. In contrast to many of the other cases discussed at this conference, El Salvador's peace process and negotiated transition did not imply a change in the government. The "transition government" was the same right-wing government that had led the country during the final years of the war. The military had not been defeated, and the FMLN was to become an important part of the political process.

I. THE TRUTH COMMISSION FOR EL SALVADOR

The international community was instrumental in facilitating peace negotiations and overseeing implementation of the Salvadoran peace accords. Unlike other truth commissions before or since, the Truth Commission for El Salvador, a product of the United Nations-brokered negotiations between the Salvadoran government and the insurgent Farabundo Martí Liberation Front, was comprised entirely of non-Salvadorans. After consultation with the parties, the United Nations named the three members of the Truth Commission: former president of Colombia Belisario Betancur, former Venezuelan foreign minister Reinaldo Figueredo, and United States law professor (and now judge of the International Court of Justice) Thomas Buergenthal.

The commissioners worked with a wholly international professional staff. The Peace Accords were signed in January 1992,[1] and the Truth Commission was created in July of the same year, at a time when FMLN combatants remained in demobilisation camps. The Truth Commission was given just six months to carry out its task.

Salvadoran civil society was not involved in the process of designing the Truth Commission, its mandate or its methodology. The United Nations and the parties to the negotiations consulted with a few key individuals in El Salvador and many more in the international human rights community. Salvadoran human rights groups provided important information to the Commission, but were not otherwise involved in the Commission's work.

The Truth Commission's mandate called for it to investigate "serious acts of violence that have occurred since 1980 and whose impact on society urgently demands that the public should know the truth".[2] The parties recognised the need to make the complete truth known and to strengthen "the resolve and means to establish the truth". The Truth Commission was designed to yield quick results "without prejudice to the obligations incumbent on the Salvadoran courts to solve such cases and impose the appropriate penalties on the culprits". The final article of the agreement establishing the Truth Commission's mandate stated that "the provisions of this agreement shall not prevent the normal investigation of any situation or case, whether or not the Commission has investigated it, nor the application of the relevant legal provisions to acts contrary to law".[3] In the final Chapultepec peace agreement,[4] the parties specifically recognised:

> The need to clarify and put an end to any indication of impunity on the part of officers of the armed forces, particularly in cases where respect for human rights is jeopardized. To that end, the Parties refer this issue to the Commission on the Truth for consideration and resolution. All of this shall be without prejudice to the principle, which the Parties also recognise, that *acts of this nature, regardless of the sector*

[1] Letter dated 27 January 1992, transmitting the entire text of the Peace Agreement between the Government of El Salvador and the FMLN, signed at Chapultepec Castle in Mexico City on 16 January 1992, UN Doc. A/46/864 – S/23501, 30 January 1992, reprinted in THE UNITED NATIONS AND EL SALVADOR (1990–1995).

[2] For descriptions and analysis of the Truth Commission's work, see Thomas Buergenthal, *The United Nations Truth Commission for El Salvador*, 27 VANDERBILT J. TRANSNAT'L L. 497 (1994); MARGARET POPKIN, PEACE WITHOUT JUSTICE: OBSTACLES TO BUILDING THE RULE OF LAW IN EL SALVADOR 109–163 (2000).

[3] Preamble to Truth Commission Agreement, Mexico Accords.

[4] Chapultepec Agreement, Chapter 1, Armed Forces, Section 5, End to Impunity.

to which their perpetrators belong, must be the object of exemplary action by the law courts so that the punishment prescribed by law is meted out to those found responsible. (emphasis added)

Thus, the apparent intent of the negotiators was not to make the Truth Commission a substitute for judicial proceedings. Nonetheless, many in El Salvador preferred to conceive of a truth commission as a substitute for justice, charged with the entire responsibility for addressing the atrocities that occurred during the period of war. According to this view, the courts would be incapable of dispensing justice and, in any case, attempting to have them do so would be destabilising to efforts to consolidate peace and include the former battlefield opponents in the new political process.

Days after the Chapultepec accord was signed, the Legislative Assembly hurriedly approved a "National Reconciliation Law", because of the need to act quickly to legalise the situation of FMLN leaders who were returning to the country and would be involved in peace accord implementation. The governing ARENA party stated its preference for a total amnesty, maintaining that national reconciliation requires forgetting and forgiving. Any attempt to prosecute for crimes of the past would, they argued, destabilise the peace process. Opposition parties urged the exemption of specific kinds of crimes from the amnesty law. The compromise agreement, which amounted to a delayed general amnesty, specifically excepted from the potential benefits of amnesty those persons named in the Truth Commission report as being responsible for serious acts of violence, so that the Truth Commission could carry out its work before the application of amnesty in all cases.[5] Because the amnesty law preceded the Truth Commission's work, the courts had no way of knowing which individuals would be named by the Commission. The Supreme Court issued a circular, supposedly to clarify this situation:

When the judge considers, upon having received a petition for amnesty, that the person for whom amnesty is sought has participated in the serious acts of violence referred to in that provision, he should ask the prosecutor's opinion, taking into consideration that in such cases the Truth Commission's report will be necessary to resolve the amnesty, and it cannot be favourably resolved until the Truth Commission decides whether such cases are included within Article 6 of the Reconciliation Law.

---

[5] National Reconciliation Law, Decree 147, 23 January 1992.

Thus the Supreme Court seemed to be saying that judges could not grant amnesty without taking into account the Truth Commission's findings. Determining which cases would be subject to amnesty was not, however, part of the Truth Commission's mandate. Despite this apparent, if peculiar, deference, the judiciary, led and dominated by the president of the Supreme Court, Mauricio Gutiérrez Castro, did not consider the Truth Commission's work to be relevant. Instead the then president of the Supreme Court belittled the peace accords as mere political agreements with no bearing on the judiciary and made no effort to cooperate with the Truth Commission's investigations.

The Truth Commission's report blasted Gutiérrez Castro for his non-cooperation. In its findings on the El Mozote massacre case, the Commission stated that he had "interfered unduly and prejudicially, for biased political reasons, in the ongoing judicial proceedings in the case".[6] The Commission found that the Supreme Court president delayed the appointment of qualified foreign experts who were to conduct exhumations. When interviewed by members of the Truth Commission, Gutiérrez Castro said that the exhumation ordered by the trial judge would prove that "only dead guerrillas are buried" at El Mozote. He further suggested that the "political implications" of the exhumation process "override legal considerations".[7]

In some cases, the Truth Commission was able to obtain court records, which usually documented that no serious investigation had been undertaken. In others, judges, heeding the advice of the Supreme Court president, failed to provide requested records. The Commission's status as a non-judicial body allowed it to receive evidence on a confidential basis "from any sources, public or private, that it deemed useful and reliable". A number of witnesses who provided information to the Truth Commission only did so on this confidential basis. To protect the confidentiality of its sources, the Truth Commission's report does not cite those it interviewed.

In its March 1993 report, the United Nations Truth Commission for El Salvador found that state agents and paramilitary groups or death squads linked to or tolerated by government forces were considered responsible for approximately 95% of the 7,000 acts of violence about which the Commission received testimony during its brief

[6] From Madness to Hope, UN Doc. S/25500, 1 April 1993, p. 121.

[7] *Ibid.*, p. 120.

mandate (a sampling of the victims of violence during an almost twelve-year civil war estimated to have left some 75,000 civilians dead). Five percent of these acts were attributed to the FMLN.

The Truth Commission investigated cases with particular resonance in El Salvador (or for the international community) as well as cases that illustrated patterns and practices of violence. Thirty-two such cases were included in the Truth Commission's report. In the cases where the Commission felt it had obtained sufficient information to make a finding, it named the individuals responsible for or complicit in specific acts of violence (including most of the high command of the armed forces, some civilians and judges, and some FMLN leaders). The Commission maintained that its mandate, which called for making the complete truth known, required it to name names, "when there is reliable testimony available, especially when the persons identified occupy senior positions and perform official functions directly related to violations or the cover-up of violations".[8] The Commission established three levels of evidence for its findings: "overwhelming" – conclusive or highly convincing evidence to support the Commission's finding; "substantial" – very solid evidence to support the Commission's finding; and "sufficient" – more evidence to support the Commission's finding than to contradict it.

The Commission sought to guarantee the reliability of its evidence by verifying, substantiating, and reviewing all statements it received. According to the Commission, no single source or witness was considered sufficiently reliable to establish the truth on any issue of fact necessary for the Commission to arrive at a finding; at least two sources were required. The Commission noted that since its report was not a judicial or quasi-judicial determination of legal rights or obligations, it was not necessarily subject to the strict requirements of due process relevant for such determinations.

The Truth Commission's decision to name names was highly controversial, both in El Salvador and for experts in the field.[9] In this regard, José Zalaquett, who was a member of Chile's Truth and Reconciliation Commission, maintains that a truth commission should never include names of perpetrators because doing so necessarily invades the judicial sphere and denies those named their right to due process protections. Juan Méndez, former president of the

---

[8] *Ibid.*, p. 25.

[9] Priscilla Hayner, Unspeakable Truths: Confronting State Terror and Atrocity 115–120 (2000).

Inter-American Commission of Human Rights, suggests that names should not be published if there is a possibility of seeking justice in the courts; however, he suggests that if the truth commission is to be the only vehicle to address impunity, names should be included in the interests of making the full truth known.[10]

The Salvadoran Truth Commission's most striking findings came in the Jesuit case, in which it found that the Minister of Defence had ordered the killings and most of the members of the Armed Forces High Command had been involved in the decision to kill the priests. (A 1991 investigation and trial, fraught with irregularities, had led to the conviction of one colonel and one lieutenant and had refused to look at who had given the orders, facilitated the crime or covered it up.) Another particularly important contribution was the Commission's reliance on forensic evidence to establish that the vast majority of the victims of the El Mozote massacre had actually been children, not guerrillas as the Supreme Court president had claimed.

In case after case, the Truth Commission included within its findings the state's failure to meet its international law obligation to carry out investigations, bring to trial and punish those responsible, and provide reparations to victims. The Commission relied on international law for its legal analysis, focusing only on Salvadoran law as something that needed to be reformed. The international composition of the Commission and the justice system's poor track record surely contributed to this approach.

In its recommendations, despite naming a number of individuals responsible for acts of violence, the Truth Commission did not call on the justice system to undertake prosecutions. An international tribunal was never seriously considered a possibility for El Salvador. While recognising the need for prosecutions, the Commission found that:

> One painfully clear aspect of that situation is the glaring inability of the judicial system either to investigate crimes or to enforce the law, especially when it comes to crimes committed with the direct or indirect support of State institutions.

> The inability of the courts to apply the law to acts of violence committed under the direct or indirect cover of the public authorities is part and parcel of the situation in which those acts took place and is inseparable from them.

---

[10] Juan Méndez, *Derecho a la verdad frente a las graves violaciones a los Derechos Humanos*, in EL RETO DE LA VERDAD Y LA JUSTICIA: JORNADAS INTERNACIONALES PARA UNA COMISIÓN DE LA VERDAD 37 (APRODEH/FIDH, 2001).

The Truth Commission found that the judiciary was not capable of fulfilling the requirements of justice. It noted that:

> The structure of the judiciary is still substantially the same as it was when the acts described in this report took place. The reforms of the judicial system agreed on during the peace process have been implemented to only a limited extent, so that they have yet to have a significant impact ..., the judiciary is still run by people whose omissions were part of the situation which must now be overcome, and there is nothing to indicate that their customary practices will change in the near future.
>
> These considerations confront the Commission with a serious dilemma. The question is not whether the guilty should be punished, but whether justice can be done. Public morality demands that those responsible for the crimes described here be punished. However, El Salvador has no system for the administration of justice which meets the minimum requirements of objectivity and impartiality so that justice can be rendered reliably.
>
> The Commission does not believe that a reliable solution can be found to the problems it has examined by tackling them in the context which is primarily responsible for them ... [A] judicial debate in the current context, far from satisfying a legitimate desire for justice, could revive old frustrations, thereby impeding the achievement of that cardinal objective, reconciliation ... the only judicial system which the Commission could trust to administer justice in a full and timely manner would be one which had been restructured in the light of the peace agreements.

While the Commission did not take a position regarding amnesty, it did endorse the Jesuits' call for a pardon for the two officers convicted for the Jesuit killings, noting that those responsible for planning and ordering the murders remain at liberty. The Commission further noted that "since it is not possible to guarantee a proper trial for all those responsible for the crimes described here, it is unfair to keep some of them in prison while others who planned the crimes or also took part in them remain at liberty".

Convinced that justice was not a possibility in the existing context, the Truth Commission focused many of its recommendations on the reform of the justice system and, particularly, the judiciary. Its recommendations built upon the reforms agreed to in the peace negotiations, but also revisited some issues discussed but not agreed to in the peace negotiations. Thus, the Truth Commission called for a rigorous evaluation of all judges by the National Judicial Council to weed out those who lacked the necessary judicial aptitude, efficiency and concern for human rights and who did not offer every guarantee of independence, judicial discretion, honesty and impartiality in their actions. The Truth Commission also called for ending the tremendous concentration of functions in the Supreme Court and its president, which seriously undermined the independence of lower court judges and lawyers, to the detriment of the system as a whole. It also emphasised the need to separate administrative from jurisdictional functions, noting that the Supreme Court should not be responsible for the appointment and removal of judges and urging that this responsibility be transferred to the Judicial Council. The Truth Commission further recommended that each judge be made responsible for administering the resources of the court under his or her jurisdiction and should be accountable for them to the National Judicial Council. Another recommendation called for the accreditation of lawyers by an independent body rather than the Supreme Court.

Based on its investigations and its own experience with the judiciary, the Truth Commission urged the Supreme Court to step down immediately (before the end of its term) to allow for the selection of a new Court under the new constitutional formula agreed to in the peace negotiations:[11]

> Given the tremendous responsibility which the judiciary bears for the impunity with which serious acts of violence such as those described in this report occurred, there is no justification for further postponing the appointment of a new Supreme Court of Justice, whose current members should make way for the immediate implementation of the constitutional reform by resigning from their posts.

The Truth Commission also recommended the destitution of the military and civilian authorities named as perpetrators in its report and urged that they be barred from holding public office for at least 10 years and permanently barred from any activity related to public security or national defence. With few exceptions, the officers named by the Truth Commission had been previously recommended for dismissal or transfer by the *ad hoc* Commission, a Salvadoran commission established under the peace accords to carry our an evaluation and purge of the officer corps. As a result of the confidential *ad hoc* Commission recommendations, reinforced by the Truth Commission's findings and international pressure from the United

[11] The constitutional reforms called for the Judicial Council to propose candidates to the Legislative Assembly, half of whom would come from an election among lawyers, who would then be elected for staggered nine-year terms by a two-thirds majority vote of the legislature. Under the prior system, justices were elected by majority vote for five-year terms that virtually coincided with presidential elections.

Nations and the United States, most of the officers named by the Truth Commission were removed or retired from military service. The government resisted implementing recommendations regarding individuals not included in the *ad hoc* Commission's review. The Truth Commission's recommendation to bar those named from public office was rejected as unconstitutional and contrary to the goals of national reconciliation.

The recommendation that the Supreme Court resign and the naming of perpetrators, including the leadership of the armed forces, served as a lightning rod for those unhappy with the Truth Commission. The head of the Salvadoran Lawyers Federation said that the report "did not even meet the requirements of the Inquisition". The entire Supreme Court took to the airwaves to denounce the violation of national sovereignty and to insist that the Truth Commission had exceeded its mandate. President Cristiani made clear that, despite the supposedly binding nature of the Truth Commission's recommendations, he would call for implementation only of those recommendations that conformed to his belief that Salvadorans needed to "eliminate, erase, and forget" the past. Before the report's publication, he had lobbied hard with the international community to try to ensure that names of perpetrators would not be included. Upon the report's publication, Cristiani called for a broad, absolute, and unconditional amnesty for all persons involved in the commission of political crimes, related common crimes, and common crimes committed by at least twenty persons prior to 1 January 1992. The amnesty was quickly approved by the legislature; it also eliminated all civil responsibility for these crimes.[12]

The Truth Commission had called for the establishment of a compensation fund for victims that would take into account the information on victims included in the annexes to the Truth Commission's report. The Commission recommended that the international community provide funds (setting aside not less than 1% of all international assistance for this purpose).

With the government flatly opposed, the political opposition more immediately concerned about other aspects of the peace accords, and relatively weak civil society organizations, there was little Salvadoran ownership of the Truth Commission report and limited constituency to demand the implementation of its recommendations. The report

[12] Decree 486, 20 March 1993.

was not widely disseminated and is not widely available in El Salvador today. The protests and objections to the report's findings and recommendations received more publicity than the Commission's actual findings. Victims found themselves essentially without representation as political actors across the political spectrum sought to position themselves for a role in post-war El Salvador.

The United Nations was charged with oversight of the Truth Commission's recommendations. In his five-year assessment of the peace process, United Nations Secretary-General Kofi Annan observed: "Reconciliation will rest on shaky foundations if the specific needs of the population that suffered the impact of the war most directly are not addressed. The measures contemplated for material and moral compensation for victims of violations of human rights ... are an area of the pending accords that casts a particularly long shadow over the recognised successes of the process as a whole."[13] According to Annan, the Truth Commission's recommendations aimed at national reconciliation "were largely ignored". He described this as a "disappointing failure to respond to the unique opportunity" to further "a climate of national reconciliation". Five years later, this situation had not changed.

In El Salvador, some of the truth was made known, some important institutional reforms were undertaken,[14] and the possibility of justice, including moral and material reparations, was effectively removed from the national agenda.

II. THE TRUTH COMMISSION'S REPORT AND SUBSEQUENT EFFORTS TO SEEK JUSTICE

How then has the Truth Commission's work contributed to the quest for justice in El Salvador? Unlike its predecessors – both comprised exclusively of nationals – in Argentina and Chile, the Truth Commission for El Salvador did not provide information to the Salvadoran justice system. Its well-founded lack of confidence in the justice system would certainly have been a bar. The Truth Commission did not establish a mechanism to allow access to any of the information it

[13] Report of the Secretary-General, 1 July 1997, para. 63.

[14] For example, as a result of the Peace Accords the former security forces were dissolved and a new National Civilian Police was created; a Human Rights Ombudsman's office came into existence, and important reforms of the Armed Forces and the Judicial Council were also mandated and implemented.

had collected. A very small percentage of the material received by the Truth Commission was explicitly designated as confidential. No system was established, however, to segregate the confidential material and permit access to the remainder. In its report, the Truth Commission proposed the establishment of a Foundation for the Truth based at a United States university, where researchers would have access to its documentation. Because of divergent views in El Salvador, this plan was never put into effect and no alternative was proposed. The Truth Commission's documents remain stored and inaccessible in a United Nations warehouse in New York. Thus, aside from the Commission's public report, none of the thousands of documents amassed by the Truth Commission has been available to anyone seeking to make further efforts to establish the truth or obtain justice.

In these circumstances, the more relevant question is the extent to which the Truth Commission's findings and recommendations have contributed to the quest for justice. The relationship between truth commissions and justice is inevitably informed by the role of civil society and, in particular, groups of victims and survivors and the legal community. In the vast majority of cases, domestic efforts to secure justice have depended on the actions of civil society groups – victims' groups, human rights non-governmental organisations (NGOs) – and judges and prosecutors capable of interpreting the law consistent with international law and their country's Constitution. A truth commission's investigations, findings, and recommendations can provide an important impetus and, potentially, critical information for such efforts. In Latin America, domestic efforts to secure justice for past human rights violations have been closely tied to the evolving jurisprudence of the Inter-American system of human rights protection as well as recent jurisprudence from the international tribunals for the former Yugoslavia and Rwanda, and the exercise of universal jurisdiction, particularly in the effort to prosecute Augusto Pinochet in Spain. While in some cases the possibility of achieving justice may be greatest at the time of transition, several Latin American examples suggest that prosecutions may become more feasible with the passage of time, a more consolidated transition and developments in the application and interpretation of international law. Thus, efforts to seek justice in Argentina and Chile that seemed completely futile 10 years ago are now yielding results, with high-ranking military officers behind bars and facing prosecution.

In El Salvador, in sharp contrast, 10 years after the peace accords were signed, no one has been prosecuted for any of the atrocities that took place during the years of armed conflict. The broad amnesty law passed in the wake of the Truth Commission's report has effectively precluded any prosecutions, and a range of political actors consider the policy of "forgiving and forgetting" to be the cornerstone of the transition from war to peace.[15] The judiciary has undergone major reforms as a result of the peace accords: judicial selection has been removed from direct political party control, the judiciary is now guaranteed 6% of the national budget, judicial salaries have increased significantly, the judicial career has been strengthened. Nonetheless, many of the Truth Commission's recommendations for the justice system were not heeded. Thus the Supreme Court still retains control over almost all aspects of the judiciary.

In September 2000, the Supreme Court's Constitutional Chamber, while declining to find the amnesty law unconstitutional *per se* and refusing to rely on international law, found that courts would need to assess in each individual case whether the amnesty law could be constitutionally applied and provided guidance for this exercise. Despite these important reforms and the Supreme Court's decision, few lower court judges appear to believe that they have the authority to determine that the amnesty law or the statute of limitations does not bar a particular investigation. In the two years since the Supreme Court's amnesty ruling, only one case has been presented to the courts. This also reflects that NGOs and victims have not been presenting cases, a reality that merits another discussion beyond the scope of this article.

To date, none of those named as perpetrators of human rights violations in the Truth Commission's report has had to face criminal proceedings, except for a few cases in which members and ex-members of the military and alleged FMLN members, almost all low-ranking, were tried before the end of the war (*i.e.*, before the Truth Commission began its work). Nor have there been advances in the search for truth. Relatives of thousands of people who disappeared during the years of armed conflict have had no official mechanism through which they could seek information about the fate or whereabouts of their loved ones.

---

[15] For further discussion of post-Truth Commissions efforts to seek truth and justice in El Salvador, see Margaret Popkin, *La búsqueda de la verdad y la justicia después de las comisiones de la verdad en Centroamérica*, in VERDAD Y JUSTICIA: HOMENAJE A EMILIO F. MIGNONE 223–258 (Instituto Interamericano de Derechos Humanos, 2001).

Since the issuance of the Truth Commission's report, the limited advances registered in the quest for justice have come primarily in international forums, notably the Inter-American Commission on Human Rights (IACHR) and a United States federal court in West Palm Beach, Florida. In its decision on the case brought regarding the Jesuit murders and the State's failure to adequately investigate the crime and bring those who ordered it to justice, the Inter-American Commission on Human Rights explicitly relied on the Truth Commission's findings. The IACHR noted that the Commission's investigation was credible because of the rigorous methodology used by the Truth Commission and the guarantee of its impartiality and good faith resulting from the manner in which its members were appointed (and in which the State itself participated).[16]

In the Jesuit case and two other Salvadoran cases,[17] the IACHR determined that the 1993 amnesty law violates El Salvador's obligations under the American Convention of Human Rights and called on the Salvadoran state to investigate and prosecute those responsible. The IACHR stressed that the Truth Commission, despite its "highly relevant" role,

> cannot be considered as a suitable substitute for proper judicial procedures as a method for arriving at the truth. The value of truth commissions is that they are created, not with the presumption that there will be no trials, but to constitute a step towards knowing the truth and, ultimately, making justice prevail. Nor can the institution of a truth commission be accepted as a substitute for the state's obligations, which cannot be delegated, to investigate violations committed within its jurisdiction, and to identify those responsible, punish them, and ensure adequate compensation for the victim.[18]

The IACHR recommended that the Salvadoran government: conduct a full, impartial and effective investigation in an expeditious manner, consistent with international standards in order to identify, prosecute and punish all the material and intellectual authors of the (murders of the Jesuits and the two women), without reference to the amnesty that was decreed; make full reparations for the consequences of those

[16] Inter-American Commission on Human Rights, Report No. 136/99 (El Salvador) (Case 10.488, Ignacio Ellacuría et al., 22 December 1999), para. 78.

[17] Inter-American Commission on Human Rights, Report No. 1/99 (El Salvador) (Case 10.480, Lucio Parada Cea et al., 27 January 1999) and Report No. 37/00 (El Salvador) (Case 11.481, Monseñor Oscar Arnulfo Romero y Galdamez, 13 April 2000).

[18] Inter-American Commission on Human Rights, Report No. 136/99, paras. 229–230.

violations, including the payment of fair compensation; adjust its domestic legislation to the American Convention on Human Rights and thereby render null and void the General Amnesty Law.

In its response to the IACHR report, the Salvadoran government maintained that "by its very nature (the Truth Commission) did not say which were the investigation sources that led them (to make conclusions about the role of other persons in killing the Jesuits) and that would have provided a basis for taking action against those indicated, *which means that the only alternative open to the judicial power was to call upon the members of the Truth Commission to say who had given them the reports, which was contrary to the restricted nature of the Commission*, and could as well have violated the international immunities or privileges of its members".[19] Using the Truth Commission's methodology as an excuse, the State thus totally abdicated its duty to investigate.

Subsequent efforts to reopen the Jesuit case to bring to justice the military commanders who ordered and facilitated the commission of the crime have encountered obstacles at every turn. The Attorney General initially maintained that he could not seek to reopen the case until the Supreme Court ruled on the constitutionality of the amnesty law; after the Supreme Court issued its ruling on the constitutionality of the amnesty law the prosecution reluctantly took the case to court to seek a definitive dismissal; the justice of the peace found the amnesty inapplicable (based on the Supreme Court's reasoning) but dismissed the case based on the statute of limitations; the appellate court blamed the representative of the victims for failing to seek justice in a timely fashion (despite the total bar posed by the amnesty law prior to the Supreme Court's September 2000 ruling); the Criminal Chamber of the Supreme Court upheld the lower court decision. In November 2001, a petition for *amparo* was filed on behalf of the victims' relatives before the Constitutional Chamber of the Supreme Court challenging the constitutionality of some of the actions taken to prevent the adjudication of the case. In December 2003, more than two years after the *amparo* was presented, the Constitutional Chamber finally issued its decision, upholding the actions taken in the case and effectively ending the possibility of pursuing justice in El Salvador against those responsible for ordering the Jesuit murders. In October 2002, the Salvadoran State Counsel for Human

[19] *Ibid.*, para. 243 (emphasis added).

Rights (or Ombudsman) issued a powerful report on the Jesuit case that called for the implementation of the recommendations of the IACHR. This report relied heavily on the Truth Commission's findings and recommendations, describing its recommendations as "a moral imperative and an imperative for justice".[20] The State Counsel considered the failure to carry out the Truth Commission's recommendations "the State's great historical debt with respect to peace". The State Counsel for Human Rights, whose office came into being through the peace negotiations, is the only state functionary to have called for implementation of the recommendations of the Truth Commission and the Inter-American Commission on Human Rights.

In July 2002, a jury in a United States federal court in West Palm Beach, Florida, delivered a stunning verdict as it relied on the doctrine of command responsibility to find two Salvadoran former ministers of defence liable for the torture of three Salvadorans by security forces in the early 1980s.[21] The case was civil in nature, filed pursuant to the Alien Tort Claims Act. In addition to the plaintiffs' accounts of the terrible torture they had suffered at the hands of the defendants' subordinates and its devastating consequences, the plaintiffs presented witnesses and experts who testified about the structure and practice of the Salvadoran military during the period at issue and introduced some of the Truth Commission's findings. In the Salvadoran press, the plaintiffs' case was depicted as vengeance that could lead to spiralling violence. How, said some, could the generals be held responsible when the guerrillas had not been prosecuted for their role in the violence. One of the country's principal newspapers declared that "verdicts of this kind truly cause far more harm than good". The notion that commanders could be held responsible for the acts of their subordinates was dismissed as ludicrous. Other commentators recalled that through the peace negotiations the future of the country was assured with the price of the past. Some noted that the Truth Commission had been designed to put an end to the discussion of the past.

---

[20] Caso Jesuitas: Informe de la Señora Procuradora para la Defensa de los Derechos Humanos, sobre la impunidad respecto de las ejecuciones arbitrarias de Ignacio Ellacuría, S.J.; Ignacio Martín Baró, S.J.; Joaquín López y López, S.J.; Amando López, S.J.; Segundo Montes, S.J.; Juan Ramón Moreno, S.J.; Elba Julia Ramos y Celina Mariceth Ramos, 30 October 2002, p. 44.

[21] *Juan Romagoza Arce* et al. v. *José Guillermo García* et al., United States District Court for the Southern District of Florida, Civil Action No. 99-8365, verdict announced on 23 July 2002; for additional information, see <http://www.cja.org/cases/romagoza.html>.

The Florida jury's verdict and the State Counsel's unprecedented report, both issued in 2002, indicate the enduring power of the Truth Commission's findings, yet they also reflect the continuing unwillingness of the Salvadoran justice system – and powerful sectors in El Salvador – to address impunity for human rights violations committed during the armed conflict.

III. SOME CONCLUDING THOUGHTS

As the preceding discussion suggests, many factors have contributed to the lack of justice in El Salvador. The parties to the negotiations were more interested in recommendations for legal and institutional reform; they sought to ensure the future but abandoned the past. By asserting the impossibility of justice in the existing context, the Truth Commission for El Salvador did not challenge the justice system to undertake investigations, and the government's negative reaction to the Truth Commission's report and the immediate passage of a broad amnesty law apparently foreclosed the possibility of justice. Essentially abandoned by political leaders and not consulted in the process of developing the truth commission or its recommendations, victims had little recourse. In this context, victims and their representatives in El Salvador have not been able to bring sufficient pressure to achieve justice or secure compensation. Despite important advances in judicial reform, the justice system has yet to rely on the Truth Commission's findings, implement the recommendations of the Inter-American Commission on Human Rights, or otherwise rely on international law developments in the struggle against impunity.

In other countries, an insistence on justice accompanied by strong civil society demand, has eventually led to victories for justice – and not because the justice system has been so thoroughly reformed (*e.g.*, Haiti, Guatemala, Argentina, Paraguay, and now Perú). Experience suggests that bringing cases may in some instances contribute to strengthening judicial independence.

The Historical Clarification Commission for Guatemala took an important step in making clear the crimes that are not subject to amnesty, and it called for prosecutions in these cases.[22] A truth commission could also address the issue of the applicability of stat-

[22] On the Guatemala Commission, see: Susan Kemp, *The Inter-relationship Between the Guatemalan Commission for Historical Clarification and the Search for Justice in National Courts*, in this issue.

utes of limitation to certain crimes. Similarly, a truth commission can suggest priorities for the justice system, thereby dispelling the notion that if it is not possible to prosecute all those responsible, no one should be prosecuted. For example, the Historical Clarification Commission emphasised the need to prosecute those most responsible in the chain of command.

It can be helpful for a truth commission to use its moral authority to recommend changes in the justice system; institutional reform may be necessary but is unlikely to be sufficient to produce a justice system capable of defending human rights. In the Americas, because of the key role played by the Inter-American system of human rights, it is important to incorporate international norms into the national legal system and implement Inter-American jurisprudence. A truth commission could emphasise the relevance and role of the Inter-American human rights system and its jurisprudence – and other relevant international standards.

A Truth Commission should be able to provide information to the justice system, if it is sufficiently reliable, and if victims want this. Experience shows that this is more difficult for international commissions. A national commission is more likely to assume that the justice system may become involved, while international commissions seem more inclined to view their task as completely separate from the responsibilities of national institutions. If information is collected on a confidential basis, as in El Salvador, a truth commission might ask witnesses whether their testimony or documentation could be provided to those seeking to carry out judicial investigations.

The experience of different truth commissions in recent years has made clear that a truth commission should normally constitute an initial step. After its work is completed, much truth remains to be uncovered and justice remains to be done. The limited time period allotted to a truth commission may lead to an unbalanced presentation of cases or a focus on responsibilities (*e.g.*, Argentina and El Salvador), that may leave little information about the fate of victims. On the other hand, a focus on the fate of victims and consequences to family (Chile) may mean less focus on the apparatus of repression. Often the truth commission is only able to uncover the tip of the iceberg. Experience has shown the need for different kinds of follow-up mechanisms to deal with cases and issues not addressed (or left unfinished) by a truth commission. Regardless of its primary focus, relying on its credibility and moral force and through its work and its recommendations, a truth commission should seek to vindicate the rights of victims. At a minimum, this means generally leaving them in a better position to exercise their rights to know the truth, to seek justice, and to obtain reparations.

KEN AGYEMANG ATTAFUAH*

AN OVERVIEW OF GHANA'S NATIONAL RECONCILIATION COMMISSION AND ITS RELATIONSHIP WITH THE COURTS

In December 2001, the Parliament of Ghana passed a law to establish the National Reconciliation Commission (the "Commission"). The law, known as the National Reconciliation Commission Act (Act 611), came into force on 7 January 2002, when it received Presidential assent. The Commission was inaugurated on 6 May 2002. The goal of the Commission is to help reconcile the people of Ghana by finding out the truth about past human rights abuses and helping those who were hurt by the abuses to deal with their pain and to move on with their lives. The Commission will also help those who participated in the abuses to come to terms with the experiences and to obtain forgiveness.

The Commission is statutorily insulated from the control or direction of any person or body, including the courts. Though chaired by a retired justice of the Supreme Court of Ghana, the Commission is essentially a fact-finding, non-judicial body subject to the laws of Ghana just like any person or body corporate. The National Reconciliation Commission Act (Act 611) – the law establishing the Commission, is fairly simple and does not hold the promise of generating any complex legal issues nor intricate practice issues with respect to the interrelationship between the Commission and the courts. In addition, the Commission has not, to date, been involved in any legal controversy and, therefore, has not yet been able to empirically gauge the courts' attitude toward it. Furthermore, unlike the situation in Sierra Leone and elsewhere, the National Reconciliation Commission of Ghana does not have another body, such as the Special Court of Sierra Leone, with similar objectives, or a competing jurisdiction or mandate.

---

* Executive Secretary, National Reconciliation Commission, Ghana.

Criminal Law Forum **15:** 125–134, 2004.
© 2004 *Kluwer Academic Publishers. Printed in the Netherlands.*

I. WHY DOES GHANA NEED A NATIONAL RECONCILIATION COMMISSION?

Ghana is a relatively peaceful country in the turbulent West African sub-region characterised by endemic ethnic and political conflicts, including armed conflicts that have wreaked untold havoc on millions of people. Relative to the Côte d'ivoire, Sierra Leone, Liberia and Nigeria, Ghana is a haven of peace and tranquility. But this picture of Ghana is a partial one concealing many terrible episodes of ethnic and political violence and hostility and gross human rights violations. Ghana has witnessed four successful military coups, with countless numbers of attempted coups and subversive activities that have marred the nation. Each of these events has provided the occasion for grave human rights violations. Various civilian regimes have also been guilty of abuse of human rights. At the moment, there are over forty flash points of ethnic conflict, most of them rooted in our pre-colonial and colonial past.

Truth and reconciliation commissions are, generally speaking, part and parcel of transitional arrangements for return to democratic constitutional rule.[1] Ghana's National Reconciliation Commission came into being eight years after the nation's return to constitutional rule. This runs against the grain of virtually all truth and reconciliation commissions, which generally emerge at the transitional phase of democratisation. Only Mexico is beginning to take similar tentative steps in establishing a reconciliation commission several years after the restoration of democracy.

In Ghana's case, the "delay" can be understood against the backdrop of partisan politics. The National Democratic Congress of President Jerry John Rawlings had no interest in creating a *special* statutory agency to pursue the goal of national reconciliation. On two occasions during his second term in office, President Rawlings publicly apologised to Ghanaians for any "excesses" which might have taken place during the convulsive reign of the Armed Forces Revolutionary Council (AFRC) in the aftermath of the June Fourth Uprising and the turbulent years of the Provisional National Defence

---

[1] It must be pointed out, however, that the world's first truth commission, established in 1974 by President Idi Amin Dada of Uganda, was not connected to any transitional arrangement. The Commission of Inquiry into Disappearances of People in Uganda was President Amin's response to mounting international pressure to confront the brutality of his regime; he remained firmly in power for several years until eventually forced out by Ugandan rebels backed by the Tanzanian military.

Council (PNDC). Rawlings was head of both governments. In the early 1990s, the civilian government of the National Democratic Congress (NDC) headed by President Rawlings also embarked on a low-key national reconciliation exercise by quietly de-confiscating the assets of key opposition politicians that were seized by the AFRC and PNDC regimes. The main opposition party – the New Patriotic Party (NPP) – viewed the apology and the selective return of a few confiscated properties to their rightful owners as hardly adequate in reconciling the nation.

For one thing, the Rawlings approach to national reconciliation was opaque, piecemeal and selective; it lacked a coherent and well-articulated structure, and was not comprehensive. In addition, the Rawlings approach did not allow for historical clarification or the writing of an accurate and complete historical record of human rights violations, and it did not involve the most critical element in any reconciliation process – the people. Finally, that approach missed the opportunity for effecting institutional reforms aimed at preventing human rights violations: the public review of the operations of key state apparatus constitutes an important method for understanding the role of state institutions in fostering human rights violations and how to prevent them.

In its Political Manifesto, the NPP promised a National Reconciliation Committee "to heal the festering sores within our body politic" and to promote national reconciliation. In his inaugural address on 7 January 2001, President John Agyekum Kufour of the NPP reiterated that commitment, and, again, emphasized it on 15 February 2001 when he delivered his maiden address to Parliament, noting that the "National Reconciliation Committee ... will be established to provide a forum for aggrieved persons to air their grievances in order to promote the goal of national reconciliation". It is plausible, based on the foregoing analysis, that had the NPP come into power sooner than 2001, the National Reconciliation Commission would probably have been established sooner, and it would thus have been seen as a part of the transitional process to democratization.

1.1. *Examples of Egregious Human Rights Violations in Ghana*

But what "grievances" and "festering sores" in the Ghanaian body politic could the NPP have contemplated in its Manifesto and the presidential speeches outlined above? What experiences of gross human rights violations and lack of redress mechanisms justify the creation of a national reconciliation commission in Ghana?

The abduction and subsequent cold-blooded murder and burning of three High Court judges (Mrs. Justice Cecilia Koranteng-Addo, Mr. Justice Kwadwo Agyei Agyepong and Justice Fred Poku Sarkodee) and a retired army officer (Major Sam Acquah) on 30 June 1982 provide ample illustration of the reality of state-sponsored disappearances, abductions and murders. Mr. Joachim Amartey Kwei, a former trade unionist, PNDC Member, and long-standing friend of Chairman J.J. Rawlings, together with five others, was arrested, tried, convicted and subsequently executed on 10 August 1983 for the abduction and murder of the four people whose charred bodies were found in the Dodowa plains (near Accra) three days after their disappearance from their homes.[2]

Despite this outcome, most Ghanaians still believe that the entire truth about the abduction and gruesome murder of the judges and the military officer has not yet been told, and that justice has not been done. It is probably impossible to tell how many ordinary people "evaporated" or "disappeared" under mysterious circumstances during the revolutionary period. It is safe to surmise that, in the heat of the revolutionary frenzy that gripped the nation between 1982 and 1986, many hundreds of people probably lost their lives through the process of *evaporation* – unrecorded capture, torture and murder of serious "problem people", including common criminals such as armed robbers and personal and political enemies of government functionaries. Journalists and lawyers were among the ranks of the many who were routinely detained and tortured.

Between June and September 1979, many wealthy and "high-time" Ghanaian women – especially market women – were routinely captured and tortured publicly. Countless numbers were stripped naked and whipped on their buttocks or in their private parts by military and police personnel with a most gruesome barbarity for allegedly selling goods above artificially-established controlled prices. Military installations, guardrooms and police stations became common centers of lengthy and unlawful detentions and torture. In the 1980s, defenseless students, worker protestors and pro-democracy forces were randomly shot at. In some cases, military personnel killed suspected "political dissidents" and common criminals with careless abandon.

These are only a few examples of the numerous cases of gross human rights violations that form part of our chequered political

[2] West Africa, 8 September 1983.

history. And many more Ghanaians are convinced that many more untold stories of extra-judicial killings, abductions, rapes, unlawful and extended detentions and confiscations of lawfully acquired properties of citizens, dotting several decades of military (and civilian) rule, from February 1966 to January 1993, remain unaddressed. Some even put the date further back to March 1957, the time of independence. Many hearts are bleeding with the pain of callous treatment and injustices meted out by Ghanaians against Ghanaians and foreign nationals in our land. And the evidence is that Ghana as a nation is a divided society urgently needing reconciliation.

1.2. *The Transitional Provisions and the National Reconciliation Commission*

The Transitional Provisions contained in the 1992 Constitution of Ghana prohibit any judicial scrutiny of, and any possibility of redress for, any actions taken or purported to have been taken in the name of the governments or operatives of the governments of the Armed Forces Revolutionary Council (4 June to 23 September 1979) and the PNDC (31 December 1981 to 6 January 1993). Thus, the possibility of redress for any wrongs during these periods is substantively and effectively foreclosed. Specifically, section 34(1) of the Transitional Provisions of the 1992 Constitution provides that

> "No member of the Provisional National Defence Council, Provisional National Defence Council Secretary, or other appointees of the Provisional National Defence Council shall be held liable either jointly or severally, for any act or omission during the administration of the Provisional National Defence Council"

The foregoing section must be read *in tandem* with Section 34(2) of the Transitional Provisions, which also provide as follows:

> It is not lawful for any court or tribunal to entertain any action or take any decision or make any order or grant any remedy or relief in any proceedings instituted against the Government of Ghana or any person acting *under the authority of the Government of Ghana* ... (emphasis added).

It is arguable that the acts or omissions precluded from judicial scrutiny in the above provisions may reasonably be construed to be those done "under the authority of the Government of Ghana".

Article 278(1) of the Constitution, which concerns the appointment of commissions of inquiry, provides that

"Subject to Article 5 of the Constitution, the President shall, by constitutional instrument, appoint a commission of inquiry into any matter of public interest where ... the President is satisfied that a commission of inquiry should be appointed...

If a matter is of public interest then the President can appoint a commission of inquiry by constitutional instrument. It is a discretionary power conferred by article 278 of the Constitution on the President.

In sum, the President has the discretionary power to appoint a commission of inquiry into a matter of public interest for good reason. The issue of healing the wounds of the past and reconciling the nation through the provision of a platform for the voices of victims of gross human rights violations to be heard, and the provision of appropriate remedies for such victims, among other lawful measures, is a matter of grave public interest in Ghana.[3]

As noted earlier, the National Reconciliation Commission is not a court; it is an investigative body with a remedial focus, and it lacks the power to determine liability, pronounce guilt on individuals or impose punishment on any person. To that end, the National Reconciliation Commission Act does not infringe section 34(3) of the Transitional Provisions of the Constitution; it seeks to provide a platform for aggrieved persons to tell their stories of victimization to a non-judicial investigative body, and to seek recompense and healing as may be appropriate.

1.3. *Structure and Operations of the Commission*

Members of the Commission are appointed by the President in consultation with the Council of State – a non-partisan body of eminent Ghanaians who advise the President. The Commission comprises nine Ghanaians distinguished for their integrity and impartiality and ability to achieve the object of the legislation.

The Commission is chaired by a retired justice of the Supreme Court of Ghana. It is supported by a Secretariat headed by an Executive Secretary. The Secretariat has five divisions: (a) Finance and Administration; (b) Public Affairs and Community Liaison; (c) Investigations and Research; (d) Counselling and Support Services; (e) Legal.

---

[3] A survey conducted in 2002 by the respected Centre for Democratic Development (CDD-Ghana) into the attitude of Ghanaians toward the creation of a national reconciliation commission in Ghana found strong support for the idea from all sectors of the society.

The applicable law requires the Commission to establish an accurate and complete historical record of human rights violations and abuses inflicted on persons by public institutions and holders of public office or persons who claimed to have acted on behalf of the state during periods of unconstitutional government. The law also requires the Commission to recommend to the President certain measures to appease the victims of human rights abuses and to prevent such occurrences in future. To find out the truth about past abuses, the Commission will take statements from members of the public, investigate those statements and conduct hearings into some of them.

To achieve its goal, the Commission has the power to: investigate the allegations of human rights abuses; investigate the circumstances, as well as the reasons if any, surrounding any particular instances of human rights abuses; recommend appropriate redress for persons who have suffered any injury, hurt, damage, grievance or who have been adversely affected by violations and abuses of their human rights arising from the activities or inactivities of public institutions and persons who held public office during periods of unconstitutional government; and recommend other measures, including changes in the way some state institutions operate, to prevent such abuses from happening in future.

The Commission has broad powers of investigation. For example, it can summon (subpoena) any person to appear before it, enter any place to conduct an investigation, and remove from any place any item or object that it believes is relevant to its investigations. Under certain conditions, the Commission may search and remove items without a warrant.

The Commission has the powers of a court in its hearings. Thus, it can call witnesses, ask them to swear an oath or make an affirmation to tell the truth, and ask them questions while they are under oath or affirmation. Although it has the powers of a court, the Commission is not a court; it is essentially a fact-finding body.

The focus of the Commission's mandate is periods of unconstitutional rule in Ghana's history since independence in 1957. Those periods are: 24 February 1966 to 21 August 1969; 13 January 1972 to 23 September 1979; and 31 December 1981 to 6 January 1993. The Commission may, on application by any person, look into alleged human rights violations or abuses committed under any period of civilian rule between 6 March 1957 and 6 January 1993.

A person who is a victim of human rights abuse may make a statement to the Commission. In addition, a person who has information about a human rights abuse may also make a statement to the Commission at any of its Zonal Offices across the country. The Commission has opened five Zonal Offices as follows: Bolgatanga for Upper East and Upper West Regions; Ho for Volta and Greater Accra Regions; Kumasi for Ashanti and Eastern Regions; Takoradi for Western and Central Regions; and Tamale for Brong Ahafo and Northern Regions.

The Commission's hearings are to be held in public. However, the Commission has the power to hear a case *in camera* (privately) if a person makes such a request, with good reason(s). The Commission may on its own decide to hear a case *in camera*. The victim is entitled to be present at the hearing, whether it takes place in public or *in camera*.

The Commission may, in appropriate circumstances, take reasonable steps to protect the identity and security of a witness. A witness before the Commission has the same rights as a witness before the High Court. This means, among other things, that the witness can have a lawyer present to assist him or her to answer questions before the Commission. The lawyer cannot, however, answer the questions for the witness.

The Commission may provide legal aid to any witness it invites to give evidence before it; it may also give such aid to any indigent or poor witness if it believes that such aid is necessary in the interest of justice. A person who complies with any requirement of the Commission cannot be sued in any criminal or civil action for complying with that requirement. If a witness complies with a request made by the Commission, any information that the witness provides cannot be used against that witness in any criminal or civil court case. However, a witness who commits perjury before the Commission may be prosecuted whether he gave evidence under subpoena or not. In addition, evidence produced as a result of the Commission's investigation or hearing, if in writing and signed by a witness, or if part of the official record of proceedings of the Commission, may be used to contradict the witness in a subsequent civil or criminal suit.

Where a person is compelled by the Commission, over his or her objection, to give incriminating evidence against himself or herself or to produce a document, such evidence or information cannot be used against that person in subsequent criminal or civil proceedings. However, if that person does not raise any objection, the Commission may receive the evidence, and the evidence may be used against him or her in subsequent criminal or civil proceedings.

The Commission is free to do its work without fear or favour. No person, body or institution has the power to control, direct or interfere with the work of the Commission. The enabling legislation guarantees the independence of the Commission.

Members of the Commission are under a legal duty to keep certain information confidential unless their work makes it necessary for them to disclose the information, or unless a court or a law requires them to disclose the information. As with all senior officers in certain sensitive public positions, members of the Commission have sworn an oath to keep certain information secret in the course of their work. Information from a private hearing shall not be published, and the records shall be kept in such a way that the identity of the victim shall not be revealed.

The Commission has a one-year time frame within which to complete its work; the clock begins to tick from the date of its first public hearing. The President may extend this time by a further six months if the Commission, on good grounds, requests for a time extension.

The Commission must submit its report to the President within three months after completing its work. In its report to the President, the Commission has a duty to describe the nature, causes and ramifications of human rights abuses on the victims.

The Commission has the power to make recommendations in its report to the President on appropriate redress for human rights abuses. They may include: individual or collective reparations for victims, including monetary and non-monetary compensation; strategies for aiding victims of human rights abuses to heal and to come to terms with their experience, including counseling; and strategies for the prevention of such violations, including institutional reforms (*e.g.*, of torture-prone state institutions and facilities), targeted human rights educational campaigns; and legal and administrative measures.

The scope of appropriate recommendations for redress of wrongs, for healing the pains of the past and reconciling the nation may cover the following: monetary compensation in appropriate circumstances, and non-monetary reparations such as the erection of monuments and naming of streets in memory of the disappeared, and establishment of scholarship schemes for the children of victims of torture and killings.

On 3 September 2002, the Commission started receiving statements of human rights violations and abuses from the public. The statements received by the Commission have covered human rights violations in the nature of killings, abductions, disappearances, detentions, torture, ill-treatment and seizure of properties.

II. CONCLUSION

The National Reconciliation Commission of Ghana has a clear and specific mandate which neither the courts nor the Commission on Human Rights and Administrative Justice possess, namely, to look into allegations of gross human rights violations committed by government officials or persons purporting to act on behalf of governments during periods of unconstitutional rule in Ghana since 24 February 1966, and to seek and promote national reconciliation. In carrying out this mandate, the Commission has the investigative powers of the police and the judicial powers of the High Court, but the Commission is not a court.

In Ghana, the issue of the interrelationship between the Commission and the courts has been couched, not in terms of jurisdictional turf and competition, but in terms of support and complementarity: the Commission is expected to perform the fact-finding, healing, reconciliation and peace promotion functions which, by virtue of the Transitional Provisions of the 1992 Constitution, the courts and tribunals are forbidden from performing during the era of civilian constitutional rule, but which, nonetheless, are essential to the maintenance of a peaceful and democratic Ghanaian body politic. That is to say, the Commission is to: (a) provide a platform for aggrieved persons to ventilate their grievances concerning gross human rights violations committed primarily under unconstitutional governments and to seek redress; (b) establish an accurate and complete historical record of such human rights violations; (c) to seek and promote healing and national reconciliation among the people of Ghana.

In a broad sense, these are activities that properly fall within the traditional purview of the courts. A judicial system that is independent, competent, efficient and courageous is an instrument for establishing accurate and complete historical records in any contested case; a judicial system anchored in justice offers strong potential for the vindication of the just but weak members of society; such a system, therefore, opens up the aperture for true healing. Justice is almost always a step toward reconciliation.

The courts are perpetual vanguards of legality and fundamental human rights; their existence assures the citizenry and the world at large that the Commission can, in appropriate cases, be taken to court if it fails to act in accordance with its enabling statute, and that the protections outlined in the enabling statute will be made substantively available to those who must come under them.

PATRICK BURGESS*

JUSTICE AND RECONCILIATION IN EAST TIMOR. THE RELATIONSHIP BETWEEN THE COMMISSION FOR RECEPTION, TRUTH AND RECONCILIATION AND THE COURTS

Exploring the relationship between the East Timorese Commission for Reception, Truth and Reconciliation and the courts requires at least a cursory look at three categories of judicial institutions relevant to the efforts to achieve accountability for the massive human rights abuses committed in the territory. The three mechanisms are a possible international tribunal for East Timor, the Indonesian *ad hoc* Tribunal on East Timor, and the United Nations-sponsored Special Panels established to try Serious Crimes in Dili, the capital of East Timor. The most relevant direct relationship for the Commission is with the Office of the General Prosecutor, and the Deputy General Prosecutor for Serious Crimes, particularly in reference to the right to relevant information and the conduct of Community Reconciliation Procedures for perpetrators of lesser crimes.

I. THE CATALYST – EVENTS OF 1999

On September 20, 1999 the INTERFET international forces arrived in Dili East Timor to find a shattered land. The programme to intimidate and bludgeon the East Timorese population into voting to remain part of Indonesia had failed (78.5% voted for independence). However the reaction of the members of the Indonesian military and their agent militias to this loss was more effective. In the period before and after the ballot result an estimated 70% of government infrastructure was destroyed, approximately 60,000 houses were burned, 500,000 civilians were displaced (250,000 to West Timor, Indonesia),

* Principal Legal Counsel, East Timor Commission for Reception, Truth and Reconciliation. (CAVR); Director of Human Rights for UNTAET and UNMISET missions, June 2000–December 2002.

Criminal Law Forum **15:** 135–158, 2004.
© 2004 *Kluwer Academic Publishers. Printed in the Netherlands.*

1000–2000 victims were killed, hundreds of women were raped and the territory was left a smoking ruin.[1]

According to Human Rights Watch, "[t]he violence was part of a systematically planned policy by elements of the Indonesian government and TNI (Indonesian national military forces), to prevent the people of East Timor from freely participating in the referendum, and to punish them for voting for independence".[2] The United Nations International Commission of Inquiry on East Timor (ICIET) visited Dili and some districts after the ballot in 1999 and in its report, made public on 31 January 2000, found evidence of "a pattern of serious violations of fundamental human rights" by the Indonesian security forces and Timorese militias, expressing a view that "ultimately the Indonesian Army was responsible for the intimidation, terror, killings and other acts of violence".[3] On 31 January 2000, the Indonesian National Human Rights Commission produced a report in which the programme was described in detail and thirty-two officials and militia leaders were named as responsible for grave human rights violations amounting to crimes against humanity.[4]

The sudden events of September 1999 had left the territory of East Timor in a vacuum in terms of government and administration. In response, the Security Council, through Resolution 1272, created an unprecedented peacekeeping mission, UNTAET, with total administrative responsibility for the territory, including the administration of justice.[5] In addition to military and police components, the job of UNTAET was to create all the structures required for a new nation: to write laws and build institutions dealing with banking and finance,

---

[1] See "Situation of Human Rights in East Timor, December 10, 1999", UN Doc. A/54/660; Komnas HAM (Indonesian Human Rights Commission), "Report of the Indonesian Commission of Investigation into Human Rights Violations in East Timor", 31 January 2000. Figures supplied by UNHCR, Dili, February 2002, indicate that a total of 60,000 housing kits were distributed to owners of burned houses by United Nations agencies and non-governmental organisations (NGOs) working in the shelter sector. Figures relating to sexual violence supplied by FOKUPERS, an East Timorese NGO working to systematically record the incidence of rape and sexual violence.

[2] Human Rights Watch, "Justice Denied for East Timor", 9 January 2003.

[3] "Report of the International Commission of Inquiry on East Timor to the Secretary General, January 31, 2000", UN Doc. A/54/26, S/2000/59.

[4] Komnas HAM, *supra* note 1.

[5] Security Council Resolution 1272 (1999) established UNTAET on 25 October 1999, granting a mandate to "exercise all legislative and executive authority, including the administration of justice".

health, education, electricity and water, taxation, immigration, border control, garbage collection law-making, policing, national defence, elections, justice, the courts and the judiciary, airports, electricity, roads and much more.

Sifting through the haze of this massive task the clear priorities were similar to many other post-conflict settings: reconciliation, reconstruction (both economic and moral) and development.[6] There was also a need to address the massive international and domestic outrage over what had taken place, and it was clear that unless the talkfests led to concrete steps to assist reconciliation between those involved in the conflict the effort and expense of reconstruction would likely be swept away by the tears accompanying renewed violence.

1.1. *Accountability for the Atrocities*

A series of independent decisions was made in response to international calls to bring those responsible for the massive human rights abuses to justice. These decisions resulted in what amounts to an uncoordinated four-tiered approach to the challenge.

At the top of the shaky pyramid is the possibility of an International Tribunal. The Report of the United Nations International Commission of Inquiry on East Timor called on the United Nations to "establish an international human rights tribunal consisting of judges appointed by the United Nations".[7] The Secretary General did not endorse this recommendation in his accompanying letter to the Security Council. Instead, his suggestion, which was accepted, was to first allow the Indonesian government to demonstrate its commitment and ability prosecute those responsible. The Secretary General stated that these efforts would be "monitored closely"[8] to ensure that they were credible and accorded with international human rights standards. On 18 February 2000 the Security Council called upon Indonesia to "institute a swift, comprehensive, effective and transparent legal process, in conformity with international standards of justice and due process of law".

---

[6] Johnny de Lange, *The Historical and Legal Origins of the South African Truth and Reconciliation Commission*, p. 7.

[7] Komnas HAM, *supra* note 1.

[8] In his letter which accompanied the Report of the ICIET to the Security Counsel, the Secretary General stated that he would "closely monitor progress" of the Indonesian domestic efforts to prosecute to ensure that a "credible response in accordance with international human rights principles" was implemented.

On 1 August 2001 Indonesian President Megawati Sukarnoputri, by presidential decree, established a "second tier" – the *ad hoc* Tribunal in Jakarta, with a mandate to bring those responsible within its territorial boundaries to justice. This decree had been preceded by Law No. 26 of November 2000, which incorporated the Rome Statute of the International Criminal Court into Indonesian law, establishing a legal basis for dealing with serious human rights violations of a widespread and systematic nature.

The third "tier" was a "hybrid court", the Special Panels for Serious Crimes within the Dili District Court, and a Serious Crimes Investigations Unit, which were given exclusive jurisdiction over serious crimes committed throughout East Timor between 1 January 1999 and 25 October 1999. Each panel must be composed of two international judges and one Timorese judge.[9] UNTAET Regulation 2000/15 which established the panels reproduced almost verbatim the substantive legal provisions of the Rome Statute. A position of Deputy General Prosecutor for Serious Crimes (which has been filled by an international expert) was established within the office of the General Prosecutor.[10] However, the Serious Crimes Panels have no powers to compel the attendance of any person indicted who is outside the territorial boundaries of East Timor.[11]

The "fourth tier" was created on 7 February 2002, with the establishment of the East Timorese Commission for Reception, Truth and Reconciliation. (Comissao de Acolhimento, Verdade e Reconciliacao de Timor Leste, or CAVR.) Although often compared to the most well-known truth commission to date, the South African model, the two are significantly different. In particular, the East Timorese Commission has no powers to consider or grant amnesty. However, the UNTAET Regulation, which created the Commission, included a mechanism which would allow perpetrators of less serious, politically related harmful acts to participate in a village-based programme of restorative justice. These Community Reconciliation Procedures (CRPs) depend upon community participation, with the objective to allow victims and the community to provide personal inputs and perpetrators to undertake "acts of reconciliation" as an alternative to the formal justice system and threats of imprisonment. The Commission was also mandated to establish the truth regarding past human rights violations committed within the context of the political

---

9 UNTAET Regulation 2000/15, s. 22. (6 June 2000.)

10 UNTAET Regulation 2000/16.

11 UNTAET Regulation 2000/15.

conflicts in East Timor between 25 April 1974 and 25 October 1999, to compile a report and to make recommendations.[12]

The structures of each one of these tiers has its own individual termites.

Many international observers consider that an international tribunal is the only mechanism which will be able to effectively target those responsible for the violence in East Timor and end the reign of impunity enjoyed by the senior ranks of the Indonesian military. However the unlikely prospect of a Security Council mandate targeting those responsible in the world's largest Islamic nation has become even more remote in the post September 11 world.

The Jakarta trial process also has jurisdiction over these "big fish" but the net appears to be full of holes. The mandate of the *ad hoc* Tribunal was extremely limited, both temporally and geographically, covering only three of the thirteen districts in East Timor during only 2 months, April and September 1999.[13] The January 2003 Human Rights Watch Report entitled "Justice Denied for East Timor" stated: "The main reason (for the failure of the Indonesian government to keep its commitments to prosecute those responsible) appears to be a lack of political will in Jakarta to prosecute senior Indonesian civil and military officials responsible for the violence".[14] The Chief General Prosecutor for East Timor has stated that these big fish may be "more like caviar – very expensive and legally protected".[15]

The third tier, the Serious Crimes Prosecution Unit in Dili has a shiny new, United Nations-funded net but its fishing waters are far from the larger predators that are its goal. After overcoming

---

[12] UNTAET Regulation 2001/10, ss. 1, 3.

[13] Law No 26/2000 on Human Rights Courts, November 2000, established the Human Rights Court as a special chamber within the Indonesian court structures. Presidential decree 53/2001 established the *ad hoc* Tribunal on East Timor, giving it jurisdiction covering abuses committed after the ballot on 30 August 1999. This was later partially expanded, after international outrage, by Presidential decree 96/2001 to cover abuses in April and September 1999 in the districts of Liquica, Suai and Dili. The mandate has been widely criticised, including by the then United Nations High Commissioner for Human Rights, Mary Robinson, who suspended the programme of technical cooperation on the *ad hoc* Tribunals between OHCHR and the Indonesian government on the basis that the mandate would not allow for effective prosecution of those responsible.

[14] Human Rights Watch, "Justice Denied for East Timor", 9 January 2003.

[15] Longuinhos Monteiro, Prosecutor General of East Timor, speaking at the Symposium on Justice for International Crimes committed in the territory of East Timor, 17 January 2003.

significant early problems largely due to poor management, the unit's performance is considered to have improved significantly after mid-2002.[16] Since the commencement of the Serious Crimes Unit in the UNTAET period, 81 indictments have been filed against 369 accused, including 37 Indonesian TNI Military Commanders and Officers, four Indonesian Chiefs of Police and 60 East Timorese TNI members. However, 281 of those 369 indictees are believed to be outside East Timor. In the Special Panels of the Dili District court, which decide on the serious crimes cases, there have been adjudications for 52 individuals, with 50 having been convicted and two defendants having been acquitted of all charges.[17]

The Special Panels consist of two international judges sitting together with an East Timorese judge. It is clear that no matter how much successful investigation is completed and however many indictments are issued, the process is unable to reach its main targets who are in Indonesia, outside its mandate of operation. There have also been reports of very serious problems in providing defendants with an acceptable level of legal assistance in trials before the Special Panels. Writing about the East Timor Public Defender's Office, which has acted on behalf of persons convicted by the Serious Crimes Panel of serious offences, including crimes against humanity, David Cohen stated:

> This heavy caseload, together with their lack of budget, investigators, and interpreters has meant that they have been unable adequately to prepare cases for trial. Unlike the prosecution, they have no budget to cover the expenses of bringing witnesses to Dili for trial. For all of these reasons the defence did not call a single witness in any of the first fourteen trials.[18]

More recently international defence counsel have acted in all trials, but a lack of sufficient resources and poor recruitment has led to a situation where some international counsel with little or no experience in serious criminal trials have acted on behalf of persons accused of committing crimes against humanity.

In an interview with the *New York Times*, the only Timorese judge to sit on the Serious Crimes Panel to date stated that

---

[16] David Cohen, *Seeking Justice on the Cheap: Is the East Timor Tribunal Really a Model for the Future?*, Asia Pacific Issues, Analysis from the East–West Center, No. 61, August 2002.

[17] Serious Crimes Unit Update, April 1, 2004.

[18] *Ibid.*, p. 5.

> [e]very individual must be responsible for his crimes. But speaking as a Timorese and not as a judge I think this system is not fair. Is it fair to prosecute the small Timorese and not the big ones who gave them orders?[19]

The International Criminal Tribunals for Rwanda and Yugoslavia and the Special Court for Sierra Leone were established with the goal of prosecuting those most responsible for massive human rights abuses. This should also be the goal in the East Timor context. However, the combined effect of the evacuation of Indonesian military and Timorese militias from East Timor in September 1999, the resistance by Members of the Security Council to an international tribunal, the problems with the *ad hoc* tribunal in Jakarta and the national limits of the jurisdiction of the Serious Crimes Unit, is that those most responsible are likely to remain outside the reach of effective prosecution.

Within this context sits the tier closest to the ground, the East Timor Commission for Reception, Truth and Reconciliation (CAVR). The mandate and goals of the Commission are not specifically focussed on providing justice for those responsible for the most serious abuses, and it is not equipped with mechanisms to directly reach them. However, it is hoped that the public hearings, research, inquiries and eventual publication of its report will provide another splinter in the fragmented and perhaps insurmountable challenge of bringing those most responsible for the massive atrocities in East Timor to justice. In addition to this, the Community Reconciliation Procedures (CRPs) programme is an attempt to deal with a proportion of the larger number of perpetrators of lesser crimes, a category whose importance is very often neglected in transitional justice initiatives.

Before dealing in greater detail with these processes and the relationship between the East Timorese courts and the Commission it is helpful to look at the issues which provide the context of this relationship.

II. HISTORICAL FACTORS RELEVANT TO JUSTICE AND RECONCILIATION

The context of the challenges for reconciliation and justice in East Timor involved two major conflicts. The first was a civil war between

[19] New York Times, 4 March 2001.

Timorese factions when the "Carnation Revolution" in Portugal led to an abrupt decision to leave its colonial post in East Timor. This decision, on 25 April 1974, created a vacuum of power in the territory which led to a messy war between two rival groups, both seeking to fill the vacuum with their own authority. It has been reported that human rights abuses were committed by both sides to this war, and there remains much ill-feeling among East Timorese as a result of the severity of actions undertaken during this period. The Fretilin party declared victory and independence of the Democratic Republic of East Timor (RDTL) on 28 November 1975. However, the second relevant conflict commenced only 10 days after independence, on 7 December 1975, when the Republic of Indonesia invaded what was formally a "Portuguese administered non-self-governing territory". Despite widespread international outcry, Indonesia declared East Timor as its twenty-seventh province on 17 July 1976.

The occupation of the territory lasted 24 years, until the fall of the Soeharto regime in Indonesia led to the United Nations-administered ballot on the issue of independence, on 30 August 1999. During this period many Timorese were involved in some way in a clandestine movement of resistance, and if caught were severely punished for this participation. A minority collaborated and assisted the Indonesian military in a horrific campaign of terror and torture designed to crush the resistance. Some human rights abuses committed by members of the resistance have also been reported. It is estimated that up to 200,000 East Timorese civilians died as a result of this struggle.[20]

The situation reached a climax during the period leading up to the ballot of 1999 when elements of the Indonesian security forces and armed groups of young, often illiterate, thugs who became East Timorese militia. Both military and militia attacked Timorese pro-independence sympathisers, with the aim of securing votes for East Timor to remain part of Indonesia, with special autonomy status.[21] The extreme violence of 1999 is often referred to by East Timorese as the "tail" of the problem which had been ongoing since 1974.

An interesting feature of this history is that throughout the 24-year period there was much mixing of the two groups. Some families were divided on the issue, marriages took place across the lines of political opinion, people changed their minds, some sat on the fence and swayed with the wind, others kept an outward appearance

---

[20] James Dunn, *Timor, A People Betrayed* (1983); J. Taylor, *East Timor, The Price of Freedom (2000)*.

[21] See UN Doc. A/54/660; David Cohen, Komnas HAM, *supra* note 1.

which denied their real beliefs and covert work. Both factions share some blame for the human rights abuses, but the apportionment of this blame is not equal and the details remain unclear. The full story of what actually took place has not been uncovered, as the territory was almost totally closed to journalists and other foreign eyes for much of the period.

III. THE COMMISSION FOR RECEPTION, TRUTH AND RECONCILIATION

In August, 2000, the CNRT (coalition of all East Timorese pro-independence parties) National Congress passed a unanimous resolution calling for the establishment of a truth and reconciliation commission.[22] Following this, a steering committee of eleven representatives of Timorese groups and the United Nations was formed and given the task of researching and formulating a mechanism which might be applicable to the needs of East Timor. The model for a Commission for Reception, Truth and Reconciliation which was finally reached (after much grass-roots consultation) was a combination of aspects found in other similar commissions, and new approaches tailored to the situation in East Timor.

Under its empowering legislation, the Commission is mandated to inquire into human rights violations which were committed between 25 April 1974 (corresponding with the decolonisation decision in Portugal) and 25 October 1999 (the date of the establishment of the UNTAET mission).[23] This period contrasts sharply with the mandate of the Serious Crimes Unit, which covers the period from 1 January to 25 October 1999. Although technically it would appear that the SCU mandate can be read to include war crimes, crimes against humanity, genocide and torture committed before 1999, practical considerations have led to a policy decision that the Serious Crimes Unit will concentrate on the 1999 crimes. The Commission's inquiries, however, will cover the 1974–1999 period. The Commission is mandated to operate for two and a half years. Its objectives include the following:

---

[22] Report of the CNRT National Congress, Dili, East Timor, August 2000.

[23] UNTAET Regulation 2001/10, On the Establishment of the Commission for Reception, Truth and Reconciliation, s. 1(c) (definition of "human rights violations").

1. To inquire into and establish the truth regarding human rights violations which occurred during the mandated period, and the factors which may have led to these violations, and to compile a Report of these findings;
2. To assist victims, promote human rights and reconciliation;
3. To make recommendations to the government;
4. To conduct Community Reconciliation Procedures, offering an alternative to court proceedings for politically related lesser crimes;
5. To refer matters to the Office of the General Prosecutor where appropriate.[24]

With regard to truth-seeking, the Commission is empowered to: make investigations and hold hearings, both public and closed; compel witnesses to attend hearings, answer questions and produce documents; search and seize relevant objects or documents (on the approval of a warrant by an investigating judge and administered by the police).

IV. THE RELATIONSHIP BETWEEN THE COMMISSION AND THE SERIOUS CRIMES INVESTIGATION UNIT

The Regulation establishing the Commission provides that nothing in that Regulation shall prejudice the exclusive prosecutorial authority of the General Prosecutor and Deputy General Prosecutor for Serious Crimes, nor the exclusive jurisdiction over serious criminal offences of the Serious Crimes Panels of the Dili District Court.[25] This provision clearly reflects the policy that although the Commission and the Serious Crimes mechanisms are intended to operate in a complementary manner, prosecution for serious crimes should not be adversely affected by the Commission, nor should it participate in activities which might impinge on the exclusive jurisdiction mentioned above.

A major issue in any jurisdiction where a truth commission has been established is whether information given to the Commission must be made available to those bodies responsible for prosecutions, or alternatively, whether it should be privileged. The issue sits at the intersection between the twin goals of justice and reconciliation.

---

[24] *Ibid.*

[25] *Ibid.*, s. 22.2.

If information is not protected by privilege it is arguable that the fundamental goal of reconciliation may be undermined, because the essential element of establishing the truth is restricted by witness's fears of prosecution flowing from admissions, and information given about past abuses. No less importantly, protection or privilege over information given to a Commission may serve to protect perpetrators who should be brought to trial. It can limit the information available to both prosecution and defence counsel, resulting in potential impunity or the denial of a fair trial for those accused.

In East Timor, after much consideration, it was decided that information given to the Commission would *not be protected by privilege*. Witnesses can be compelled to appear and answer questions under oath, and to produce documents of items requested.[26] However they cannot be compelled to give answers which may incriminate themselves, their spouse, parents, children or relatives in the second degree. In this way witnesses cannot be forced to give information which might incriminate themselves, but if they choose to do so this information is not protected and could be used to prosecute themselves or others.

A number of factors particular to the setting in East Timor tipped the balance in making the above decision. As the Commission was designed at a time which was very soon after the period of intense violence and destruction, there was little grassroots acceptance of provisions which might limit the potential for prosecuting those responsible for serious crimes. In addition, an entirely new legal system was being set up, in a context where there was no existing public confidence in the law. It was felt that the procedures of the Commission should not affect the development of this fragile process, as a strong and independent legal system is perhaps the most fundamental building block in the construction of the new nation. Maintaining full support for these principles outweighed the degree to which this decision might hinder the truth-seeking goals. At the same time it was felt that if witnesses were able to be compelled to appear and answer questions they must enjoy the fundamental right not to incriminate themselves.[27]

The Commission was given powers to accept information on a confidential basis.[28] Such information must be passed to the Office of the General Prosecutor (OGP) if requested, but the Regulation

---

[26] *Ibid.*, s. 14.

[27] Notes from Steering Committee meetings, Sept–Oct, 2000.

[28] *Ibid.*, s. 44.

specifically states that the Commission shall not be compelled to release such information except on the request of the OGP.[29] Although it appears that information which is given to the Commission must be passed on to the OGP if requested, there is no requirement that clearly compels the Commission to pass information to the OGP as a matter of course (without a specific request) or any reference to the time at which such information or recommendation for prosecutions should be given. Thus it would seem to be within the mandate of the Commission's truth-seeking function to investigate material, receive information and maintain it confidentially, until decisions are made concerning whether such material should be part of its final report and recommendations. If during this period specific requests are made by the OGP to supply information, however, such requests cannot be resisted. It should be noted that it is only the OGP which has the power to compel the CAVR to disclose confidential information. No department within the government, the office of the President etc., has a similar power.

V. COMMUNITY RECONCILIATION PROCEDURES

At the time that the Commission was designed, a number of factors, many common to other post-conflict situations, made it clear that a new solution should be sought to the problem of the thousands of less serious crimes which had been committed during the period of violence. Such a mechanism would be complementary to the work of the Serious Crimes Unit, with its mandate to target those responsible for more serious crimes. This focus was especially important as there were significant difficulties facing prosecution of those most responsible and it was felt that without some practical, achievable mechanism aimed the majority of perpetrators (those involved in lesser crimes), the unresolved anger of victim communities may lead to renewed violence directed at those within their own communities who had participated in the programme of abuses.

There are several factors relevant to the development of this new mechanism. The infant legal system was stretched dealing with new crimes and the most serious of the past crimes. The 60,000 houses

[29] *Ibid.*, s. 44(2). At the discretion of the Commission, any person shall be permitted to provide information to the Commission on a confidential basis. The Commission shall not be compelled to release information, except on request of the Office of the General Prosecutor.

which were burned in September 1999 were added to thousands of crimes such as assault, thefts, etc., to provide a massive caseload of lesser crimes. There was simply no possibility that these matters could be effectively completed by the available legal mechanisms. Almost none of the small pool of lawyers in the country had any practical experience. Inexperienced new judges and prosecutors had been appointed and were being trained whilst at the same time struggling to deal with the caseload of new crimes demanding their attention each day. The inclusion of the old politically related cases added a huge and, in practical terms, valueless (*i.e.*, they could not practically be judicially completed) pressure to a level which was already at breaking point. In addition, as there was no capacity to deal with these cases, there would be a *de facto* amnesty or situation of impunity for those responsible. This would undermine the efforts to establish a credible justice system, with no acceptable answer available to citizens who ask why they should be punished for new offences, which others in their own communities had committed in the recent past with no repercussions.

In East Timor the majority of perpetrators came from the same villages as the victims. This was a significant difference to many other situations, for example the majority of cases dealt with by the Truth and Reconciliation Commission in South Africa. In East Timor it was not a case of perpetrators and victims facing each other at a public hearing and then moving back to their own communities hundreds or even thousands of kilometres away. The militia had been recruited from available young males in villages and in many cases had attacked persons whom they had known since they were children, had attended school with, etc. If there is to be peace and reconciliation in East Timor, the future is one in which victims and perpetrators must be part of each other's daily lives. Regular, face-to-face confrontation mixed with unresolved anger is a formula for renewed conflict. Moreover, even if the courts did have the capacity to deal with these thousands of crimes, it would not solve the problem perpetrators have within their own communities. Prison sentence served in far-away Dili could not buy acceptance, safety and reconciliation with the persons they needed to live with, day by day.

Evidence of these different needs includes the fact that a number of persons who were convicted and served their sentences in prison contacted the CAVR to request participation in a CRP process following release from prison. It has been commonly stated by persons involved in CRP hearings that the most important aspect of reacceptance into the communities is the requirement of perpetrators to admit their actions in front of the whole community, listen face to face to the anger and comments of victims, publicly apologise and then live with this social readjustment on a day to day basis.[30]

The goals of the formal criminal justice system are different and do not include these factors. Criminal justice models are designed to deal with individual crimes against the state, and victims do not usually have any opportunity to speak to perpetrators, or *visa versa.* The acts committed by many East Timorese needed to be understood also in relation to the damage they created to social relationships, the torn social fabric which needed to be repaired and the different nature of identity of those who live in communal groups. This required mechanisms designed both for justice – to punish those responsible, but also to repair the destroyed social fabric which is the guardian of social order and peace.

Accountability for crimes committed during the relevant period was a muddy pool. Many perpetrators had been manipulated or forced to join in the pro-autonomy programme, drugs had been distributed to some involved in the violence, a massive project involving pressure and intimidation to accept a particular political view had been imposed, there had been much offering of favours, rewards, honour, etc., to simple villagers unable to detect the level of manipulation. A significant proportion had played a mixed role with outward actions directly opposed to those of their "secret" life. Apart from the legal technical difficulties these factors presented, it was felt by many that the formal justice system's effectiveness in the specific context was limited. In order to achieve an acceptable level of justice, promote much-needed reconciliation, and ensure that the huge caseload was not simply ignored a new tool was needed. The new tool would need to be cheaper, faster and more community-based than existing procedures within the formal justice sector.

In order to find a solution to these issues, the Steering Committee held widespread public consultations, during which it became clear that the overwhelming majority of East Timorese wanted a process which included strict legal punishment for the most serious offenders but also provided a more lenient, community-based mechanism to deal with perpetrators of less-serious crimes. In addition, it was felt that both the traditional justice systems and the formal justice system should be in some way involved. The traditional systems were designed for dealing with relatively simple cases that arise in the

[30] Interviews conducted with participants in CRP hearings, Oct–Dec, 2003.

day-to-day village life; not large-scale offences of the type and magnitude of those committed in 1999. The justice system was too rigid and lacked capacity but, by taking elements of both, a workable solution to deal with this particular caseload might be reached.

In Part IV of UNTAET Regulation 2000/10, the Commission was given powers to hold Community Reconciliation Procedures (CRPs).[31] These procedures seek to achieve an agreement by perpetrators to undertake community service or other acts of reconciliation after a community-based hearing, which airs the views of all parties and requires an admission and apology from a perpetrator. This agreement will be then registered with the nearest District Court. When its terms are completed the threat of criminal and civil liability for the actions of the perpetrator will be forever removed.

Each step of these procedures is set out in the Regulation. They include significant co-operation and interaction between the Commission and the Office of the General Prosecutor (OGP). In particular, the decision as to which matters are appropriate to be dealt with the Commission remains with the OGP. The statement of each perpetrator who wishes to take part in a CRP which is received by the Commission must be forwarded to the OGP, who will decide if the matter will proceed as a prosecution or is an appropriate matter for a community hearing. If during the hearing of the CRP credible information is given of a deponent's participation in a serious criminal offence, the hearing must be adjourned and the matter referred back to the OGP.[32] After the hearing, the Community Reconciliation Agreement must be forwarded to the nearest District Court. "Unless the relevant District Court considers that the act of reconciliation specified in the CRA exceeds what is reasonably proportionate to the acts disclosed or that the CRA violates human rights principles",[33] the Agreement will be registered and a temporary stay of prosecution comes into force over those acts included in the deponent's statement. When the deponent has completed all of the acts of reconciliation agreed to he or she will no longer hold any criminal or civil liability for acts disclosed in the Agreement.

Perhaps the best way to illustrate how they apply in practice is by an illustrative example, which includes many aspects of CRP hearings already held. Perpetrator A returns from West Timor, having previously been part of a group which burnt two houses in September

[31] *Ibid.*, Part IV.
[32] *Ibid.*, s. 27.5.
[33] *Ibid.*, s. 28.2.

1999. During the same period he also beat four people in his village and stole a motorbike. He is afraid that he will be subjected to payback violence and wants to reintegrate with his community. He is accompanied by B and C who were forced to join a militia group in 1999, later became caught up in their activities and were involved in intimidation and minor assaults.

The three young men contact and give statements to the local representatives of the Truth and Reconciliation Commission which briefly outline the wrongful acts which they wish the Commission to deal with. Before giving this statement the deponents must be clearly informed that information included in these statements may be used against them in future legal proceedings. The statements are sent to the CAVR National Office where a Statements Committee reviews them and passes them on to the Office of the General Prosecutor with a recommendation as to whether the case is considered appropriate for a CRP. The Office of the General Prosecutor checks the facts against its own files to decide whether to initiate proceedings, to ensure that the perpetrators are not implicated in more serious crimes and check that there is no information contradicting the content of the statement. The Prosecutor General signifies the matters are appropriate to be dealt with by CRP and the files are returned to the Commission, within two weeks of receipt. If the OGP intends to exercise jurisdiction over a matter, the file is not returned to the CAVR but remains in the office of the Prosecutor.

A Community Reconciliation Process in the perpetrators' village is then arranged, presided over by a panel of three to five leaders, including a local catechist from the Catholic Church, a traditional spiritual leader and elders, including two women. It is chaired by a Regional Commissioner. The perpetrators publicly state what they have done, ask for forgiveness and renounce the use of violence for political ends. Victims and the community give their views, including telling the perpetrators face to face how their actions have affected the victims' lives. An agreement is then brokered by the Panel whereby A agrees to assist in rebuilding of a local school, return of the motorbike and to provide one pig and a small amount of cash to specific victims. The community indicates that the public apology from the other two perpetrators is sufficient. Traditional ceremonial practices, including communal chewing of betel nut on a large mat are used to achieve and settle the Community Reconciliation Agreement. The Agreement is then registered with the District Court whereby criminal and civil liability of the two perpetrators of the more minor crimes is extinguished. When A has completed his payments and work on the school he also will no longer be held legally liable for the actions declared in the CRP.

5.1. *Results of the CRP Program*

At the end of March 2004, the CAVR completed its programmes in the districts of East Timor, including the CRP programme. It is generally considered by both national and international observers that the CRP programme has been a resounding success. When the programme was planned there was a stated goal of 1000 cases to be completed. Although at that time this was thought to be too high to be practical, in fact by the close of the programme more than 1500 statements had been taken and forwarded to the General Prosecutor – more than 50% over the initial goal. A total of 1404 perpetrators had successfully completed CRP district hearings, with 111 cases remaining with the General Prosecutor for possible future legal action.

No comprehensive analysis of the impact of the programme on communities has yet been undertaken. However, the CAVR had conducted a mid-programme follow-up programme of interviews with participants to ascertain the level of community satisfaction with the program. This series of interviews, conducted with perpetrators, victims, communities and panel members produced the following general conclusions:

- Over 90% of all those interviewed stated that the process had been a positive one and that they had been satisfied with its results.
- A major proportion of perpetrators interviewed also stated that the CRP process had produced a "significant positive effect" on their day to day lives.
- Every perpetrator interviewed stated that the process had assisted in repairing the relationship between themselves and their community. Many stated that they were now free to move freely within their communities whereas this had been restricted before.
- The majority of victims interviewed stated that after the CRP hearings they felt more respected within their communities and there had been a change of relationship with the perpetrator in that the victims' status had been elevated.
- Many victims answered that the process had helped them to understand the motivation and circumstances surrounding the actions of the perpetrator. There were many comments which

> recognised that the acts had been perpetrated during a time of war, and this made them more understandable.[34]

One extremely interesting finding from the survey was that victims did not consider that the nature or degree of punishment, or "act of reconciliation" which the perpetrator had to carry out, was of crucial importance. Victims stated overwhelmingly that the most important determining factor in whether a perpetrator should be accepted back into the community was the strength of their public admission and apology. If the admissions were full and did not avoid responsibility and the apology was considered to be heartfelt then the major block to acceptance was removed. Acts carried out in furtherance of the agreement were of lesser importance. In fact in many cases victims and communities demanded only a full confession of responsibility and apology. On the other hand in a number of cases reconciliation and acceptance could not proceed because victims stated that they did not believe the apology was real.[35]

Despite the positive nature of responses to the CAVR survey, more independent research undertaken after an intervening period will be needed before conclusions can be drawn. However, some concerns of victims have been received by the CAVR in relation to the CRPs. These include feelings of discontent related to their continuing situations of poverty, exacerbated in some cases by the fact that perpetrators may be economically better off, increasing feelings of injustice. In addition, many victims have expressed serious concerns flowing from the fact that the major perpetrators of the human rights violations remain free and prosperous in Indonesia whilst they struggle to rebuild their lives in East Timor. Also unclear is the degree to which the community's desire to settle matters and reintegrate perpetrators may have influenced or pressured the acceptance, often without significant sanction, by the victims.

The procedure has many advantages. It is faster, simpler and much cheaper than having the case investigated by police, prepared by prosecutors, defended and finalised by a court, leading perhaps to a prison sentence. In the context of East Timor it replaces what is realistically no process, as there are insufficient resources to deal with any significant number of these cases. Thus whatever level of success is achieved is more than that which would otherwise have been reached.

---

34 Report of Ben Larke, adviser to the CRP programme of the CAVR, June, 2003.
35 *Ibid.*

The CRP programme allows victims and the community to give their views and participate in the process, and thus own both the procedures and the results. It is more effective in reaching a solution which is community-based and therefore reflects what those affected actually want, taking into account all the underlying factors of which only they are aware. It can be much more effective in providing protection for perpetrators, as the local leaders of the particular community are involved in brokering the agreement. Thus if someone decided that they would beat the perpetrator even though he has complied with the agreement the aggressor would himself be in opposition to his local leaders. The level of security gained by involving the local structures involves community sanctions and disincentives, which operate 24 hours per day, 7 days per week. Police coverage cannot even approach this, particularly in remote mountain regions. It includes and utilises the strength of local spiritual and traditional practices. In the absence of the reach or respect for a formal justice system such practices hold significant strength and meaning.

Perhaps the greatest evidence of the success of the programme is the degree to which communities have utilised it. More than 1500 perpetrators have volunteered to participate and a recent survey on the justice sector of East Timor indicated that all districts wanted the CRP programme to be continued. However the programme is not just targeted at perpetrators, its goal is to repair community relationships. It is estimated that from a total population of fewer than one million people, between 30,000 and 40,000 community members have attended and participated in a CRP procedure. It would seem that the scope and support given to the programme has been a major factor in deterring the predicted payback violence, which has failed to materialise.

5.2. *Negative Aspects and Challenges to the CRP Programme*

The implementation of the CRP programme in the villages of East Timor revealed a number of problems, some of which related to the design and drafting of the Regulation, others due to the nature and complexity of the issues. Among these problems were:

1. The legal challenge of defining a "serious crime" were never fully addressed. For example, UNTAET Regulation 2001/15 gave the Office of the General Prosecutor exclusive jurisdiction over "serious criminal offences". These offences included crimes against humanity, genocide, war crimes, murder, sexual offences

and torture. However, a relatively minor act, such as a beating, or a house-burning, if committed against a political group (pro-independence supporters) could fulfil the elements of, for example, the crime of persecution as a crime against humanity. Thus, although the legislation and implementation of the CRP programme is centred on the fact that it should not address "serious criminal offences", in fact technically many of the cases dealt with could fall within this definition, even though they may involve relatively minor acts. The solution undertaken when this problem was realised was to set out in a Schedule to Regulation 2001/10 "Criteria for Determining whether Offence appropriately dealt with in a CRP". These criteria included the nature of the offence, with examples of theft, minor assault and arson, the total number of acts committed, the perpetrator's role, and a statement that "[i]n principle, serious criminal offences, in particular murder, torture and sexual offences, shall not be dealt with in a Community Reconciliation Procedure".[36] In fact the original schedule had stated that "under no circumstances" could a CRP deal with a serious criminal offence, but for the reasons stated above this was later amended to "in principle". This allowed the Prosecutor to decide not to exercise jurisdiction over matters which may technically have constituted serious criminal offences. Thus, at the point where the OGP returns the matter to the CAVR for hearing there is no indication that the matter is not a serious crime, only that a decision has been made not to exercise jurisdiction.

2. The justice system did not develop as quickly as expected and in fact is falling further and further behind. At the time of writing there was a caseload of over 1000 new matters of "less serious crimes" to be decided by the Dili District Court with only three sitting judges, none of which has significant experience. Although it had always been anticipated that the courts could not deal with the huge number of past cases it is now obvious that no past cases, even those which are close to the border of jurisdiction as a "serious criminal offence" will be addressed. This has removed any incentive of the threat of prosecution from potential participants in the CRP. Although this may be seen as a very positive sign of success, in that so many volunteered to participate without such threat, communities reported that the major

[36] Regulation 2001/10 Schedule 1.4.

problem with the programme was that many who should have participated did not. This was because these persons were either in West Timor or chose not to attend.

3. Some legal standards have been compromised in the interests of practicality. Because it was obviously impossible for all participants to be advised by lawyers the process was designed as an entirely voluntary undertaking. However, the admissions made in the statements are admissible in court and deponents are not advised by a lawyer before making such admissions, although they are informed of the potential uses. This is a serious issue, which provides a major hurdle to the design, as a fundamental aspect is the consideration of cases by the OGP, all of which involve admissions. The result is that, notwithstanding the likelihood that the cases will be proceeded with, following the close of the CRP programme the statements and admissions of 111 deponents, all taken without legal advice, remain with the OGP.
4. It now appears that the Serious Crimes Unit will not be able to complete investigation of all 1999 cases of murder, rape and torture before its mandate is completed and funding is no longer available. This leaves a potentially significant caseload of matters which have may "fall between the cracks" of the two procedures, more serious than those dealt with by CRP's and yet potentially not dealt with at all. This will produce the dangers of impunity for these offences and the accompanying threat of vigilante justice.
5. Because the goal of the process is reconciliation and reacceptance of the perpetrator into the community there is some concern that individual victims' wishes, although freely expressed, may be affected by pressure from the community as a whole. In this context all communities have also been victims, but care should be taken not to manipulate the agreement of individuals. This duty of care may not have been sufficiently recognised.

5.3. *Other Programmes of the CAVR*

At the close of the CAVR's field operations on 31 March 2004 it was clear that it had provided a substantially greater focus on grass roots reconciliation initiatives than any previous truth and reconciliation commission. In addition to the approximately 1500 CRPs, 52 public hearings dedicated to victims had been conducted in most of the subdistricts, three-day healing workshops had been conducted for hundreds of the worst affected victims, also providing them with a small sum as symbolic reparation, 262 community mapping exercises in the worst affected villages had produced, through participatory process, community profiles of human rights abuses in each of these communities, 7200 victim statements had been collected, and eight major thematic public hearings had been held in the capital, Dili. Programmes have also been run in the refugee camps in West Timor.

The thematic public hearings, covered nation-wide by television and radio, have had been extremely well received by the population. Despite earlier fears that they may provoke violence by uncovering old wounds. In an unprecedented event, in December 2003, all major national leaders, including the President, Prime Minister, President of the Parliament, Chief of the armed forces, heads of all major political parties, and a number of serving Ministers gave public evidence of the events of the civil war, in which they had participated. The event included significant public evidence given by these leaders of the roles, which they played in the conflict, acceptance of responsibility, apologies to victims, and previously unreconciled leaders hugged and wept together on national television. The leading Portuguese journalist on East Timorese affairs, who had covered almost the entire period of the conflict, wrote the following after this public hearing:

> I do not know what the Timorese felt. But I, who had become a friend of these men and women – these men and these women who had more illusions and dreams than I have hair – felt during those moments that this was the most magnificent point, in human terms, that I had witnessed in the history of Timor–Leste... I believe that the whole world, once again, was distracted when the Timorese were giving it, as well as all of us, a lesson in humanity.[37]

VI. CONCLUSIONS

Justice and reconciliation in countries recovering from widespread human rights abuses are two complementary tools with the same objective. The goals are in no way in competition with each other. Those responsible for the past horrors must be brought to account. But accountability processes will have only limited success in healing community wounds. A different, widereaching and practical programme is needed to address this post-conflict reality.

The work of the East Timor Commission for Reception, Truth and Reconciliation is separate but inextricably linked to the various legal mechanisms focussed on accountability for the human rights

[37] "A Lesson in Humanity", Adelino Gomes, Publico newspaper.

abuses committed in the territory between 1974 and 1999. Its truth-seeking, research and investigation procedures will, it is hoped, pull together information from a wide variety of sources to produce the first historical account of that period. The resulting report of the Commission will inform the international debate concerning the need for an international tribunal, and may recommend domestic prosecutions. It will also, it is hoped, inform the Indonesian public on a special chapter in their national history, and in doing so assist the progress from the abuses of the New Order military dictatorship towards a society based on democratic principles.

The CRP programmes implemented by the CAVR have provided a valuable mechanism which communities report has significantly increased their sense of harmony and reconciliation. The much predicted large scale of pay-back abuses since 1999 have not taken place, and in fact there has been surprisingly little violence meted out to former perpetrators of abuses. In addition the CRP programme has been the only face of justice that many East Timorese have seen since their country became independent. This is as much a negative report on the difficulties and failures of the formal justice system as it is evidence of the CAVR's success. Much more needs to be urgently done to ensure that the nascent justice system overcomes these difficulties so that it is able to present a uniform and effective system of law of law to the population. In this regard the programmes of the CAVR have been a valuable transitional tool which must now be built into a more permanent and comprehensive legal approach.

The four-tiered approach which has unfolded in the context of East Timor is, as mentioned earlier, infested at each level with termites which undermine the potential for success.

(i) The international tribunal is the only mechanism which can bring those most responsible for the massive human rights abuses to justice. Although it may seem to be perhaps closer to a dream at this point in history, it is no more fantastic than any commentator's prediction in, say, 1995, that East Timor would be free and independent before the end of the millennium.

(ii) The Jakarta *ad hoc* Tribunal process in many respects falls far short of internationally acceptable standards, and has been described by Human Rights Watch as "Indonesia's Sham Prosecutions".[38]

[38] Human Rights Watch, *supra* note 2.

(iii) The Serious Crimes panel in Dili has indicted hundreds of perpetrators, including those at the most senior levels of the Indonesian military service. This is a valuable and important contribution, but unfortunately most of those indicted remain outside the SCU mandate. The Special Panels of the Dili District court have handed down a substantial number of convictions for serious crimes, but these have been able only to target mid-level militia group leaders and members, a significant number of which had previously been illiterate farmers.

(iv) The CAVR has provided a restorative form of justice at the village level, which has assisted reconciliation and averted renewed violence. But the CRP programme also has not been able to include the most serious perpetrators within its potential mandate. Other CAVR grass-roots programmes have also made a major contribution to reconciliation and the Final Report will hopefully add to the level of justice achieved by exposing the truth and publicly shaming those responsible. This Report is due to be presented to the national President and to the Secretary General of the United Nations in October 2004.

Any solution or partial solution put forward in the context of reconciliation and justice in a post conflict environment can very easily be criticised. In fact such criticism has become somewhat of an armchair industry. East Timor, like other fragile new democracies, does not have the luxury of working only with lofty theoretic ideals of justice and reconciliation. If the choice is to move forward then the choice is to work in the mud – to somehow find ways to proceed, however slowly, in a creaking under-resourced wagon, carrying the almost overwhelming weight of complicated historical conflict saturated in highly charged, inflammable emotion. As in all similar contexts there will never be clear solutions, which satisfy all parties and sufficiently take into account all relevant principles. The available choices are to do nothing, holding smugly to a clean book of rules, or to face the real challenges and find new ways to make some progress, maintaining momentum, balance and morale whilst inevitably moving sideways and sometimes even backwards, with eyes firmly focussed on the road ahead.

MARTIN IMBLEAU*

INITIAL TRUTH ESTABLISHMENT BY TRANSITIONAL BODIES AND THE FIGHT AGAINST DENIAL

Denial of gross human rights violations is usually a disguised form of racism. Deniers argue that *apartheid* in South Africa was a moderate and justifiable national policy; that there was no such thing as a policy of disappearance and torture in Chile under Pinochet; that the genocide in Rwanda was an exaggerated event, the 1994 death toll actually resulting from a typically trivial African ethnic war; that the Holocaust is a giant hoax, that it never took place, that the only thing gassed at Auschwitz and Treblinka were lice and that the six million Jews supposedly killed were actually alive and wealthy in Israel or in the United States. Deniers also support Milosevic's version of recent history, *i.e.*, that the Srebrenica massacre that killed 7000 people was prepared by the Muslims themselves. This subtler, but just as efficient form of racism, aims at attacking the historical truth. It does so notably vis-à-vis the first official records of the violations, in most cases those established by transitional bodies such as the International Military Tribunal (IMT) at Nuremberg. The deniers' intent is to justify the criminal behaviour of regimes condemned by such bodies, to rehabilitate these regimes and to eliminate, in public opinion, the barrier those past events represent for the resurgence of criminal policies.

---

* Martin Imbleau obtained his bachelor in Law diploma from the Université du Québec à Montréal where he is now a lecturer, and his Master degree in Law at the Université de Montréal. He practices law in Montreal, Canada. He is also an independent researcher, mainly on the interplay between massive human rights violations and the establishment of historical truth. He is the author of *La négation du génocide nazi – Liberté d'expression ou crime raciste?*

Criminal Law Forum **15:** 159–192, 2004.
© 2004 *Kluwer Academic Publishers. Printed in the Netherlands.*

A typical fair-minded reader[1] might unfortunately believe those allegations. What allows their rejection and potentially the prosecution of deniers is that the events are historical facts established by judicial bodies such as a court of law, or by a quasi-judicial transitional body like a truth commission. Thus, they cannot be denied by anyone acting in good faith. This is the first, and remains the most important, obstacle facing those who deny historical facts like the ones mentioned above. The Shoah, for example, was established by the IMT[2]and the Srebrenica massacre by the International Criminal Tribunal for former Yugoslavia (ICTY).[3]

It is our society as a whole that is under attack when crimes of such magnitude, having affected us as human beings, are denied. A transitional body,[4] whether a court of law or a truth commission, aims at establishing the truth. It can be set up for a single crime or have a broader scope, as is usually the case for investigations concerning gross human rights violations. When looking at events like genocide, crimes against humanity, *apartheid* or a widespread disappearance policy, the truth obtained by transitional bodies will have more than one facet. Immediate justice, or other forms of accountability, is certainly a goal and a pressing need. The establishment of a truth, a historical one that will serve as a point of reference now and in the future, is also an objective for transitional bodies. Besides more short-term goals, the truth these bodies establish and share may very well serve for longer periods

---

[1] In the Irving case against Professor Lipstadt, the judge used the expression to evaluate the effects of deniers'propaganda on readers: "My task is to arrive, without over-elaborate analysis, at the meaning or meanings which the notional typical reader of the publication in question, reading the book in ordinary circumstances, would have understood the words complained of, in their context, to bear. Such a reader is to be presumed to be fair-minded and not prone to jumping to conclusions but to be capable of a certain amount of loose thinking." See *Irving* v. *Penguin Books Limited and Lipstadt*, High Court of Justice, Queen's Bench Division, n° 11996-I-1113, 11 April 2000; Mr. Justice Gray.

[2] *France* et al., v. *Goering* et al., (1946) 22 IMT 203.

[3] *Prosecutor* v. *Krstic* (Case No. IT-98-33), Judgment, 2 August 2001.

[4] The expression "transitional bodies" is used in this text to describe judicial, quasi-judicial or inquiry bodies used at the end of a conflict or in cases where serious and systematic human rights violations have taken place. In most cases, the mission of these bodies is to come to terms with the past. The expression encompasses courts of law, special courts, international courts, truth commissions (with or without a reconciliation mandate) and inquiry bodies. See Alexandra Barahona De Brito, Carmen Gonzalés-Enriquez and Paloma Aguilar, *Introduction*, in THE POLITICS OF MEMORY – TRANSITIONAL JUSTICE IN DEMOCRATIZING SOCIETIES 1 (2001).

and may be used as foundations to preclude past criminal behaviour from reappearing. This truth may shape our future. When trying to define the advantages and the risks associated with establishing the truth in periods of transition by bodies that have been established, in whole or in part, for that purpose, we ought both to realise and to take into consideration the long-term reasons for undertaking such a process in the first place. In this paper, we will explore this long-term effect of a transitional body's mandate and the prophylactic function of the historical truth they establish.

There is today, if not a consensus (since some argue that forgetting may sometimes be the only option), at least some generally shared belief that past violations should be looked at.[5] Transitional bodies offer the first possibility to do so, because they are the initial forums for truth establishment following a troubled period. Their acts and decisions influence not only the first phase following the collapse of an exiting regime and the transition, but they also have an impact on the historical record itself. In this text, we look at the possibility for transitional bodies to establish a truth that can serve not only the present but that can be considered historical. We will consider some constraints those bodies face and certain traps they need to avoid for their record to be considered a foundation for historical truth. Transitional bodies are not in a position to investigate all crimes and to provide conclusions on every abuse. They rather tend to concentrate on the most vicious forms of criminality, as for example the policies behind such criminal behaviour. In doing so, they establish not an exhaustive record but a higher level of truth, a macro-truth that looks at perpetrators and certain victims and that may choose representative cases. In general, it is likely that a truth commission will be chosen over trials or at least that it will be part of transitional institutions. In this context, we focus more on truth commissions but nonetheless consider the implications a criminal trial can have.

I. THE TEACHING VALUE OF HISTORICAL TRUTHS

People cannot and must not lack historical memory. Before turning the page on events, a population needs to know *what* it is turning the page on. Amnesia, forced upon the people by the State, does not do

---

[5] P. HAYNER, UNSPEAKABLE TRUTHS – CONFRONTING STATE TERROR AND ATROCITY 11 (2001).

any good.[6] How can something new be initiated, a new phase in a country's history, if the population is not aware of the preceding period? Large scale, state-sponsored massacres or massive human rights violations should not be interpreted in multiple ways. Before engaging in any debate about who is responsible for what and who is to be held accountable, and before trying to understand the lessons learned from the past, the facts must be known. No society, no transformation can be built on contested empirical claims about historical truth.[7] This is the short-term effect of truth establishment.

The establishment and the protection of events like the Holocaust, *apartheid* and the Rwandan genocide is necessary because their elimination from our history has an objective: the elimination of their importance in the collective conscience. All crimes are not equal and do not have the same impact or significance. Accountability for disappearances, state-sponsored torture, crimes against humanity, or genocide has a prophylactic function. These events can be projected beyond themselves and in some instances govern the acts of the present. For example, no citizen of South Africa can now deny the country's past. Presenting the truth has been an essential step in implementing a new regime. Acknowledgement and rejection of the racist system that prevailed was a prerequisite.

The same is true of many other cases. This recognition is vital if, in the future, the circumstances of the present are ever used to justify a re-interpretation, or especially if a complete denial of the past should surface. The reappropriation of the dead for different causes and needs is not an isolated event, quite the contrary. It is a widely shared temptation.[8] The truth links the past to the present, the population to the victims. This is the long-term effect of truth establishment.

History is the only tool to deal with deniers of gross human rights violations. The very first and most efficient way to adequately fight these hooligans is to know the truth, to share it and to ensure it lasts. Only a demonstration based on facts can repel deniers. The ways of referring to history in order to fight deniers

---

[6] P. Aguilar, *Justice, Politics and Memory in the Spanish Transition*, in THE POLITICS OF MEMORY, *supra* note 4, at p. 102.

[7] Mark J. Osiel, *Making Public Memory, Publicly*, in HUMAN RIGHTS IN POLITICAL TRANSITIONS: GETTYSBURG TO BOSNIA 240 (Carla Hesse and Robert Post, eds., 1999).

[8] JEAN-MICHEL CHAUMONT, LA CONCURRENCE DES VICTIMES – GÉNOCIDE, IDENTITÉ, RECONNAISSANCE 14 (2002).

may vary from one set of circumstances to another, though. For example, prosecuting them for what they are truly trying to do, that is, the reinstatement of racist state-sponsored behaviour, is an option in some countries.[9] The most active, and without a doubt the most pernicious movement has been that of the Holocaust deniers, or revisionists, as they falsely refer to themselves. Briefly, the philosophy behind prosecution and criminalization is intended to protect the veracity of the Holocaust in order to block deniers' intentions to eliminate the historical fact as a whole, so they can rehabilitate the national-socialist philosophy and thus allow a new wave of anti-Semitism to reappear.

The first obstacle deniers face is that the event has been established by various sources, notably by the ITM at Nuremberg and by the other trials conducted under the Allied Control Council Law No. 10. Consequently, as long as the Holocaust exists, people will be resistant to implementing discriminatory measures against Jews. The Holocaust has a tremendous bearing in our lives. The event is *the* point of reference for evil acts. Therefore, as long as the event exists, public opinion represents an insurmountable obstacle for deniers. But if it does not exist, if the parapet disappears, nothing precludes the resurgence of racist measures.

It is the teaching of such events, their prophylactic role, that deniers want to erase and that ought to be protected. By eliminating the event from our consciousness and our history, deniers want to influence the present. We may agree or not on the role legislation plays in historical truth protection, and it is not the purpose of this text to argue that point. But in any case, the truth must have a point of reference. In the case of the Holocaust and other gross human rights violations, that record which serves as a reference comes to a large extent from that of a judicial body, either national or international, like the Nuremberg Tribunal, or from that of quasi-judicial or inquiry bodies like truth and reconciliation commissions. Such transitional bodies can legitimately generate this point of reference. They establish themselves as historical authorities and go to some extent beyond the more traditional legal aspects such processes imply.[10]

---

[9] Many European countries have adapted legislation to deal with either Holocaust deniers specifically, the case of France, Germany and Austria, or with denial of gross human rights more generally, as in Switzerland.

[10] See DONALD BLOXHAM, GENOCIDE ON TRIAL – WAR CRIMES TRIALS AND THE FORMATION OF A HOLOCAUST HISTORY AND MEMORY 221 (2001).

II. THE ROLE OF TRIBUNALS OR QUASI-JUDICIAL BODIES IN TRUTH ESTABLISHMENT

Deniers, but also scholars, view judicial truth establishment as biased and limited and argue that it shall therefore never serve the purpose of historical truth establishment. The question is whether it should be the role of a tribunal or of quasi-judicial bodies like truth commissions to establish the truth in the first place, or whether this should exclusively be part of the responsibility of historians, as some claim. Historical narratives can be produced by different means such as trials of the old regime, quasi-judicial or ad hoc bodies created for that very purpose, or by historians. But if trials are adequate to debate a specific historical issue, such as the development of a crime, is this still the case when judges or commissioners are faced with massive human rights violations? We tend to believe that this is even more the case, especially for truth commissions. History is not the sole property of historians.[11] Dealing with historical research and truth establishment should of course not be improvised and collaboration between truth commissions and historians is certainly necessary in some cases.[12] But for a more comprehensive, complex and contested research in countries where massive human rights violations have occurred, historians genuinely depend on documentation accumulated during trials and by truth commissions. In cases of genocide, crimes against humanity or other massive violations of human rights or humanitarian law, the quasi-totality of historical sources comes from the judicial forum, at least during the initial period following the crime. The Nuremberg trial is a good example.[13]

For crimes such as those under investigation by transitional truth-seeking bodies, evidence is sometimes not easy to gather without some imposing investigation work that requires the collaboration of

---

[11] A. B. De Brito, *Truth, Justice, Memory and Democratization in the Southern Cone*, in THE POLITICS OF MEMORY, *supra* note 4, at p. 160.

[12] In South Africa, before the establishment of the Truth and Reconciliation Commission some 24 historians considered the challenges it would face in trying to establish an objective record about past violations. The objective was, as Alex Boraine has noted, to provide accurate and professional records of some human rights violations that had already been documented by various sources throughout the country and by the international community. ALEX BORAINE, A COUNTRY UNMASKED 50 (2000).

[13] See F. Brayard, *Juges et Historiens – Sur un segment et deux triangles*, in LE GÉNOCIDE DES JUIFS ENTRE PROCÈS ET HISTOIRE 1943–2000 14 (F. Brayard, ed., 2000).

many constituents. Victims are held at secret detention centres, their bodies are disposed of secretly and security forces, supported by the state, are denied any access to information.[14] In previous decades, South America faced a continent-wide policy of disappearance where violence ordered or hidden by the authoritarian regimes was clandestine.[15] Unlike the situation in South Africa where legislation authorized some of the acts of government and the security forces, the systematic violence political systems had put in place in South America was covered up and completely denied. Abductions were carried out in absolute secrecy. The truth that emerged from the transitional bodies revealed state implication in the crimes and the impunity that went along with it. Added to the destruction or disappearance of any material evidence, this problem of evidence leads to the use of truth commissions in one form or another.[16] Historians can follow up and pursue more thorough investigations of the established facts but in cases such as those involving disappearance policies, in-depth research by historians would not have provided the basis that is necessary for further research to be undertaken. The report of the Chilean truth commission, issued in the early 1990s, was the very first genuine public manifestation of what had really happened in the country since 1973.[17] For the first time the military were no longer able to ignore and deny the crimes. The establishment of such truth is not possible without some national research such as the one undertaken by a truth commission.

For some authors and scholars, historical truth does not equal judicial truth. The latter faces only two possibilities, the guilty and the innocent. Court are not propitious for the hatching of historical truth[18] because trial content and that of an historical exposé differ in the fact that in the former, the image of the past results from the confrontation between the accusation and the defence and not from an elaborated account or an accumulation of evidence and arguments following a very precise methodology.[19] The trial, they argue, does

---

[14] A. Neir, *Rethinking Truth, Justice, and Guilt after Bosnia and Rwanda*, in HUMAN RIGHTS IN POLITICAL TRANSITION, *supra* note 7, at pp. 39–52

[15] See A. B. De Brito, *supra* note 11, at p. 119.

[16] RUTI G. TEITEL, TRANSITIONAL JUSTICE 78 (2002).

[17] A. B. De Brito, *supra* note 11, at p. 131.

[18] See T. TODOROV, MÉMOIRE DU MAL TENTATION DU BIEN, ENQUÊTE SUR LE SIÈCLE 301 (2000).

[19] Michael R. Marrus, *L'Histoire et l'Holocauste dans le prétoire*, in LE GÉNOCIDE DES JUIFS ENTRE PROCÈS ET HISTOIRE, *supra* note 13, at p. 43.

not call upon science but instead uses the confrontation of different versions of history in a contradictory forum which must always respect any and all rights of the defence. In that context, to render justice is not simply to come to a logical conclusion but to exercise power. Judgment is then not a logical conclusion of the inquiry. For such critics, the difficulty lies in the structural parameters of the trial process, which is a reduction of the past, based upon the need to establish the provable rather than the probable.[20] Thus, there is not only one version of the events but two or more, the tribunal inevitably endorsing one or another version of the competing historical accounts. Time does not affect the two professions in the same way. Historians can always suspend their research or pursue it later, whereas judges usually can't.[21] According to this vision, these forums are ill-suited to establish a proper historical representation since they only offer a limited view, a limited examination of facts.

The controversy is understandable but in our opinion remains academic. One must go beyond this perception and look at the real role and implications of trials and quasi-judicial bodies in those debates. Judges and truth commissioners always have the obligation to decide upon the facts that are being presented to them. The fact that the events are considered to be historical ones should be of no importance here to them. Contrary to the allegations made by some who oppose the role of trials or quasi-judicial bodies in the search for historical truth, the conclusion reached by a truth commission or a trial is not opposed to that which historians would otherwise establish through their research. Just like historians, before agreeing to an argument, judges or a commission must previously agree on the facts. The obstacles they meet in doing so are not fundamentally different from those encountered by historians.[22] In fact, comparing the roles of a truth commission or a judge to that of historians allows us to establish common denominators[23]; both have a third-party position with regard to the event and, if acting in good faith, both intend to establish the same truth. For the former, the research is carried out in the court whereas for the latter it is done in the archives and the records. The accounts provided by witnesses are essential elements for both professions in their quest for truth. Their concern with the

[20] Donald Bloxham, *supra* note 10, at p. 221.

[21] Antoine Prost, *L'Historien, le Juge, le Témoin et l'Accusé*, in LE GÉNOCIDE DES JUIFS ENTRE PROCÈS ET HISTOIRE, *supra* note 13, at p. 291.

[22] See Mark J. Osiel, *supra* note 7, at p. 238.

[23] See PAUL RICOEUR, LA MÉMOIRE, L'HISTOIRE, L'OUBLI 413 (2000).

evidence and with the credibility of witnesses is also very much present in the two instances.[24] There is also usually the same complementary aspect between the oral account provided by witnesses and the material evidence provided either by experts or independently, the same perspicacity in trying to reveal and detect contradictions, inconsistencies or improbabilities, and finally the same attention is given to omissions, forgery, lies and allusions.[25] When the evidence is not complete, both must accept the risk of guessing following logical steps to conclusion.[26] Both should be experts in the revelation of forgery and fakes and in the manipulation of suspicion vis-à-vis what is before them. In historical debates, one can sometimes avoid responding to a question in an adequate way. This is absolutely impossible before a tribunal and represents a fundamental aspect of transitional justice. Even if we doubt the absolute convergence between the methodology of the historian and that of the judge or of the commissioner, one must recognise that they do not inquire from much different perspectives. Of course the judge has to judge, which is his or her prime function. He or she has to conclude and to settle the question. That aspect, in and of itself, does not justify the rejection of judicial processes for historical truth establishment.

But the mandate and the obligation of the truth commission is not only gathering facts. The idea is not only to establish truth in a vacuum but to do it in the context of transition. The truth commission's role, like the historian's role, is to clarify among public opinion the what, the how, and the why of acts. But truth commissions as well as courts of law are generally publicly accepted and authoritative fact-finders.[27] That is something historians lack. They do not have the same impact in that their findings are not available in the same timeframe.[28] Truth, or the perceived truth, may not always be the same as history in the eyes of the public. Transitional trials go beyond that by establishing not only an individual but to some extent also a

[24] Some truth commission, like that of El Salvador, have relied on the two source rule (the standard used by historians and journalists) that implies two credible and independent sources. In South Africa, the Truth and Reconciliation Commission's Investigative Unit ensured that the factual accounts provided by the perpetrators were accurate and that the full disclosure concept was met. See Priscilla Hayner, *supra* note 5, at p. 130.

[25] See Florent Brayard, *supra* note 13, at p. 14.

[26] Oscar Handlin, Truth in History 119–120 (1979).

[27] Mark J. Osiel, *supra* note 7, at p. 223.

[28] Ruti G. Teitel, *supra* note 16, at pp. 74–75.

collective responsibility. Historians simply do not have that ability, and certainly in the timeframe available to them. In addition, findings by historians may be the right ones but establishment of truth does not stop there. The process leading to the truth, its acknowledgement by the public and its dissemination are key aspects. The success of a country's transition may depend on it.

III. LIMITATIONS AND RISKS

Even if the need for and the requirement of truth establishment are rarely contested, truth recognition still needs to be done in a proper way. Truth can be either contested or simply not known. Therefore, it is preferable that the process leading to truth recognition be handled by a recognised and unbiased third party. A court or a truth commission can play that role. If its importance as well as its teaching values are to be served and maintained, historical truth establishment has to be done correctly and its process needs to be recognised by as many constituents as possible: the victims, the population and preferably the perpetrators themselves. Constraints imposed on transitional bodies or those that are intrinsic in their way of operating have to be known and taken into consideration.

Truth established by transitional bodies is often subject to criticism in that it is considered an imposed version and thus more of a state truth than a historical one. The fear of historical manipulation is real, and recent history is full of examples where states did manipulate historical facts: the history of the Gulag in the USSR, the role of the Japanese Army in the Rape of Nanking, and the complete denial of the Armenian genocide by the Turkish State, to name a few. Judicial or quasi-judicial truth finding must not be a disguise for political motivations, or the conclusions will not stand the test of time. Even if limited, truth establishment has to be done adequately. Respecting essential rules for truth establishment and being aware of the potential traps a transitional body may fall into will push back allegations of truth manipulation for political purposes.

3.1. *Some Constraints and Limitations*

Truth will be defined and influenced by factors surrounding the creation of truth commissions and the latitude they will have. Negotiations between an exiting regime and its opposition, or the lack thereof, inevitably affect the choice of vehicle and the constraints it will have and can thus the scope of truth. When the prior regime has been overthrown, the scope for prosecution is usually wider since almost no political limits are present. In cases where a peace agreement defines the compromises between two opposing groups, negotiations usually try to set rules for amnesty, which will then influence the options for dealing with the past.[29] In the case of South Africa, the African National Congress would probably never have been in a position to negotiate the transition with the sword of Damocles that criminal trials represent hanging over the government representative's head. When the outgoing regime participates in the negotiations and therefore helps to end its own rule, limitations for accountability are usually a topic at the top of the negotiation list, especially when the two groups have committed many crimes.[30] On the other hand, a strong position, like the one that African National Congress was in, can further or even cause negotiations to take place. The Truth and Reconciliation Commission in South Africa was created in favourable conditions and resulted from successful negotiations between historically opposed groups.[31]

Unless the mandate is ridiculously restricted, these constraints will not have an impact on the meaning of the facts which are being presented or investigated, and truth will be established within the scope of the mandate.[32] But the limitations in which a truth commission operates, as well as its environment, do have an impact. Limited time, procedural constraints (search and seizure, subpoena, etc.) and budget, to name a few, will affect the number of cases examined. For example, the Chilean Truth and Reconciliation Commission did not have a mandate to investigate the many cases of torture, kidnapping and other criminal acts that did not result in the death of the victim, so truth was not established for those cases. The South African Truth and Reconciliation Commission was not able to investigate all human rights violations. Indeed, some important features of *apartheid* were deliberately set aside. Fundamental economic right deprivations like housing and education were excluded. The act creating the commission provided a narrow definition of gross violation:

> ... gross violation of human rights means the violation of human rights through (a) the killing, abductions, torture or severe ill treatment of any person or (b) any

---

29 Christine Bell, Peace Agreements and Human Rights 286 (2000).

30 See P. Hayner, *supra* note 5, at p. 12.

31 A. Boraine, *supra* note 12, at p. 264.

32 See P. Hayner, *supra* note 5, at p. 72.

attempt conspiracy , incitement, instigation, command or procurement to commit an act referred to in paragraph (a), which emanated from conflicts of the past and which was committed during a period 1 March 1960 to 10 May 1994 within or outside the Republic, and the commission of which was advised, planned, directed, commanded or ordered by any person acting with a political motive.[33]

The mandate of the South African Truth and Reconciliation Commission basically concerned cases exceeding the already very wide latitude of criminal behaviour permitted by legislation. In addition, racist acts engaged in outside political movements, or the day-to-day racial criminal acts against the black majority were not part of the mandate either.[34] This dichotomy between "legalised" criminal acts and "real" and "illegal" acts may have created a sense of betrayal among the population and the victims. One of the most patent examples of limitation was the inability to look at forced removals authorised by legislation. But not adhering to this narrow definition, as Alex Boraine notes, would have meant that the Truth and Reconciliation Commission would probably still be in existence today.[35] This observation does not in any way reduce or undermine the important effects of the *apartheid* policy. The only thing it does is reduce the scope of the investigation for efficiency purposes and because the mandate was obtained through negotiation between parties. Nothing prevents any other body from being established in the future or any independent research from further investigating the other components and effects of the said policy.

Cut-off dates like the ones imposed on the International Criminal Tribunal for Rwanda (ICTR) (between 1 January 1994 and 31 December 1994) or those applying to South Africa also limit the scope of inquiry but are nonetheless necessary. In Rwanda this has created a huge controversy about the investigation of the cause of the genocide and the acts of the Armée patriotique rwandaise (the Tutsi Army that seized power in 1994) between 1990 and 1994. Truth is certainly partial, but not necessarily biased. Truth will still be established for the facts falling within that scope. The mandate of the ICTR is limited and it ought to be recognised as is instead of being considered an unrealistic mandate to establish the complete and

[33] Section 4 of the South African *Promotion of National Unity and Reconcilation Act*.

[34] See Richard A. Wilson, *Justice and Legitimacy in the South African Transition*, in The Politics of Memory, *supra* note 4, at p. 207.

[35] A. Boraine, *supra* note 12, at p. 107.

definitive Oxford-type history of the Tutsi–Hutu relationship. It is what we describe as a portion of the macro-truth.

As for procedure, truth commissions that have the power to search and seize as well as powers of subpoena can actually compensate for the lack of voluntary evidence. This is an important aspect when facing a dysfunctional legal system since perpetrators who do not fear prosecution will not come forward by themselves. Historians evidently do not have that power. The South African Truth Commission did. Sierra Leone also has the ability to compel anyone to testify. Finally, the speed at which a transitional body fulfils its mandate is a double-edged sword. The excellent survey done by Priscilla Hayner shows that truth commissions will usually have a mandate of between one and two years.[36] If a truth commission proceeds too fast in establishing the truth in order to quickly inform about what has happened, some will use this excuse to argue that the result of the trial or the truth commission was so pedagogy-oriented that facts were manipulated and that truth was distorted. On the other hand, if actions take too long, society may lose the benefit of obtaining quick knowledge of past abuses, which may be fundamental in a period of transition.

3.2. *Myth Making and Moral Equivalence*

Truth establishment runs two very common opposing risks which can create the perception of political truth-making and thus lead to the rejection of the findings: first, that of creating a myth about the past and second, that of doing the converse by diluting the truth and the evils. The first reason is that the truth has been established by the successor and that it is biased. The Holocaust denial movement relies heavily on those arguments to convince all of us that the truth established at Nuremberg ought to be rejected. The objection is that there is a relationship between the construction of collective history and today's politics. When politics and history are so closely intertwined, the building of history is not necessarily some truth building but the creation of a myth[37] to promote the new regime. The new regime may try to demonstrate that the establishment of a collective memory is actually based on records and that it is collective history

[36] See Richard A. Wilson, *supra* note 4, at p. 204, and the survey of Priscilla Hayner, *supra* note 5 at p. 5.

[37] See Ruti G. Teitel, *supra* note 16, at p. 70 and Alexandra Barahona De Brito, Carmen Gonzalés-Enriquez and Paloma Aguilar, *Introduction*, *supra* note 4, at p. 36.

while it is actually a truly biased collective memory creation. This is a myth-making process: truth commissions and courts of law are not free from all suspicion. Both can indeed become opportunities for myth making when they are set up to impose a vision, and to manipulate the public and thus the historical record. One example of myth-making would be to exaggerate past wrongdoings in order to attenuate those perpetrated by the new regime. Manipulation can prove to be a very powerful tool by directing our perception toward recently committed and state-sponsored abuses.

Once established, the new regime may also try to preclude further research so that there can be no questioning of the myth. Institutions shall in no case be set up or used to "create" memory and myths about the past to justify the present, the future or other political motivations. When manipulated, truth will not remain and will be challenged in the future. Myth is obtained when truth is forced or imposed upon people, or where government or special interest groups prohibit research on cases examined by the transitional bodies. In that sense, findings by the court or the truth commission shall in no way be perceived as a prohibition of parallel investigation. On the contrary, a truth commission report is not an imposed closure concerning the examined period;[38] it is merely a starting point.

The purpose of transitional bodies in the context of public truth establishment and acknowledgement is that once the conclusions about the mandate have been reached and made public,[39] everyone knows the atrocities really occurred and is aware of the main facts leading to such a conclusion. Consensus, although a goal, will not be achieved in most cases, however. But the big picture, the macro-truth, is then established and cannot be denied anymore. That is the starting point. But it shouldn't be the end point. A record like the one obtained through the IMT does not represent a definitive record, even if it is a permanent one with regard to the facts. It may be partial, but it is still an established record on which lawyers and historians keep relying.[40] The partial picture of past repression implies a continued need for research. As for the Holocaust, dozens of studies and books are written and published each year. The same is true for the

[38] A. B. De Brito, Carmen Gonzalés-Enriquez and Paloma Aguilar, *Introduction*, *supra* note 4, at p. 35.

[39] Some truth commission reports were never released. This is notably the case for the Haitian Commission. Others are not widely distributed. Some, on the other hand, have become best-sellers, the case of Argentina.

[40] Ruti G. Teitel, *supra* note 16, at p. 73.

Rwandan genocide. Criticism is vital to the community.[41] Myth-making is diametrically opposed to a truth commission mandate and to the purposes of truth establishment and protection. It also favours the appearance of denial movements.

Creating history that only depicts the oppressor's regime as the evil one without concentrating too much effort on the actions of the liberators is understandably frequent. Certainly not desirable, but common nonetheless. Not many Americans, Britons or Russians were prosecuted after the World War II. Maybe the bombing of Dresden would have justified prosecution. It definitely would have been worth some public inquiry and an acknowledgement of the event. No action of that sort was taken. The bombing of Dresden by the Allied forces was a terrible event but it did not take on the scope of a continent-wide campaign designed to eliminate one group from the face of the earth. It is morally inadequate to put the two on the same level. This is not to create a billboard of sufferance, it is to qualify the event based on facts and legal definitions, which is what transitional bodies should do. But with truth commissions as well as with trials, well-balanced history may be told.[42] The danger, or dilemma, is to *force* the establishment of well-balanced or sanitised history. There is indeed a risk of politicising history. In the case of negotiations paving the way for a peace agreement, opposing parties may agree upon certain powers for a court or for a truth commission. Those powers can constrain the independence of that body and eventually undermine the historical inquiry it conducts. The process leading to the truth should not fall into the trap of moral equivalence, of censored and neutral history. In most transition situations, the oppressor partly or totally loses influence. If given the opportunity, the oppressor will previously influence the truth-seeking process in a way that not only its involvement in the violations but also the crimes committed by the other party or parties will be investigated. This can be done through negotiations leading to a truth commission mandate as mentioned above, but also through the international community defining the powers of an international tribunal like the ICTR or the ICTY, or by a willingness of the truth commission's members to address any and all kinds of violations. South Africa was faced with that dilemma when the Truth and Reconciliation Commission looked at crimes

---

[41] O. Handlin, *supra* note 26, at p. 111.

[42] Ruti G. Teitel, *supra* note 16, at p. 86.

committed by the African National Congress and by the Zulu-based Inkatha Freedom Party supporters.[43]

Truth commission and court mandates originating from negotiations can be described in such a way or have such constraints that even if fundamentally different in proportion, crimes committed by both parties are somehow assimilated. When happening on both sides, violations should be investigated on both sides.[44] We cannot simply set aside the crimes committed by a liberation army because the cause it was defending was a just and noble one. On the other hand, it is morally inadequate to equate the struggle for liberation of a population under a discriminatory regime with the acts of those who put the regime in place and who defended such criminal policy. It is always difficult and rather unpopular to criticise a liberation movement for its acts.[45] We cannot treat *apartheid* as if it were the same as the liberation struggle, as the National Party in South Africa wanted to do.[46] But that does not mean that the African National Congress was entitled to commit human rights violations, even though it was fighting a just war: truth commissions, when the mandate allows it, ought to deal with criminal behaviour on all sides, but without putting everything on an equal footing. It was agreed upon during negotiations in South Africa that actions of the African National Congress would also be looked at by the Truth and Reconciliation Commission. In fact, the African National Congress had twice put in place commissions in order to research and shed light on abuses committed by its members. But this is an unusual set of circumstances. And even then, the African National Congress attempted to block the final report, even though it had nothing to hide.[47] The African National Congress was concerned about the danger of concentrating too much on those exceptional acts and felt that the armed struggle against *apartheid* should not be treated as a crime against humanity and that it was therefore not analogous to *apartheid* policy itself. The African National Congress argued that its actions had to be evaluated in the context of a desperate struggle for liberation. The

---

[43] See A. Boraine, *supra* note 12, at p. 53.

[44] See Amy Gutmann and Dennis Thompson, *The Moral Foundations of Truth Commissions*, in TRUTH VS JUSTICE – THE MORALITY OF TRUTH COMMISSION 34 (Robert I. Rotberg & Dennis Thompson, eds., 2000).

[45] A. Boraine, *supra* note 12, at p. 259.

[46] ERNA PARIS, LONG SHADOWS – TRUTH, LIES AND HISTORY 279–280 (2000).

[47] A. Boraine, *supra* note 12, at p. 156.

Inkatha Freedom Party also tried to block the release of the final report for similar reasons.

The explanation seems to be that truth is more easily accepted when all parties are blamed. Because of that perception, there is incitement to deal with the gravest violations committed by the "right" side, by the victors. Doing so can however dilute the true sense of the oppressors' crimes. It is not easy to obtain a balance. Prosecuting or holding truth commission hearings on the most important, and probably the most publicised crimes of the new regime is sometimes the option in trying to achieve that delicate balance. A good example of the necessity to deal with the most visible cases is the Truth and Reconciliation Commission hearing of Winnie Mandela. The high profile of Ms. Mandela and the allegations were so omnipresent that in terms of credibility it would have been suicidal for the process as a whole not to investigate and to make findings about her case.[48] Overall, the South African Truth and Reconciliation Commission seems to have reached equilibrium in managing these difficulties and ensuring its independence and therefore its credibility.

Both perceptions can exist at the same level and with regard to the same institution. This seems to be the case for the ICTY. On the one hand, the Serbs perceive the tribunal as biased against them.[49] The Croatians, on the other hand, think that any attempt to prosecute Croatians is an unscrupulous endeavour to balance history and to place Croatians and Serbs on the same moral level. The recrimination of the Serbs is that rather than establishing the truth, the tribunal only considers part of the evidence and that its work aims at recreating myths and falsehoods created initially by the enemies and which the international community now reproduces. From the Croatian perspective, the ICTY tries to create a moral equivalence between the crimes. For example, General Janko Bobetko, Croatia's top military commander during the 1991–1995 war for independence and a war hero in his country, has recently been charged by the ICTY with the killing of ethnic Serbs during a military operation to regain rebel-held territory in central Croatia. According to Bobetko himself, the aim of the tribunal is to equalise the victim and the criminal and to mix up Serbian and

[48] Winnie Mandela was found to be both a victim and a perpetrator. She never applied for amnesty.

[49] N. Roht-Arriaza, *The Role of International Actors in Accountability Processes*, in THE POLITICS OF MEMORY, *supra* note 4, at p. 58.

Croatian crimes.[50] The tribunal is perceived as placing Croatian troops and Serbian "oppressors" on the same moral level. Since the perception is that of a pure victim with clean hands, any comparison between the horrors committed by Serbs and the struggle for freedom by Croatians is considered outrageous. A regional truth commission would definitely be of some help in that regard.

The arrival of Carla Del Ponte as Prosecutor for both the ICTR and the ICTY coincided with a renewed interest in trying to prosecute members of the Front Patriotique Rwandais, who defeated the Hutu *genocidaire* army and the Interahamwe militia in 1994. This has put enormous pressure on the ICTR. The Rwandan government has subsequently become very reluctant to allow its nationals to leave the country for Arusha, Tanzania, seat of the ICTR, and has created obstacles in order not to co-operate with the tribunal. Again, the view of Paul Kagame's regime is that the cause was a just one and that assimilating their acts to the genocide downplays the magnitude and the importance of the genocide.[51]

Never agreeing to the type of arrangement that allows truth commissions to look at crimes committed on both sides may lead to the necessity to go through a more judicial process, such as a trial of the perpetrators. Members of the outgoing group will definitely oppose that type of process. This dilemma has the potential of bringing the whole transition to a stop.[52] This is to say that establishing the truth is not an easy task, but it also makes us aware of the manipulation of truth establishment processes for immediate and political needs. All evils are not equal and trying to paint them as if they were is obscene. Artificial even-handedness[53] is no better than myth-making and the political truth discussed above.

3.3. *High-level Truth Establishment or Macro-truth*

Truth commissions have a limited mandate, both in time and in scope. A truth commission's mission is not to provide complete details of all cases of abuse over the time period under investigation. The complaint about the truth being political simply because it is

[50] See *Croatia: Country in Crisis Following UN Indictment of War Hero Bobetko*, 25 September 2002 <www.balkanpeace.org/hed/archive/sept02/hed5227.shtml>.

[51] See Hirondelle News Agency, *UN Prosecutor rallies UK Support to Investigate Rwandan Army,* 3 December 2002.

[52] See Ruti G. Teitel, *supra* note 16, at p. 87.

[53] Expression used by A. Boraine, *supra* note 12, at p. 306.

partial ought to be rejected, considering the context and mandate of transitional bodies. It can provide details about a certain number of cases or even cite a lot of cases. But the mandate of the commission goes beyond simply accumulating facts and pieces of evidence. When they are established, commissions usually evolve in an environment where recent history is either contested or unknown but certainly not generally acknowledged. In that sense, a truth commission, just like a trial, is a form of public historical accountability.

Transitional bodies are not in a position to find the whole truth about every single element and fact related to the crimes under investigation. Actually, truth establishment never really ends because research can always contribute to the overall truth. What transitional bodies will establish is the "big picture truth". The mandate of transitional bodies is to identify the patterns of violations as well as the broader aspects of the previous regime's policy and of the crimes that regime committed. Its goal is to demonstrate that the atrocities were indeed committed and to identify, by naming the individual or the regime as a whole, the person(s) responsible. This is what we call "macro-truth". Priscilla Hayner calls it "global truth".[54] It is a limited truth, not in the sense that crucial facts have not been taken into consideration but in the sense that truth commission reports do not look at every single piece of evidence, hear every witness, investigate all abuses and make findings about all of the above. The big picture aims at establishing a consensus about the intolerable. Truth commissions will shape this tool called history which teaches all of us that atrocities were committed and that we should learn form them, for immediate need and for the future.

The South African legislation provided for the establishment of the Truth and Reconciliation Commission with the objective of establishing "as complete a picture as possible" of the causes, nature and extent of the gross human rights violations committed between 1960 and 1994. Investigating a 34-year period represented almost an impossible task. The work of the TRC was not to investigate isolated events but rather to establish and describe the big picture as completely, as objectively and as accurately as possible.[55] José

[54] P. Hayner, *supra* note 5, at p. 85.

[55] See A. Boraine, *supra* note 12, at p. 63, and R. A. Wilson, *supra* note 34, at p. 204.

Zalaquett shares a similar view about the limits of such processes.[56] As for Sierra Leone, the mandate of the commission was to "get a clear picture of the past"[57] and to investigate to "the fullest degree possible" the abuses and the context in which they were committed.[58] The objective is to centralise, in a relatively short period of time, as much evidence as possible in order to surround the outline of the pattern of abuse.

History obtained through transitional bodies is not shaped by a particular or biased account of the state's past. Accounts of events like *apartheid*, disappearance policies or genocide cannot themselves be shaped to fit one's vision. The macro-truth that has been established is a forensic truth, an objective truth impossible to deny. For example, no one could ever object to the factual truth that *apartheid* was a state policy and that P.W. Botha was behind that discrimination policy. From whatever angle one looks at it, the truth will forever remain unquestionable. Again, we are not talking about a small criminal case but about systematic human rights violations. It is inevitable that changes will occur in the interpretation of the facts over time. An interpretation is never 100% neutral and objective, but facts are. The truth commission will create official records of facts but not of interpretations and will thus limit (although probably not eliminate) counter-accounts of historical accounts.

We are often told that there is never just one truth. This is an easy answer in a paranoid post-modernist world that likes to believe in gigantic conspiracies. The findings of transitional bodies eliminate, or

---

[56] See N. Roht-Arriaza, *The Need for Moral Reconstruction in the Wake of Past Human Rights Violations: An interview with José Valaquett*, in HUMAN RIGHTS IN POLITICAL TRANSITIONS: GETTYSBURG TO BOSNIA, *supra* note 7, at p. 200.

[57] "A Truth and Reconciliation Commission shall be established to address impunity, break the cycle of violence, provide a forum for both the victims and perpetrators of human rights violations to tell their story, get a clear picture of the past in order to facilitate genuine healing and reconciliation." Art. XXVI (1) of the *Peace Agreement between the Government of Sierra Leone and the Revolutionary United Front of Sierra Leone*, Lomé, 7 July 1999.

[58] Section 6 of *The Truth and Reconciliation Commission Act 2000*, Supplement to the Sierra Leone Gazette Vol. CXXXI, No. 9, states : "(2) Without prejudice to the generality of subsection (1), it shall be the function of the Commission – (a) to investigate and report on the causes, nature and extent of the violations and abuses referred to in subsection; (1) to the fullest degree possible, including their antecedents, the context in which the violations and abuses occurred, the question of, whether those violations and abuses were the result of deliberate planning, policy or authorisation by any government, group or individual, and the role of both internal and external factors in the conflict..."

at least limit, this offload of responsibility vis-à-vis history. The key to true and useful intellectual history is fact. The interpretation that follows is another step. Usually, there is no single and definitive understanding of history. This interpretation may depend upon political or social context, or upon many other variables. But contrary to interpretation, facts are outside reasonable historical debate once they have been established. Facts are facts and truth is truth. The account is what it is, no more and no less. If it is true that scholars' or judges' conceptions are subjective, at least to the extent that their point of observation, interest and preconception shape what they believe and therefore what they can portray, the past has its own reality independently of who attempts to view and describe it. History is a body of knowledge.[59] It is independent of any affiliations or loyalties. Historians, scholars and judges all need to recognise the social and intellectual constraints under which they will operate in establishing truth.

But even when they are established, when no one can deny the revealed facts, we will always find some who will try to reject the findings on the basis that they are incomplete or politicised. The past is a burden for the present and it can remain a subject for debate for an unimaginable period of time. The Algerian War, Pétain's Vichy government in France or the Armenian genocide are good examples of events stuck in never ending debates not about new interpretation, but about their very existence. The reports of transitional bodies aim at blocking those denial movements by establishing the truth about such events right away.

3.3.1. *Choice of Forum*

As Richard Wilson notes, truth commissions may be the best forum created so far to ensure truth establishment in an independent and timely manner when judicial systems are not working adequately, which is almost always the case in countries that are looking at ways to deal with past state-sponsored wrongdoings.[60] It is rarely the mission of a tribunal to analyse all the historical, political, sociological and economic causes that converged and gave rise to a conflict. When they do get involved in such debate, they do so only from the specific angle of criminal responsibility. The tribunal cannot generally accomplish the work of memory required in cases like the one mentioned above.

Generally speaking, criminal courts used as transitional bodies are less common than truth commissions for different reasons, mostly

[59] O. Handlin, *supra* note 26, at pp. 1 and 41.
[60] R. A. Wilson, *supra* note 34, at p. 211.

pragmatic ones. Recent examples tend to confirm that a system of cohabitation between the two bodies seems to emerge nevertheless, Sierra Leone and East Timor being the most recent examples. The context dictates this choice. Since in most transitions, the local judicial system does not function properly and since creating a single purpose court like in Rwanda and former Yugoslavia is a giant task, a truth commission is a more commonly used vehicle for truth establishment purposes. But after seeing the horrors, each society will react differently according to its history, its internal dynamics and its psychological blockage. Thus, there is a myriad of possibilities as far as the choice of forum to act as transitional bodies is concerned: ordinary national courts, single purpose or special national courts, international tribunals, truth commissions, inquiry commissions, etc. Each has its own internal dynamics. We believe, as others, that the specific context, history and social background of each country where trials or truth commissions have been put into place to deal with past state abuses are such that it is nearly impossible to establish universal parameters to determine which one ought to be put in place and in what circumstances.[61] The magnitude of the violence, the way criminal acts were perpetrated, their proximity in time, the power and confidence of the new regime are all factors affecting the choice of the vehicle, its mandate, its power and the scope of the report it will render.[62] For the purpose of the text, and based on past experiences, we can however identify certain guidelines.

The nature of criminal law policies influences both the needs for a transitional justice vehicle and its characteristics. The choice of forum will be affected by the legacy of the past regime. The longer the authoritarian or criminal regime was in place and the more victims it generated, but also if records were removed or destroyed, the less the population will have a chance to see the truth be revealed by normal processes. If most victims were killed, tortured or otherwise assaulted publicly or with everyone knowing about them, then the establishment of public truth may be less of a goal, and a more direct justice using normal parameters may be adequate. On the other hand, repressive acts carried out secretly will bring about a more pressing need for a public establishment of the truth.[63] For example, disap-

---

[61] A. B. De Brito, Carmen Gonzalés-Enriquez and Paloma Aguilar, *Conclusion*, in The Politics of Memory, *supra* note 4, at p. 303.

[62] P. Aguilar, *supra* note 7, at p. 99.

[63] See A. B. De Brito, Carmen Gonzalés-Enriquez and Paloma Aguilar, *Introduction*, *supra* note 4, p. 19.

pearance policies like the ones in South America or hidden torture like in South Africa do not require the same answer as daylight massacres such as those perpetrated in Rwanda. Research on disappearances which actually confirm the existence of crimes will most of the time require a truth commission approach. Without it, there is little chance truth can be obtained. The more clandestine the criminal acts and methods were, the more truth establishment and public acknowledgement will be required to exist, paving the way to the creation of a truth commission.[64]

When the past regime simply collapses and no real negotiations take place, a trial is often a quicker way of dealing with the past. Stated simplistically, the less the old regime will retain power in the transition, the greater are the chances for the trial option to be chosen. But an authoritarian regime, even if replaced by a democratically elected representative, may remain very influential and unofficially pull the strings of the new regime. Trials will not be the preferred option in this case and we can assume that the military will have taken great care to preclude that option before transferring power.[65] But past situations cannot automatically be reproduced and provide guidance. Sierra Leone is in that regard a confusing case since negotiations took place between opposing groups and since both a truth commission and a single purpose Special Court were established.

Gaining access to official information (state or military records for instance) is, if not vital, at least helpful for truth establishment. But examples like Nazi Germany where the official records where found intact and spoke for themselves about the criminal intentions are rare. The opposite rather seems to be the rule. Argentina and Chile are two countries in which officials destroyed the records. Since these pieces of evidence are in some cases the only ones linking state activities to atrocities, their destruction directly hampered the discovery of the full truth. But that fact, *i.e.*, the systematic destruction of records, can in turn become a central piece in the establishment of past state abuses. The South African Truth and Reconciliation Commission reports mentioned an extensive practice of official document destruction. This conclusion is a truth in itself. It implicitly proves the victims to be right, even though the authorities deny this

---

64 A. B. De Brito, Carmen Gonzalés-Enriquez and Paloma Aguilar, *supra* note 61, at p. 310.

65 *Ibid.*, pp. 304–306.

fact, and forms part of the macro-truth. It would most probably be harder for a court of law to reach the same conclusion.

The magnitude of a regime's criminal acts may preclude a tribunal from sufficiently going into detail in order to establish a truth that could be used to establish a pattern. Truth about dramatic events may not be recoverable from one single trial but it may take several trials to establish it, especially when several people are involved in having committed the crime. In this case, dozens and dozens of judgments would be necessary to obtain the pattern. Consequently, it may take many years for the victims but also for the population to know what really happened. The limited truth established on a case-by-case basis may ultimately form the big picture the population needs and is looking for, but not in a timely manner. Allied trials but also national ones in Germany lasted for years after the end of the World War II. But as early as 1946, German society as well as the victims benefited from judgment by the IMT of the most notorious Nazi leaders. In cases where the judicial system, other than not being credible, simply cannot cope with all the caseload covering a certain number of years, truth commissions can compensate. Since courts focus neither on the patterns nor on the system underlying the criminal acts, but on individual involvement, the rationale they will develop will be more limited. Maybe the court will look at broader implications such as the context of the crime, but the facts upon which the case is decided are only those in which the defendant took part.[66] Finally, in cases of state-sponsored atrocities and violations, covered up by state legislation, it is almost impossible to know exactly whom to prosecute before obtaining important and credible pieces of evidence first. If a trial is the preferred option, we then have to face the question of who and how many people should be prosecuted. In Rwanda, few will be prosecuted by the international tribunal, and as for those still detained in Rwanda, no one knows.[67]

[66] P. Hayner, *supra* note 5, at p. 8.

[67] At time of writing, close to 115,000 persons were still detained in Rwanda as suspects of the 1994 genocide. The vast majority of them have not been judged before a court of law and are still presumed innocent. Until recently, most of them had not seen their prosecution file. Rwanda announced, on 1 January 2003, that those who had confessed to their crimes (excluding ringleaders) during the genocide, minors aged between 14 and 18 at the time of their alleged crimes, elderly prisoners, sick prisoners and those accused of ordinary crimes would be released. The measure also applied to those who run the risk of being imprisoned for longer than provided for under the law.

The truth commission approach may offer a better prospect for truth establishment since it can play a broader role. It can notably work with exemplary cases from the different aspects of the criminal policy in place at the time in order to obtain information on how representative that policy was. The exception to this rationale may be tribunals created to prosecute top officials such as top military officers. Macro-truth seems indeed to be obtained via a court of law when very high level officers, the ringleaders or the big fish, are prosecuted. That was the case for Nuremberg. It is also the case, although to a lesser extent, for the trial of Kambanda by the ICTR.[68] The Milosevic trial before the ICTY may provide another example. But those are not frequent and the Nuremberg reference may be even more exceptional since all the "available" big fish were grouped in one giant trial with the very intent of establishing not only the criminal acts but the intent, indeed the conspiracy that preceded the crime of aggression. But prosecution of high-ranking representatives does not automatically lead to adequate truth establishment. Direct evidence may not be available or was destroyed by the accused themselves. It is not always easy to establish, without any reasonable doubt, the perfect link between the political leadership and the offences or atrocities committed. South Africa is a good example. And if the leaders of past regimes are brought to trial for crimes that are not the gravest because most of the evidence was destroyed voluntarily by the leaders themselves, there is a risk for the trial to become a political one, a show trial to convince the public that at least something is being done.[69] The selection of individuals to be prosecuted in the hierarchy of past regimes affects the public acknowledgement of the truth established. The Milosevic case and the Kambanda conviction are exceptions, as mentioned earlier. It would otherwise be unacceptable, as Zalaquett mentions, to prosecute only the subordinates, the scapegoats, simply to show the population that at least some action is being taken.[70] Transitional trials can do justice (for the population) but be unfair to the accused. Besides due process constraints, the simple selection of exemplary cases raises many questions about the fairness of the process.[71]

---

[68] *Prosecutor* v. *Kambanda* (Case No. ICTR 97-23-S), Judgment and Sentence, 4 September 1998.

[69] See Ruti G. Teitel, *supra* note 16, at p. 43.

[70] N. Roht-Arriaza, *supra* note 49, at p. 208.

[71] On the issue of fairness in picking exemplary cases, see Alexandra Barahona De Brito, Carmen Gonzalés-Enriquez and Paloma Aguilar, *Introduction*, *supra* note 4, at p. 28.

Throughout the hearings of the Amnesty Committee in South Africa, government agents defended themselves by arguing that they were only following instructions while, on the other hand, officials and senior government representatives were pleading that they were not aware of the acts of their subordinates.[72] The first group was trying to convince the Truth and Reconciliation Commission that they had received clear instructions and that politicians were of course aware of the context that allowed them to torture and to plan their assassinations. Political leaders denied any knowledge of those procedures carried out by the security forces. In a trial, each and every case would have to be dealt with by using the Yamashita rule[73] for some and by accepting or refusing the superior orders defence for others. This may sound appealing in legal theory but can be very complex, if not impossible, to achieve under normal circumstances. In these cases, a TRC may help avoid those difficulties. Truth commissions can be equipped to deal with such constraints. In assessing all the facts presented to them and by making the necessary link, notably in the chain of command, truth commissions possess a latitude that courts will only exceptionally have. Instead of having a specific number of successive trials, the truth is established all at once in one forum. With the truth commission approach, it is this global truth that is being looked at. One example of a widespread technique was the use of "wet bag" torture in South Africa.[74] The accumulation of evidence about such practices allowed the Truth and Reconciliation Commission to reveal the secrets of the wet bag procedure. It may very well not have been possible to reach such a conclusion in a court of law. In that sense, truth commissions may secure more information than the trial.

It is common for truth commissions to turn to representative or key cases in order to establish the truth in their report but also to provide some public description or hearing and thus acknowledgement of past wrongdoings by a larger audience. Complete and exhaustive research is improbable and public hearing of all investigated cases for public acknowledgement is unfeasible. To accomplish its mandate, a truth commission can rely on exemplary cases. In South Africa, it was of course impossible to have hearings for all

---

[72] See A. Boraine, *supra* note 12, at p. 126.

[73] On this dichotomy, see D. Cohen, *Beyond Nuremberg: Individual Responsibility for War Crimes*, in HUMAN RIGHTS IN POLITICAL TRANSITION: GETTYSBURG TO BOSNIA, *supra* note 7, at pp. 53–92.

[74] A. Boraine, *supra* note 12, at p. 345.

individuals who intended to provide statements of violations. Thus, some screening process was established before public representation took place. Statements were chosen to be representative of a group based on types of victims, places or other factors, so that a mix of violations could be heard in public and shared with the rest of the population. An Investigative Unit was asked to corroborate the essential facts of the statement. To add to the seriousness of the method, a Research Department was created to prepare briefings on the background of certain human rights violations that had occurred in order to explain in which context the violations had taken place. The El Salvador and Guatemala commissions both limited their investigations and relied mainly on exemplary cases.[75] After hearing thousands of testimonies and once sufficient evidence was on file to establish the pattern of violations, representative cases were picked by the El Salvador Truth and Reconciliation Commission for detailed analysis.

People expect truth commissions to establish a full and uncontested truth. This is unrealistic, as truth reports can contain a great number of details and refer to thousands of cases like in South Africa. Truth commissions will still not be able to circumscribe facts about any and all human rights violations. Putting aside facts or not considering all criminal acts, but instead concentrating on the worst manifestations of past abuses, can marginalise more banal forms of criminality. Criminal acts not accounted for isolate their victims. But the truth commission simply cannot do everything. The debate should instead be shifted toward the choice of representative cases. The macro-truth we are referring to is not a botched one, but neither is it complete. Depicting a truth commission report as an exhaustive exercise may undermine its credibility and the acceptance of its findings. The South African Truth and Reconciliation Commission collected more than 21,000 statements and worked on corroborating each of them. It produced findings on a majority of what were more than 20,000 cases.[76] One could say that this is more than a macro-truth. But still, some cases, even high profile ones, were not completely solved. The death of Steve Biko is probably the most notorious incident. This is an example where only partial truth was established.[77] The TRC concluded that Biko died in the custody of

---

[75] Ruti G. Teitel, *supra* note 16, at p. 86.

[76] Richard A. Wilson, *supra* note 34, at p. 207.

[77] Erna Paris, *supra* note 46, at p. 296.

law enforcement officials and that "the probabilities are that he died" as a result of injuries sustained during his detention.[78]

Again, a cookie-cutter answer seems not to exist. These elements certainly do not constitute an exhaustive list of criteria and reasons to be taken into consideration in choosing the proper vehicle to try to establish the historical truth. But they can, hopefully, provide high levels of understanding of the main differences in contexts and goals.

3.3.2. *Naming Names*

The problem of naming the perpetrators does not exist with a criminal tribunal but is very much present in a truth commission's mandate. But a macro-truth is not established with vague statements and blame. Individual accountability for direct violation is critical. Individual guilt is necessary so that collective guilt can be removed from the whole group. Naming names prevents the entire group from being stigmatised. It also reduces the chance of arbitrary revenge on any member of the opposing group. In Rwanda, individual accountability is an important feature for that very reason. Naming the perpetrators is necessary for determining accountability and providing part of the sanctions, even a moral one,[79] like having one's name figure on the list of perpetrators in a truth commission report. Removing this possibility reduces the mandate of the truth commission and affects the credibility of the process, which is also to provide in part for some accountability. It may result in the rejection of the findings since no one seems to be accountable for any of the abuses. Naming only those who agreed to testify in exchange for an amnesty is a way to get around this difficulty. But senior representatives who do not fear the judicial system will not volunteer to testify. Not naming them, especially in cases where they are not only the ones who executed the plans but where they were also the masterminds of the abuse pattern, the Bothas, the Pinochets, the

[78] Even if the Biko family did not ask the Commission to make a finding on his death, the Truth and Reconciliation Commission reached the following conclusion: "The Commission finds that the death in detention of Mr Stephen Bantu Biko on 12 September 1977 was a gross human rights violation. Magistrate Marthinus Prins found that the members of the SAP were not implicated in his death. The magistrate's finding contributed to the creation of a culture of impunity in the SAP. Despite the inquest finding no person responsible for his death, the Commission finds that, in view of the fact that Biko died in the custody of law enforcement officials, the probabilities are that he died as a result of injuries sustained during his detention." From the Truth and Reconciliation Commission of South Africa report, published by Macmillan, March 1999.

[79] See P. Hayner, *supra* note 5, at pp. 29 and 108.

Karadzics and the Bagosoras of this world, will leave a feeling of incompleteness. This can be a fatal flaw for truth establishment purposes. Stating the violations without conclusions about who is responsible is not great progress. The families of the victims and society at large may know that a certain disappeared, was tortured or killed. In the case of Stephen Biko in South Africa, what we wanted to learn is not that security forces took him and beat him in custody. Everybody knew that. We needed to learn what had really happened and who had ordered the crime.

Obtaining the truth, naming the names while still ensuring due process rights, is not an easy task. Truth commissions will sometimes state in their report that their conclusion concerning a person's involvement does not constitute a legal judgment of the accused's liability.[80] But the stigmas of being named in a report that will be widely distributed are so huge that high precautions should be taken. Even if a truth commission is not considered a judicial body, those mentioned should have the right to respond to accusations. The South African example, in which the truth commission had to provide a 21-day prior notice offering a chance to those to be mentioned to respond to the allegations, represented a well-balanced approach. Respect of that obligation may increase the complexity and reduce the number of perpetrators mentioned, thus limiting the scope of the report. But that is the price to pay for respect and long term acceptance.[81] The choice does not always exist, because the negotiations of terms of reference of a commission may simply eliminate that possibility at the roots. In the Sierra Leone case, it seems to be left to the discretion of the commissioners to decide on that issue once they complete their work. In other words, there is no initial limitation. Would more persons come forward and offer testimony in this case? This remains to be seen.

3.3.3. *The Macro-truth and its Reuse*

Is partial truth better than none? In most instances, even if it is partial, an unbiased and properly carried out truth establishment is preferable to not being able to benefit from a public acknowledgement of past wrongdoings. Although the effect of a such a partial truth may not be clear immediately, the long-term necessity of acknowledging past abuses commands the creation of a public

---

[80] *Ibid.*, p. 108.

[81] See Ruti G. Teitel, *supra* note 16, p. 30, and Alex Boraine, *supra* note 12, p. 113.

process with the mandate to obtain some form of recognition of the crimes committed.

The portion of the truth established by transitional bodies cannot be denied any longer. But truth commission reports are not a closure with regard to the past, they are an opening for further research and potentially even for future prosecution, in other words, further truth establishment. Without the initial phase, there are no guarantees that there will be a second one. Reports by truth commissions are summaries of accounts of the past, and several years after their release the accounts they provide can be used and relied upon in other forums, serving different purposes – among others to prosecute perpetrators and even those who were granted amnesties. In that sense, truth inquiries may be a prelude to a more judicial alternative ultimately leading to individual punishment.[82] Recent examples have demonstrated that history does not simply fall into oblivion and may hunt perpetrators for a very long time.

Before leaving power, the Argentinean junta of the early 1980s granted itself an amnesty and even issued a decree ordering the destruction of evidence that linked the military to acts of repression. But a truth commission was nonetheless created. The amnesty was later repealed and the files of the truth commission, as well as its report, were provided to the authorities for prosecution. The evidence in this case helped to condemn high-level military officers. Besides assisting the immediate transition, the initial compromise was instrumental in even broader truth establishment. In Guatemala, Rigoberta Menchu asked the Spanish judicial authority to undertake an investigation based on the report of the truth commission and to prosecute José Efrain Rios Montt for his involvement in killings and disappearances. In El Salvador, names of perpetrators were mentioned in the report but a few days after its release, an amnesty law was passed. A challenge to the law remains possible. Chile offers a very interesting case. An amnesty was passed by Pinochet, who also agreed to a forum designed to investigate the past, but with a fairly limited mandate. For example, the mandate excluded torture cases that did not result in death. So no truth concerning thousands and thousands of tortured people could be obtained.[83] At the time the Commission was

[82] Ruti G. Teitel, *supra* note 16, at p. 89.

[83] For more details on these examples, See P. Hayner, *supra* note 5, ch. 4.

created, many saw its mandate as a symbolic one. The future would provide another interpretation. The report of the truth commission contributed to opening a gap so truth could find its way into courts and into the population. Notwithstanding the amnesty law, dozens of cases were reopened against generals, the military junta and retired officers.[84] Tribunals have since then been active in trying to prosecute perpetrators. Even the political right in Chile now admits the existence of a disappearance policy under Pinochet's regime, something which was unthinkable not long ago.

In the South African process, if amnesty was not granted, nothing prevented criminal courts from taking up cases already considered by the Truth and Reconciliation Commission. The Biko family unsuccessfully tried to fight the Truth and Reconciliation Commission on grounds that an amnesty would eliminate the possibility of redress in criminal court. The killers of Steve Biko were later denied amnesty. They could then be brought to justice where it was possible to establish a more complete truth.

Those are some examples showing why we reject the dogmatic vision that transitional body processes sacrifice justice only for immediate purposes and that truth commissions are a second-best option. Truth in itself does not always lead to reconciliation, but there cannot be solid and lasting reconciliation without a common truth being established. Zola said that a society is strong only when it sheds light on the truth, when it deals with it. In the case of peace agreements where granting amnesty is the only way out, where it is the absolute compromise to initiate the transition, the establishment of a truth commission in exchange for amnesty may seem too big a compromise. But it can also be a way of obtaining an immediate departure of the oppressors, leaving hope for future prosecution based on the information that the new regime will gather through the truth commission process. Amnesty can protect a criminal from future prosecution, but on the other hand, it can also allow families and the society as a whole to know what happened to their relatives. And as we have seen, truth commissions can pave the way for justice and further truth establishment. In that sense, truth commission reports served as a basis, not as a conclusion. As time goes by, other trials, as well as the work of historians, journalists and others will detail the facts.

[84] See A. B. De Brito, *supra* note 11, at p. 153.

IV. CONCLUSION

Some link truth commission processes to the construction of a collective memory that is necessary in times of radical transformations such as political transition. But truth does not always equal collective memory. For the Armenian genocide, the official Turkish truth is completely opposed to the collective memory of Armenians. With truth establishment by transitional bodies, what is at play is much more the construction of truth and history, rather than that of memory. Because truth was established by transitional bodies, no one can argue any longer, at least not in good faith, that *apartheid* was a justified national policy, that there was no such thing as a disappearance policy in Chile, that the 1994 death toll in Rwanda resulted only from a war and that the Shoah is a myth. The intent of the deniers of those facts is to eliminate them from our memory and most importantly from history in order to preclude us from referring to them in the present. Tragic events like these form an exemplary memory, a memory that is present in our lives and that help the events to keep producing their effects. This memory transforms the society, and it affects all individuals by changing their points of reference and their behaviour through the introduction of these crimes in their lives. Large-scale human rights violations need to be established and protected so that they will not be eliminated from our collective consciousness and so that they will continue to link our present to our past. The elimination of these events or their non-establishment may lead to the resurgence of the rational condemning those crimes. Without truth establishment, there is a strong chance for them to be manipulated in one way or another or to be completely denied for state purposes like in Turkey or in schoolbooks like in Japan.[85] Truth establishment is a requirement, not a bonus. The need may not be clear in a period of transition where the wounds are still fresh, but in the long run not acknowledging the facts is very likely to be detrimental to peace.

---

[85] A controversy exploded in 2001 over schoolbooks that grossly downplayed the magnitude of the crimes committed by the Japanese Army in World War II, notably the Rape of Nanking.

Large-scale massacres or massive state-sponsored human rights violations like the Srebrenica massacre[86] or the Rwandan genocide are not the type of events in regard to which we should allow any interpretative version to circulate.[87] Our obligation is one of history. Truth commissions, criminal trials and other transitional bodies can do part of that job. Control over the narrative of the past means control over the construction of narratives for an imagined future.[88] Knowledge and public acknowledgment allow all of us to resist the temptation to rewrite history. The obligation is one of history, but of a history that should avoid the trap of biased memory-making, be it by creating a myth or by attenuating past abuses. We ought to recognise, as a starting point, the limits imposed upon such processes and we must not overestimate the scope of the truth to be established by transitional bodies. These forums will establish the most obvious and patent cases of abuses and in that regard will generate a public and collective historical truth for such cases or even of the scope of criminal policy as a whole. Such establishment is the only efficient way to resist to attempts to rewrite history.[89]

Truth established by transitional bodies is the one that will delineate the transition and represent the shift from illegitimate to legitimate rule. It can also be considered as a limited criminal function. Even the simplest public establishment of wrongdoing has the potential of stigmatising the perpetrators' ideology and of preventing its reappearance. Justice in case of massive human rights violations

---

[86] The Srebrenica massacre is the most recent case of denial and is quite disconcerting. Some are suggesting the Srebrenica massacre was a hoax. More than 7,000 Muslims were killed in Srebrenica in July 1995. Most of them were either rounded-up and summarily executed or hunted down in the woods. Bosnian Serb General Radislav Krstic was convicted of genocide over the Srebrenica massacre by the ICTY and the tribunal went into details about the event (*Prosecutor* v. *Radislav Krstic*). According to Milosevic, though, the massacre plot was hatched during a meeting at the home of a Muslim municipal official and executed by Muslims, a mercenary unit and the French intelligence services as a pretext for military engagement. In addition, the Serb Government released a report which stated that only between 2,000 and 2,500 Muslims had died in the Srebrenica massacre and that most of them were soldiers, suggesting that the Muslims had imagined or fabricated the massacre. These people are not reinventing the wheel, they only use techniques developed by Holocaust deniers. See *Milosevic denies Srebrenica blame*, CNN.com/World, 27 September 2002, at <www.cnn.com/2002/WORLD/europe/09/27/hague.milosevic/index.html>.

[87] Mark J. Osiel, *supra* note 7, at p. 239.

[88] A. B. De Brito, Carmen Gonzalés-Enriquez and Paloma Aguilar, *Introduction*, *supra* note 4, at p. 38.

[89] A. Neir, *supra* note 14, at p. 39.

passes through two major stages: truth establishment and accountability. The second phase is of course critical but the first one is a prerequisite. Truth establishment for events like massive human rights violations is one of the primary objectives of transitional bodies. In fact, the establishment of historical truth may be the most significant contribution to the emergence of international justice,[90] which has an impact by mainly following large-scale human rights violations. Such truth is the nail in the coffin of so-called revisionists and deniers. Transitional bodies can play that role. In fact, we depend to some extent on that first acknowledgement of past abuses, both for transition purposes and for long-term needs. Justice is needed in these instances, but a lasting truth is even more important. The truth obtained by transitional bodies will serve as a point of reference.

[90] William A. Schabas, *Clémence et vérité historique*, DIPLOMATIE JUDICIAIRE, published on the internet, <www.diplomatiejudiciaire.com/CPI/CPI14.htm>.

TRISTRAM HUNT

WHOSE TRUTH? OBJECTIVE TRUTH AND A CHALLENGE FOR HISTORY

I would like briefly in this paper to look at some areas of tension between the proliferation of truth commissions and state-sponsored investigations into historical controversies and the challenge it poses for historians. My contention is that we are in danger of alliding the political good and nation-building which such inquiries indubitably achieve with their ability to count as unchallengeable records of historical worth.

Increasingly, the conclusions of truth commissions and tribunals are being presented as the official truth of a country. Nowhere is this search for historical consensus more the case than in post-conflict societies, such as Rwanda or Latin America, where the rulings of historical commissions are vital in forging a new "national memory". In these contexts, the truth behind a nation's history can be hedged, adjudicated by judges, and signed-off by committee for the greater good of political progress and reform of the security and military apparatus. Judge Richard Goldstone has argued that the great benefits of truth commissions lie in their capacity to "construct an official and irrefutable history of the dark past".

I think this frankly hubristic approach to history and truth is mainly the fault of a laudable ambition on behalf of those conducting the investigations, but also a more fundamental chasm which exists between the legal and historical professions as they currently operate. Partly due to a degree of naivety but also a shade of arrogance within the legal world, there is a belief that what is recorded within the court room or inquiry hall can constitute the irrefutable history of the past. This is both intellectually circumspect and historically dangerous.

There is first of all an intellectual supposition behind the claims made for truth commissions which understands the nation as – in the words of Benedict Anderson – an imagined political community forged by cultural artefacts. The identity of a nation can thus be created and recreated through the invention of traditions and the

Criminal Law Forum **15:** 193–198, 2004.
© 2004 *Kluwer Academic Publishers. Printed in the Netherlands.*

creation of memories. There are two primary objections to such a starting point.

The first is one raised by Michael Ignatieff, when he asked whether nations, like individuals, have unitary psyches and an ability to come to terms with their pasts; whether they have the capacity to exorcise their demons by establishing the official truth of a period. But can we honestly speak of nations "working through" a civil war or other atrocities? For nations are made of individuals and in numerous societies – especially post-conflict societies – the primary identity can be religious or ethnic rather than a fabricated national conception. Notions of "truth" about the past are indelibly linked to these competing identities. What you believe depends on who you are. Today, in the former Yugoslavia, Serbian identity is regrettably linked to Slobodan Milosevic's warped sense of history – what else can account for the fact that in a recent poll 42% of Serbs questioned gave Milosevic five out of five for his performance at the Hague trial?

If a fractured, sub-national, competitive identity is the first problem, the second is the dangerous precedent established when lawyers and judges boast of creating a national memory. In his superb recent autobiography, Eric Hobsbawm has warned of history being created in ever greater volumes. Whether it was Franjo Tudjman in Croatia or the BJP in India, new histories are being forged for sectarian and political reasons and with little regard for the truth. Now, of course, Truth Commissions and historical inquiries (like the huge revisionary work about to begin in Belgium into the colonial crimes of King Leopold and his henchmen in the Congo) are often established precisely to counter wilfully misleading interpretations of the past. But I think it is well to be aware of the danger and misappropriation of such language when well-meaning lawyers and investigators talk of forging new memories and creating official histories.

If those are my broader intellectual concerns, my more practical concerns about the role of truth commissions and the writing of history were first sparked by the case of the former Rwandan army colonel Theoneste Bagosora. In April 2002, he tried to boycott his trial at the International Criminal Tribunal on the grounds that the court's investigation had unfairly focused on his activities to the exclusion of the broader Hutu–Tutsi conflict (as well as other issues including the withholding of documents). And while I wouldn't want to comment on the horrific crimes he is accused of as a former Defence ministry official, Bagosora's lawyers raised an interesting historical objection to the inquiry process. That is, the elevation within the historical terrain of those moments, peoples or acts under investigation against the broader canvas.

Historical events, particularly contentious events, need always to be seen within their appropriate context. The atrocities of Bloody Sunday, for example, are best understood with a wider appreciation of the Troubles in Northern Ireland, the sectarian prejudices of the British army, and political fears of terrorist insurgency. Indeed, some have argued they are more accurately understood within a far broader history of partition and nationalism. Although, one has to hesitate about extending the timeframe too far back: once controversial events are reduced simply to ugly eddies in the great ocean of history, attributions of individual or governmental responsibility become ever more difficult to make as a cultural defence is so readily proffered.

Yet the point remains that tribunals staffed by lawyers, such as the Saville Inquiry, are usually highly adept at discovering the limited narrative truth – who shot whom, what was hidden where – but can fall down when attempting to explain the more fundamental issues of causation and responsibility. Why something happened; who was responsible; what were the hidden cultural or social triggers – these basic historical questions can be lost within the confines of a courtroom. Some have termed this a distinction between the factual truth and the moral truth – a notion which seems to have some currency.

But just as importantly, the focus on a specific event, in a trial or inquiry, can itself alter the historical terrain elevating the importance of one moment, say, Bloody Sunday, from a broader, historical context, such as the mainland terror campaign of the IRA. Even though, that was, in part a reaction to what happened in Londonderry. Of course, the actions of a state have a wholly different moral and legal framework to those of a terrorist organisation. But when former terrorists then join a legitimate government – as Adams and McGuinness have done – and then have some potential capacity for influencing the process (through their willingness to give evidence, public pronunciations etc.) this can create an interesting tension in the quest for truth.

But the very process of a judicial inquiry by its generous resources and legal powers of compulsion generates a wealth of data available to future historians. This will inevitably ensure the events have greater prominence within the historical landscape. Which is, of course, the far-sighted intention of many agitators behind the call for inquiries. The creation of martyrs is essential to any historical struggle.

My second objection flows on from the point concerning the potential influence of politicians on inquiries into recent history. Officially sanctioned accounts of the past are something historians usually have good reason to be wary of. Leaving aside Archbishop Tutu's brave confrontation with Winnie Mandela, there were many who thought the South African Truth and Reconciliation Commission too readily gleaned over some of the less palatable episodes of the African National Congress in the armed struggle against *apartheid.* Alternatively, in correspondence I have had on this issue, it's been suggested that the Commission wholly failed to deal with the sexual crimes of the *apartheid* era and so failed to illuminate the full culture of terror. Again, an omission in an official historical record.

However much commissions profess their independence (and much of the time this is genuinely the case), they do operate within a broader political context. The Chilean playwright Ariel Dorfman has also spoken admiringly of truth commissions as "able to establish certain truth in a public way, to become part of official history". This even though Chile's National Commission for Truth and Reconciliation was little more than a pro-Pinochet whitewash. So is it fanciful to suggest that we will come to regard some of today's truth commissions and inquiries in the same light as we now regard the Widgery inquiry of the 1970s? Again, I think Ignatieff puts it well when he suggests that the best historical inquiries can do is to reduce the number of lies in circulation.

While truth commissions can force a nation to face its history, however guarded by official authorities, trials of war criminals can close off the past. When one individual is prosecuted for the broader crimes of a state, then with their personal guilt and incarceration the historical slate can be wiped clean. Following Nuremberg, there was scant public debate in Germany about the cultural and political roots of the Holocaust right up until the late 1970s. If Slobodan Milosevic is found guilty at the Hague war crimes tribunal, few in the Serbian political elite will have the resolve to look into the fundamental ethnic fissures behind the 1990s genocide. By focusing guilt on the single individual, war crimes tribunals skewer the historical picture absolving the broader mass of silent, willing executioners. The International Criminal Tribunal for Rwanda has so far (I believe) convicted eight genocide suspects – so perhaps encouraging the broader Hutu community to shirk its responsibility for the deaths of fellow Tutsis.

The study of history and law has always been intimately linked. The modern Western European historical profession grew out of the world of legal scholarship – the so-called German Historical School of Savigny and Niebuhr in the early 1800s. But today's lawyers have lost touch with their historical confreres. Some seem to entertain a rather naive approach to the discipline of history. In his summing up of the David Irving – Penguin books libel case, Judge Charles Gray accused Irving of being a historian with a "political agenda". Join the club. Where Irving, of course, went horribly wrong was then to "manipulate the historical record in order to make it conform with his political beliefs".

Yet in numerous truth commissions and trials, the historian is now wheeled in as an impassionate, independent, scientific expert – like a forensics specialist in a homicide case. Well, we know how badly forensics can get it wrong. Despite their best efforts to rigorous, objective impartiality, every historian brings their own inimitable agenda to a case. Each side can choose their own historian. Where this situation becomes more fraught is when lawyers and expert witnesses have exclusive access to historical documents. With exclusivity comes the closing off of debate and the creation once more of a suspect, legally sanctioned historical past.

There is a broader question about historians being involved in affixation of guilt. Surely it is up to historians (like journalists?) to provide a proper historical context and not stray into judgement on an individual facing criminal sanction? A good case can be seen in the 1964 Auschwitz trials in Frankfurt. A team of historians from the Institute for Contemporary History, Munich, wrote briefing papers on "Command and Compliance in the SS" which provided an analysis of the SS cultural context. It was left to other to sift the evidence and ascribe guilt.

Professor Richard Evans, lead witness in the case against David Irving and professor of modern history at Cambridge University, has argued that the historian should never be involved in questions of guilt or innocence. Conversely, Evans has also pointed out the danger of the language of the courtroom in turn structuring the practise of history. In the study of Nazi Germany, Evans has pointed to a worrying "judicialisation of history" with legal categories such as "perpetrator", "victim", and "bystander" being applied to complicated social conditions. Such crass categorisation, he believes, is more of an obstacle than an aid to historical understanding. This perhaps points to a deeper issue about the methodology of the lawyer as opposed to the historian and the tension between a focused search for guilt or innocence and the more diffuse challenge of presenting a historical synthesis.

In short, can the dialectical method of examination and cross-examination really yield a nuanced analysis of the past? Here the lawyers are generally more bullish. Richard Rampton QC, who led the defence against David Irving, has suggested there is little difference between the approach of the civil lawyer and the historian. Both are searching for truth on the balance of probabilities. The virtue of the court is that it speeds the process up, exposes mavericks and puts to the test opposing arguments. Michael Mansfield QC, who is involved with the Saville Inquiry, regards the two disciplines as complementary, with the lawyer establishing a clear chain of events to which the historian can then (if they want) add their own necessarily subjective analysis. The lawyers do the hard grind of discovering the factual truth while (as he puts it) fanciful discussions of moral truth can be left to the historians.

There is little doubt that through the process of rigorous investigation, legal sanction to summon witness and unearth documents, and the dialectic of the courtroom enormous strides can be made through truth commissions into helping historians understand the past. The great wealth of documents and witness statements produced by the Nuremberg trials were vital for historians dissecting the Third Reich – as some of the evidence unearthed by Saville will be an excellent conduit into 1970s Ulster.

Yet I do think we should be circumspect about truth commissions' grandiose claims to establishing official and irrefutable histories. For all the reasons I have cited – elevation of historical moments from the broader canvas; lack of understanding of cultural contexts; political pressures on the process; the dialectic of the courtroom; the judicialisation ethos – they are to be treated with caution.

I think perhaps a more nuanced approach by historians to truth commissions would regard them not as historical sources (except in a limited way), but rather historical *events*. Truth commissions are perhaps best approached not as an archive, but as an element – generally a concluding element – in the historical period that is (as lawyers put it) "under investigation".

ANGELA HEGARTY*

TRUTH, LAW AND OFFICIAL DENIAL: THE CASE OF BLOODY SUNDAY

The recovery of truth has become one of the abiding concerns of the resolution of conflict in the modern era. Those who have suffered as the result of conflict look to law as a means of asserting their grievances and achieving accountability for the wrongs done. Yet the question remains whether law is capable of providing that accountability and arriving at some form of truth. In many places conflict has been resolved through regime change and the creation of new institutions that provide the backdrop for this search for truth and justice. There, the old state is gone and those who were responsible for abuses are no longer in power. Using law to arrive at truth and justice has some prospects for success there. But those places are rare, as even where there is apparent regime change, the actors involved in the conflict often remain.[1]

In a number of other places the state remains largely intact, despite attempts to transform it through political negotiations. In Northern Ireland, for example, despite the Good Friday Agreement, there has been limited significant alteration to the institutions of justice. This makes the search for the truth about the conflict and in particular the use of law to assert grievances quite problematic. The

* Transitional Justice Institute, University of Ulster. Parts of this paper were presented at seminars and symposia organised by the Centre for the Study of Human Rights and Equality, University of Ulster and the Irish Centre for Human Rights, National University of Ireland, Galway. I am grateful to Prof. Fionnuala Ní Aoláin, Prof. Christine Bell and Dr. Robbie McVeigh for their very helpful comments on various drafts of this paper. I am grateful also to John Coyle, BL and Eamon McKee, whose willingness to argue ideas and theories with me in the past few years has been invaluable.

[1] There is a wealth of literature on the difficulties of lustration. See, for example, Stanley Cohen, *Crimes of the State: Accountability, Lustration and the Policing of the Past*, 20 LAW AND SOCIAL INQUIRY 7 (1995); Maria Los, *Lustration and Truth Claims: Unfinished Revolutions in Central Europe*, 20 LAW AND SOCIAL INQUIRY 117 (1995); Naomi Roht-Arriaza, *Conclusion: Combating Impunity*, in IMPUNITY AND HUMAN RIGHTS IN INTERNATIONAL LAW AND PRACTICE (N. Roht-Arriaza, ed., 1995); Juan Mendez, *Accountability for Past Abuses*, 19 HUMAN RIGHTS Q. 255 (1997) 255; II TRANSITIONAL JUSTICE: HOW EMERGING DEMOCRACIES RECKON WITH FORMER REGIMES (Neil Kritz, ed., 1995).

Criminal Law Forum **15:** 199–246, 2004.
© 2004 *Kluwer Academic Publishers. Printed in the Netherlands.*

old discourses, of official denial remain strong and the institutions which furthered those discourses, are largely still in place. This article considers those problems and examines how they manifest in one key case, that of Bloody Sunday, when 13 civilians were shot dead by the British army during a civil rights demonstration on 30 January 1972.

I. LAW AND THE ENDS OF ACCOUNTABILITY

One characteristic feature that may be observed about law is that it is the principal method by which accountability can be achieved. Yet the practical experience for many is very different. Law may be capable of delivering the accountability and truth sought by victims of human rights violations, but it is also often the tool employed by states to avoid or deny responsibility. This is the case in Northern Ireland, where throughout the long history of the conflict, the legitimacy of the state and the use of law has been at issue.[2] In the more recent phase of that conflict, which began in 1968, there have been numerous allegations about the role and activities of the state. During the conflict and despite the validation of many of those allegations by international human rights bodies,[3] the state has

---

[2] There are numerous histories of the conflict. See for example, David McKittrick, Making Sense of the Troubles (2000); John McGarry & Brendan O'Leary, Explaining Northern Ireland. (1995); Padraig O'Malley, The Uncivil Wars: Ireland Today (1997); Thomas Hennessy, A History of Northern Ireland, 1920–1996 (1997); Michael Farrell, Northern Ireland: the Orange State (2nd ed., 1980).

[3] These include the United Nations Human Rights Committee (1991 and 1995), the United Nations Committee Against Torture (1991 and 1995), the United Nations Commission on Human Rights (1993, 1994, 1996, 1998, 1999 and 2000) and the Sub-Commission (1992, 1993, 1994 and 1996); the European Committee for the Prevention of Torture (1994). See CAJ Submission to the United Nations Committee Against Torture (Comments on the Third Periodic Report by the United Kingdom to the Committee Against Torture) September 1998, <http://www.caj.org.uk/keydocs/CAT.htm>. See also Julia Hall, To Serve Without Fear Or Favor: Policing, Human Rights and Accountability in Northern Ireland 14-24 (1997); Amnesty International, Political Killings in Northern Ireland (1994); Amnesty International, United Kingdom: Human Rights Concerns (1991); British Irish Rights Watch, Intimidation of Defence Lawyers in Northern Ireland (1996); British Irish Rights Watch, Conditions in Detention in Castlereagh (1995); CAJ, Submission to the United Nations Committee Against Torture (1996); Human Rights Watch/Helsinki, Children in Northern Ireland: Abused by Security Forces and Paramilitaries (1992); Lawyers Committee For Human Rights, At the Crossroads: Human Rights and the Northern Ireland Peace Process (1996).

sought to portray itself as neutral, as an arbitrator between "two warring tribes".[4] This portrayal was, as McGarry and O'Leary observe, "not novel": the British had done the same in other conflicts in which they were involved.[5]

An important aspect of this neutral presentation of the United Kingdom in Ireland was the criminalisation of those who opposed the state. The conflict was thus presented as a breakdown in law and order rather than as a war of liberation. Key to this characterisation was law and the legal system through which it was applied and enforced.[6] Successive United Kingdom governments introduced ever more stringent and draconian emergency legislation, escalating an erosion of civil liberties. Special rules were created for detentions without trial, using techniques of interrogation that brought a finding from the European Court of Human Rights of inhuman and degrading treatment.[7] Several different types of legal innovations were instituted, including the use of "supergrasses",[8] special no-jury courts[9] and sweeping changes to the normal rules of evidence.[10] There are continuing and substantiated allegations that the state security apparatus colluded with loyalist paramilitaries to murder catholic civilians.[11] Amongst the most controversial of the state's activities has been its involvement in a large number of disputed killings, involving the use of lethal force by police officers and soldiers.[12] The

---

[4] See Roy Greenslade, 'The Damien Walsh Memorial Lecture', 4 August 1998, available at <http://cain.ulst.ac.uk/othelem/media/greenslade.htm> (visited 10 February 2003).

[5] Brendan O'Leary & John McGarry, The Politics of Antagonism: Understanding Northern Ireland 183 (1993).

[6] See Kevin Boyle, Tom Hadden & Paddy Hillyard, Law and State – The case of Northern Ireland (1975) and Ten Years on in Northern Ireland: The Legal Control of Political Violence (1980).

[7] *Ireland* v. *United Kingdom* (1978) 2 EHRR 25.

[8] See Steven Greer, Supergrasses: A Study in Anti-Terrorist Law Enforcement in Northern Ireland (1995).

[9] See John Jackson & Sean Doran, Judge Without Jury–Diplock Trials in the Adversary System (1995).

[10] See Kevin Boyle, Tom Hadden & Paddy Hillyard, Ten Years on in Northern Ireland – The legal control of political violence (1980); Report of the Northern Ireland Human Rights Assembly, Broken Covenants – Violations of international law in Northern Ireland (6–8 April 1992) (1993).

[11] See Sir John Stevens, Stevens Enquiry 3: Overview & Recommendations (2003).

[12] See Fionnuala Ní Aoláin, The Politics of Force: Conflict Management and State Violence in Northern Ireland 29–71 (2000).

largest single loss of life in such an incident throughout the conflict was on Bloody Sunday. It was also through law, however, that many of those who objected to the activities of the state sought to assert their rights and to reclaim the rule of law, which in their view had been so wholly undermined by the legal innovations introduced by the state during the conflict. As Stephen Livingstone observes, "law … has been a contested site for most of the past thirty years".[13]

This is an illustration of law's paradox: it is the principal method by which offending governments are held to account, whilst also being a vehicle through which those governments have criminalised and imprisoned their opponents. For those opponents and others who are the victims of state wrongdoing, the law is part of the state, is used to validate state abuses and is identified with state ethos and culture. Thus in Northern Ireland, where the state is opposed through various means by Irish nationalists, the law is that of the United Kingdom replete with all the badges and emblems of the colonial power.[14] That is why the reshaping of law and state and the development of new legal processes are such central aspects of political transition.[15] Without legal reform, the law is still the property of the state that carried out the violations and thus remains deeply distrusted by those subjected to them.

Progressive legal change has been an important aspect of the social change in Northern Ireland during the conflict: not all legal innovation has been repressive. Law was used to bring about important changes in electoral reform,[16] employment practices[17] and housing,[18] which had important effects in alleviating some of the worst aspects of the conflict. These illustrate the importance of legal change, which creates the circumstances where allegiance to the legal system can become much more widespread. It also signals a willingness to acknowledge the faults of the past and the abuses they spawned. Legal change can take many shapes, moving upwards from simple

[13] Stephen Livingstone, *And Justice for All? The Judiciary and the Legal Profession in Transtition*, in HUMAN RIGHTS, EQUALITY AND DEMOCRATIC RENEWAL IN NORTHERN IRELAND 131 (Colin Harvey, ed., 2000).

[14] The Criminal Justice Review, set up under the Good Friday Agreement, recommended change to some aspects of court ethos (Recomendation 141, REVIEW OF THE CRIMINAL JUSTICE SYSTEM IN NORTHERN IRELAND: REPORT OF THE CRIMINAL JUSTICE REVIEW GROUP (2000)).

[15] See RUTI G. TEITEL, TRANSITIONAL JUSTICE 66–7, 197–211, 223–228 (2002).

[16] *e.g.*, ELECTORAL LAW ACT (NORTHERN IRELAND) 1969.

[17] *e.g.*, FAIR EMPLOYMENT (NORTHERN IRELAND) ACTS 1976 AND 1989.

[18] *e.g.*, HOUSING EXECUTIVE ACT (NORTHERN IRELAND) 1971.

institutional change to lustration, where those who participated in the offences of the past are replaced by new personnel; accountability, where those offences are laid to rest, in the form of trials, truth commissions, public inquiries etc; and change to the content of the law itself, involving, for example, new constitutional guarantees, equality measures and repeal of emergency measures.

However, with the advent of such change, the state risks losing control of the law and thus of a primary means by which its policies and activities can be validated. This explains why in Northern Ireland change to the legal and criminal justice systems remains so controversial. Increasingly, however, those who are the victims of human rights abuses and those who represent them have realised the opportunities presented by law as a way of advancing the truth of those abuses, whilst at the same time becoming ever more aware of the dangers of engaging with official discourse. This tension creates a complexity in the relationship between victim and law, epitomised in the case of Bloody Sunday, where victims are both suspicious of the legal process and yet also demand from it an outcome that validates their experience. Key to understanding this issue is the role law has played in supporting the state in Northern Ireland and those with power in the state, when challenged about their activities. Victims of those activities are largely powerless: their experiences are denied, invalidated or used as political weapons in the conflict.[19] For a significant number in Northern Ireland their powerlessness also results from their political allegiance – many are from a political tradition that is opposed to the existence of the state and the primary public dialogues are pre-disposed towards the state's version of events.[20] This is acutely so in the case of the Bloody Sunday dead and their relatives. Yet, they, like many other victims continue to seek redress though the legal institutions and processes of the state: the interesting question is why?

These struggles lead to other important questions, which are at their most apparent in the case of Bloody Sunday. For example, how can the official discourse of law, which may have been used to deny the existence of abuses be the means whereby justice and truth are achieved?

[19] See MARIE-THERESE FAY, MIKE MORRISEY & MARIE SMYTH, NORTHERN IRELAND'S TROUBLES: THE HUMAN COSTS 202–205 (1999).

[20] See Simon Cottle, *Reporting the Troubles in Northern Ireland: Research and Media Propaganda*, 14(3) CRITICAL STUDIES IN MASS COMMUNICATION 282–296; THE MEDIA AND NORTHERN IRELAND (Bill Roulston, ed., 1991); LIZ CURTIS, IRELAND: THE PROPAGANDA WAR. THE BRITISH MEDIA AND THE BATTLE FOR HEARTS AND MINDS (1984).

How does a liberal, western state such as the United Kingdom use law to address or to deny its own failings and transgressions? Can it do so, or are its legal processes simply too formal, too rigid or too partisan to accommodate alternative narratives about the role of the state during a violent political conflict? As Campbell, Ní Aoláin and Harvey observe, "[a] British constitutional law discourse, underpinned by centuries of domestic tranquillity, has had no need to develop doctrines on the resolution of serious internal political violence".[21]

This article considers these issues by looking at the case of Bloody Sunday, where the allegations against the state are clear but have never been accepted by it. It examines the role of law in the successive attempts to make the state address those allegations. Those attempts include two public judicial inquiries, one under Lord Widgery, which reported in March 1972, and the other, under Lord Saville, which began in 1998 and which has yet to report. I consider the themes that arise from that examination and consider the relationship between truth, law and official denial in the case of Bloody Sunday. I conclude that this case poses questions about the meaning of truth and the possibilities for justice through law in Northern Ireland. Those questions remain unresolved, as the Saville Inquiry has yet to report, but a number of principal themes can already be identified and explored.

II. THE ROLE OF LAW IN TRUTH FINDING

One way to resolve law's paradox is to see law's role as threefold, as investigatory, expository, and as validation. Thus, the methodology of the legal process may provide for access to information that might otherwise be unavailable: the nature of many types of legal processes is suited to such an investigatory approach. Second and despite its limitations, law is one of the very few mechanisms by which the state may be made accountable for its actions by individuals: this is law as exposition. Finally, the law provides a means of "drawing a line" under difficult or controversial events and stamping a final authority upon a version of those events, by acknowledging what occurred. In that acknowledgement is the minimum form of accountability that is necessary for the rule of law to prevail and the validation which victims of abuses seek. It is for this reason that many of those who have been abused by legal processes still seek legal redress, arguing that the

[21] Colm Campbell, Fionnuala Ní Aoláin & Colin Harvey, *The Frontiers of Legal Analysis: Reframing the Transition in Northern Ireland*, 66 MODERN LAW REVIEW 317, 326 (2003).

wrong done in the shape of the law may only be undone by the law. It is also for this reason that the state chooses to make use of legal processes: law, despite its rigidity, provides the official version it desires.

Since the end of World War II there has been a marked growth in the priority given to accounting for human rights violations generally. Despite this, genocidal conflicts and gross violations of human rights persist.[22] As Eide argues, the development of human rights has three stages – idealisation, positivisation and realisation.[23] It would appear, therefore that the evolution of the international human rights machinery is somewhere between stages two and three. There has been an increase in the acceptance of international human rights norms, as evidenced by the increasing accession by states to international human rights treaties, the proliferation of treaties on specialised areas and the expansion of "soft law". But the challenge, as Michael Posner notes,[24] is no longer to persuade states to sign up to human rights declarations, but rather to ensure that they adhere to them. The increased concern with truth-finding and law has coincided with a growth in the international standards. These have inevitably increased the understanding of the usefulness of international law and especially human rights norms amongst the legal profession. It has been amplified in the United Kingdom by the incorporation of most of the European Convention on Human Rights into domestic law by the Human Rights Act 1998, which it has been said will exercise "a magnetic effect" on United Kingdom law.[25]

The discourse of human rights has become more popular with governments, but many continue to commit serious human rights abuses despite their treaty commitments to protect rights. States now use the language of rights and the international mechanisms to cover their tracks, "offering legalistic defences, drawn from the accredited human rights discourse".[26] This gap between rhetoric and practice has led to a greater focus upon accountability and investigation. If a

---

22 M. Cherif Bassouini, *Searching For Peace And Achieving Justice: The Need For Accountability*, 59 LAW & CONTEMP. PROBS 9, 10 (1996).

23 Asbjørn Eide, *Dynamics of Human Rights and the Role of the Educator*, in FRONTIERS OF HUMAN RIGHTS EDUCATION (A. Eide & M. Thee, eds., 1983).

24 M. Posner, *Human Rights & Non-Governmental Organisations; Foreword*, 66 FORDHAM L. REV. 627, 627–628 (1997).

25 Anthony Lester, *Human Rights and The British Constitution*, in THE CHANGING CONSTITUTION 109 (Jeffrey Jowell & Dawn Oliver, eds., 4th ed., 2000).

26 STAN COHEN, STATES OF DENIAL: KNOWING ABOUT ATROCITIES AND SUFFERING 107 (2001).

state agrees to be bound by international human rights treaties, then those treaties create a normative standard against which that state may be judged. Thus there has been an increase in the type and volume of mechanisms addressing human rights violations, although the issue of their effectiveness remains unresolved. Other factors have served to focus attention upon the need to address serious human rights abuses, not least the tumultuous world events of recent years, which have focussed more attention on the practice of human rights. As a result of the upheavals in Southern Africa and Eastern Europe, the role of the promotion of human rights in the democratisation of states has become increasingly important. The attempts to resolve self-determination disputes, such as those arising from the break up of the Soviet Union, have permitted the wider disclosure of violations committed by previous regimes. The political agreements arrived at in resolving some of these conflicts have also involved, as part of the condition of the deal, an accounting for the violations committed by the prior regime.[27] The emergence of evidence of such gross violations and the perceived need for some formal legal response to them have led to the creation of both *ad hoc*[28] and permanent structures[29] to address the violations. These institutions are themselves subject to criticism of their effectiveness and their reach,[30] but their formation can be seen as another step towards the full "realisation" of rights.

III. LAW AND OFFICIAL DENIAL

The disposition of the state and the manner in which law was employed to partisan political ends during the conflict have become part of the critique offered by those who oppose the state in Northern Ireland and by those who object to its human rights record. This role of the state remains a matter of dispute and the events that flowed

[27] See Christine Bell, Peace Agreements and Human Rights (2000).

[28] For example, the International Criminal Tribunal for the former Yugoslavia and the International Criminal Tribunal For Rwanda:

[29] Such as the International Criminal Court (*Rome Statute of the International Criminal Court*, UN Doc. A/CONF.183/9).

[30] See Payam Akhavan, *Justice And Reconciliation In The Great Lakes Region Of Africa: The Contribution Of The International Criminal Tribunal For Rwanda*, 7 Duke J. Comp. & Int'l L. 325 (1997); Virginia Morris & Michael Scharf, The International Criminal Tribunal for Rwanda (1998); Mary Griffin, *Ending the impunity of perpetrators of human rights atrocities: A major challenge for international law in the 21st century*, 838 Int'l Rev. Red Cross 369 (2000); William Schabas & Michael Scharf, Slobodan Milosevic on Trial: A Companion (2002).

from that role are also still contested. The difficulties encountered during the current Inquiry under Lord Saville demonstrate that and say much about the problems with finding truth and achieving accountability, when doing that may require domestic institutions to acknowledge unpalatable facts about the nature of the state and its activities, which they have hitherto denied.

More than 30 years on, Bloody Sunday, remains a source of controversy, debate and pain. It casts a long shadow in contemporary Irish history and was compounded for many by the outcome of the Widgery inquiry into the events that effectively exonerated the state. The failure of Widgery to properly investigate Bloody Sunday and to apportion blame appropriately caused great damage to the legal process and the rule of law in Northern Ireland and was symptomatic of the state's response to the conflict. It was also a breach of international human rights law,[31] although that was not an avenue that was much explored at the time.[32]

Out of the experience of Widgery and the current Bloody Sunday Inquiry emerge a series of themes that illustrate the problems with truth finding in a domestic context. The abuses such inquiries purport to investigate have taken place partly because of the contestation of politics, history and identity which remains unresolved, despite the advances of the Northern Irish peace process. What happened on Bloody Sunday and what occurred afterwards in the legal and political systems are dramatic, grand scale illustrations of British security policy in Northern Ireland, but the nature of that policy remains contested. That has an effect in the present and affects the ongoing search for truth and justice. Like any state that both denies the truth of its policies and activities, and is in a position to implement that denial, it seeks to eternally obstruct that truth emerging. Yet like any liberal democracy faced with prima facie evidence of serious violations of human rights and harried by adverse international comment and reaction, it has to be seen to do something to address those allegations. Thus, Bloody Sunday and its aftermath is a case-study in a state's denial of its own offences. Stan Cohen's typography of "official denial" is relevant here:

> Each variant of official denial appears in the official discourse: *literal* (nothing happened); *interpretive* (what happened is really something else) and *implicatory* (what happened is justified). Sometimes these appear in visible sequence: if one

---

[31] See SAMUEL DASH, JUSTICE DENIED: A CHALLENGE TO LORD WIDGERY'S REPORT ON 'BLOODY SUNDAY (1972); Bryan McMahon, *The Impaired Asset: A Legal Commentary on the Report of the Widgery* Tribunal VI LE DOMAIN HUMAIN 3 (1974).

[32] See note 102 *infra* and accompanying text.

> strategy does not work, the next is tried. If "literal denial" is countered by irrefutable evidence that something indeed happened ... the strategy may switch to legalistic reinterpretations or political justifications.[33]

Faced with large amounts of film evidence from the numerous journalists present and hundreds of other eyewitness accounts, the state could not "literally deny" Bloody Sunday. It therefore moved swiftly into interpretive and implicatory denial: the soldiers only shot gunmen and bombers, they came under intensive fire from Irish Republican Army (IRA) snipers, they killed gunmen whose bodies were spirited away. Like other states "with democratic credentials sensitive to their international image",[34] the United Kingdom had to provide some justification for its response. Its strategy in Northern Ireland was thus to set up judicial inquiries that were dominated in their crucial elements by it or its allies.[35] This was the case with the Widgery Inquiry and may yet transpire to be the case with the Bloody Sunday Inquiry.

Both the Widgery and Saville Inquiries are the progeny of the British political and judicial systems that operate normative but conservative views of democracy and law and which have been supportive of the state's security policy in Northern Ireland. The interpretation of the standards that govern the Bloody Sunday Inquiry has been played out in the succession of judicial reviews and challenges to its rulings that have been adjudicated by a judiciary that may be incapable of reading rights in a proactive way. Thus the attempt to uncover the truth of Bloody Sunday may founder on the rocks of the British legal tradition and mindset, which have historically been reluctant to acknowledge human rights abuses committed by the state in Northern Ireland. The constraints of the British legal model are complicated by the changing political background, that of the Irish peace process, which allowed the second inquiry to become possible. As Campbell, Ní Aoláin and Harvey observe

> To what extent, for example, does the [British] constitutional legal paradigm blunt gains made through politics? ...A problem arises when legal technique is unable to capture the complexity of the political context. In particular, when the dominant legal paradigm undermines novel political solutions.[36]

---

[33] Stan Cohen, *supra* note 26, at p. 103.

[34] *Ibid.*, p. 107.

[35] See Angela Hegarty, *The Government of Memory: Public Inquiries and the Limits of Justice in Northern Ireland*, 26 FORDHAM INT'L. L. J. (4) 1148–1192 (2003).

[36] Colm Campbell, Fionnuala Ní Aoláin & Colin Harvey, *supra* note 21, p. 322.

IV. THE EVENTS OF BLOODY SUNDAY

In order to understand the issues raised by the attempts to publicly examine the events of Bloody Sunday, some discussion of the events themselves is necessary. They are well known and are widely documented. What is not at issue is that on 30 January 1972, in the city of Derry[37] in Northern Ireland, the British Army shot and killed thirteen men who were taking part in a civil rights protest march against internment,[38] a demonstration that had been banned by the Northern Ireland government.[39] Thirteen other men and one woman were wounded by army gunfire and one man died later as a result of his wounds. Many other civilians were injured, alleging ill treatment by the army.[40] No soldiers were injured by civilians, although there were allegations at the time that this had occurred.[41] There were hundreds of eyewitnesses to the events, which took place in a small section of the Bogside, a working class nationalist[42] area in the centre of Derry.

---

[37] The city is officially named Londonderry, but the addition of the prefix "London" in 1613 has never been accepted by the majority nationalist population of the city. Throughout this article I refer to the city as Derry, although an alternative employed by other commentators is "Derry/Londonderry". For a brief history of the vexed history of the city's name see BRIAN LACEY, SIEGE CITY: THE STORY OF DERRY & LONDONDERRY (1991).

[38] The Northern Ireland government had invoked a section of the Special Powers Act 1921 the previous summer. On 9 August 1971, they allowed the use of the internment provision, a power that allowed for arrest and detention without charge or trial.

[39] At the time Northern Ireland had its own provincial government. This government was suspended, partly as a result of the aftermath of Bloody Sunday in March 1972. See BRENDAN O'LEARY & JOHN MCGARRY, THE POLITICS OF ANTAGONISM: UNDERSTANDING NORTHERN IRELAND 175–177 (1993).

[40] Statements taken by Northern Ireland Civil Rights Association 31 January-3 February 1972. See DON MULLAN, EYEWITNESS BLOODY SUNDAY 240–256 (1997). Many similar statements have been made to the new Bloody Sunday Inquiry.

[41] One soldier accidentally shot himself in the foot but lied about how the injury had come about. See Bloody Sunday Inquiry Transcript, DAY 305, pp. 27–31 (4th March 2003) and Statement of Soldier Inq No. 1255, paras 12–13.

[42] The nomenclature of Northern Ireland's political identities is complex. The following is a useful explanation: "Protestants are largely Unionists – people who want to maintain the union with the United Kingdom. Most Catholics, on the other hand, are Nationalists, who wish to reunite with the Republic of Ireland, which has a population of about 3.5 million, of whom 95% are Catholic. Some Unionists call themselves 'Loyalists', some of whom support the use of violence for political ends. Some Nationalists call themselves 'Republicans', some of whom support the use of violence for political ends." HELSINKI WATCH, HUMAN RIGHTS IN NORTHERN IRELAND 1 (1991).

What is contested is the purpose of the military operation and whether or not the British army present had opened fire after being fired upon by IRA gunmen. The British military authorities have always maintained[43] that the intent of the military operation was to arrest rioters and that firing by the army was in response to a sustained attack upon them by the IRA, the illegal republican paramilitary organisation.[44] They said that they had shot gunmen and bombers, a claim that outraged the civilian population.[45] There was anger throughout Ireland and abroad at the killings and there were boycotts, protests and demonstrations of this outrage.[46] The funerals were attended by many dignitaries and hundreds of ordinary people from all over Ireland.[47]

Aware that the seriousness of the situation was such that some form of investigation was necessary, the United Kingdom government announced a public inquiry into the events. It invoked the Tribunals of Inquiry (Evidence) Act 1921) ("the 1921 Act") and placed before Parliament a resolution to institute a Tribunal of Inquiry,[48] the most judicial form of inquiry.[49] In setting up the Tribunal, the government did not feel itself bound to refrain from comment on the issue, although it expected this of others. In the

---

[43] The British Army issued a number of press statements and briefings, as did the United Kingdom government in the wake of the killings. See, for example, Philip Howard, *Press Given Detailed Account of Arrest Force's Actions*, THE TIMES, 1 February 1972, p. 4; Dick Grogan & Martin Cowley, *Army Commander Describes Shooting as Defence Action*, IRISH TIMES, 31 January 1972, p. 1.

[44] There are numerous histories of the IRA, for example, J. BOWYER BELL, THE SECRET ARMY: THE IRA 1916–1979 (1989); TIM PAT COOGAN, THE IRA (1987); BRENDAN O'BRIEN, THE LONG WAR: THE IRA AND SINN FÉIN FROM ARMED STRUGGLE TO THE PEACE PROCESS (1995); PATRICK BISHOP & EAMONN MALLIE, THE PROVISIONAL IRA (1987); ED MOLONEY, A SECRET HISTORY OF THE IRA (2002).

[45] Simon Winchester, *Bogsiders Bitter in Condemnation*, THE GUARDIAN, 1 February 1972, p. 1; *It Was Wilful Murder, Say Priests,* DERRY JOURNAL, 1 February 1972, p. 1.

[46] *Impartial Inquiry Demanded; Reactions to Mass Derry Killings*, IRISH NEWS, 31 January 1972, p. 1.

[47] *Powerful Response to Day of Mourning,* IRISH TIMES, 3 February 1972, p. 1. See also Michael Farrell, *supra* note 2.

[48] The United Kingdom's legal system allows for a range of public inquiries, *ad hoc*, judicial and statutory. The Tribunal of Inquiry is regarded as the most serious of these and is set up to "inquire into a matter of urgent public importance" (s. 1(I) of the 1921 Act).

[49] Barry K. Winetrobe *Inquiries After Scott: The Return of the Tribunal of Inquiry*, [1997] PUB. L. 18, 19.

debate in Parliament following the tabling of the resolution it robustly defended the army's version of events. As Christopher Clarke QC, Counsel to the Bloody Sunday Inquiry observed in his opening statement, "Lord Balniel, spoke, in effect, on behalf of the army and put forward their version of events. His speech would be regarded by some as perfectly justified in the light of the charges made and widely publicised against the army of massacre, and by others as an attempt to get the official line of *[sic]* the public eye before the Inquiry began, just in time to avoid the restrictions imposed by the Law of Contempt."[50]

The Prime Minister at the time was Edward Heath, who appointed Lord Widgery, then the Lord Chief Justice of England and Wales, as the sole member of the Tribunal. His terms of reference were very narrowly drawn by Parliament[51] and Widgery himself was keen to "emphasis[e] the narrowness of the confines of the Inquiry".[52] The establishment of the Inquiry was an important element of the United Kingdom government's strategy: the laws of contempt were at that time so stringently interpreted that the institution of the Tribunal silenced public debate about the matter in the United Kingdom. As one newspaper ruefully observed, "until the Lord Chief Justice completes his inquiry, nobody may offer to the British public any consecutive account of the events in Derry".[53] This may be interpreted as over-zealousness in protecting the propriety of the legal process, but it also fits with the critique of law as a way of denying

[50] Bloody Sunday Inquiry Transcript, available at <http://www.bloody-sunday-inquiry.org/> (hereinafter 'Inquiry Transcript'), day 41, p. 124, lines 3–10. A number of Labour MPs tabled a Commons motion calling for Balniel's resignation as a result of his conduct during the debate, alleging he had "attempt[ed] to prejudice the outcome of the inquiry" (*Calling for Balniel's Resignation*, IRISH TIMES, 3 February 1972, p. 8).

[51] The terms of reference were: "That it is expedient that a Tribunal be established for inquiring into a definite matter of urgent public importance, namely the events on Sunday 30 January which led to loss of life in connection with the procession in Londonderry on that day" (INQUIRY INTO THE EVENTS ON 30 JANUARY 1972 WHICH LED TO LOSS OF LIFE IN CONNECTION WITH THE PROCESSION IN LONDONDERRY ON THAT DAY: REPORT OF THE TRIBUNAL APPOINTED UNDER THE TRIBUNALS OF INQUIRY (EVIDENCE) ACT 1921 (THE WIDGERY REPORT), H.L. 101, H.C. 220, April 1972, para. 1).

[52] *Ibid.*, para. 3.

[53] *The Problems Facing Widgery: Can He Get the Facts?*, SUNDAY TIMES, 6 February 1972, p. 13. The Sunday Times Insight investigation was spiked, when Lord Widgery himself phoned its then editor, Harold Evans. (Cal McCrystal, *In Cold Blood*, THE INDEPENDENT, 18 January 1992, p. 20 (Weekend).

human rights violations. Thus the law provides an apparently independent process by which allegations of abuses can be examined, but by its very nature is a mechanism which can be manipulated by the powerful – in this case the state. Law in this instance is therefore not a tool by which truth can be uncovered and justice achieved, but precisely the opposite – it becomes the means whereby the state can ensure that does not happen. This was the jaundiced view of many in Northern Ireland at the time, where some public debate took place about the usefulness of co-operating with Widgery. Some, who felt that it might arrive at the truth, argued for reluctant participation in the Inquiry.[54] Others, less sanguine about the prospects for justice from the state, given the long history of its involvement in Ireland, took the view that it was simply a "whitewash" and that taking part was a futile exercise.[55]

Widgery's approach was flawed from the start. He refused to hear evidence from most of the civilian eye-witnesses or from all of those who had been wounded on the day,[56] and declined to conduct proceedings in the largely nationalist city of Derry, preferring instead to sit in the predominantly unionist town of Coleraine, some 40 miles away.[57] He also allowed soldiers to give evidence anonymously and whilst disguised. Other problems with the Tribunal's approach only emerged years later: for example the discovery of the soldiers' original statements, which had not been made available to the relatives of the

[54] EDWARD DALY, MISTER ARE YOU A PRIEST? (207–208) 2000.

[55] *Cardinal, Bishop Demand Inquiry*, IRISH NEWS 31 January 1972, p. 1; *SDLP and Nationalists Will Boycott Inquiry*, DERRY JOURNAL 4 February 1972, p. 16; *Widgery Unacceptable for Inquiry – SDLP*, IRISH TIMES, 3 February 1972, p. 9. See also EAMONN MCCANN, BLOODY SUNDAY IN DERRY: WHAT REALLY HAPPENED 91–92 (1992); Eamonn McCann, Statement to the Bloody Sunday Inquiry, (Inq Statement no AM77), para. 2.

[56] He took evidence from seven of the 13 wounded.

[57] A memo uncovered years later in the Public Records Office, documenting the meeting between the then prime minister, Edward Heath, the Lord Chancellor Hailsham and Lord Widgery records that there were objections to the Tribunal sitting in Derry. "Memorandum of a meeting at 10 Downing Street on 31 January 1972" (hereinafter "Downing Street Memorandum"), reproduced in Don Mullan, *supra* note 40, & pp. 269–273). The Guildhall in Derry, where the Saville Inquiry held its hearings, is described as "on the wrong side of the [River] Foyle", *i.e.*, in a Nationalist area. There was a history of the state preferring Coleraine over Derry; a few years earlier, Coleraine had been controversially chosen as the site for Northern Ireland's second University, a decision which was viewed as politically discriminatory and which led in part to the outbreak of the modern phase of the conflict in 1969.

dead, in the Public Record Office at Kew revealed that these had been altered.[58] These changes had the effect of making the actions of the soldiers concerned less likely to attract criminal charges and reduced the discrepancies between their various accounts.[59] This material had never been made available to the legal representatives of the families of the dead and the wounded.

To the surprise of few, Widgery's verdict, delivered a few weeks after Bloody Sunday, supported the state's version of events. He found no significant fault with the army's behaviour and no "general breakdown in discipline",[60] although he did speculate that at one point the army firing "bordered on the reckless".[61] To the general outrage of the local nationalist population[62] and the particular hurt and offence of the families of the dead and the wounded, Widgery determined that whilst "[n]one of the dead or wounded is proved to have been shot whilst handling a firearm or bomb …there is a strong suspicion that some…had been firing weapons or handling bombs …and that yet others had been closely supporting them".[63]

The question is no longer whether Widgery was a satisfactory and independent process but whether its flaws were deliberate or accidental. It may be that Widgery's flaws were simply a product of a conservative, rigid legal system, peopled by individuals who were by experience and class more likely to support the army's version of events.[64] The alternative is the version widely believed throughout Ireland, that the Widgery Inquiry took the course that it did in order to collude with the state in denying that the killings were murders.

The matter of what was the real purpose of Widgery's Inquiry is raised in part by the contents of a memo unearthed in 1997 from the United Kingdom Public Records Office. It was an official record of a meeting between Lord Widgery and Edward Heath, Prime Minister at the time of Bloody Sunday. The memo recorded that at the meeting,

---

[58] Dermot Walsh, The Bloody Sunday Tribunal of Inquiry: A Resounding Defeat for Truth, Justice and the Rule of Law 9 (1997).

[59] *Ibid.*, pp. 54–55. Prof. Walsh's report analyses the statements found by solicitor Patricia Coyle in the Public Records Office in 1996.

[60] Widgery Report, *supra* note 51, Summary of Conclusions, no 11.

[61] *Ibid.*, p. 8

[62] See Daly, *supra* note 54, at pp. 211–212; McCann, *supra* note 55, at p. 94

[63] Widgery Report, *supra* note 51, para. 10.

[64] Widgery was himself a former British army officer. See CAIN, Biographies of People Prominent in the Conflict, at <http://cain.ulst.ac.uk/othelem/people/biography/wpeople.htm>. He was flown in and out of Northern Ireland in a British Army helicopter.

Heath had warned Widgery to "never forget it is a propaganda war we are fighting."[65] Twice in the memo, the civilian case is referred to as "the other side",[66] which tends to suggest a less than neutral approach.

Widgery's report, rather than laying the issue to rest, simply inflamed matters. The boycott of public institutions by nationalists that had begun the previous year in response to the introduction of internment intensified[67] and there were other moves at an international level to raise the matter of the killings and of discrimination and injustice in Northern Ireland generally.[68] The civil rights marches organised by NICRA continued,[69] but the wave of violence engendered by the Bloody Sunday killings engulfed NICRA and its campaign petered out.[70] Instead, large numbers of young people joined the IRA, because, as Niall Ó Dochartaigh notes, "to many in Derry, the army appeared to have carried out a calculated massacre of unarmed rioters, deliberately escalating the conflict".[71] Widgery's report provides evidence for the view that the purpose of state investigations of human rights abuses, however judicial, are simply another way to frame official discourse to legitimise those abuses. In considering this view it is worth reflecting on the different ways in which law can respond to such violations.

V. THE PUBLIC INVESTIGATION OF HUMAN RIGHTS VIOLATIONS: TRUTH COMMISSIONS AND PUBLIC INQUIRIES

Law can respond to and seek to address human rights abuses in a number of ways and there are various processes by which individuals and states can be made accountable for such violations. It can be done either by a criminal or a civil process: former dictators and generals can

---

[65] "Downing Street Memorandum", *supra* note 57, at p. 270, para. (e).

[66] *Ibid.*, at (vi) and (viii)

[67] Farrell, *supra* note 2.

[68] Chris Glennon, *Fr. Daly Tells the Derry Story to the US*, SUNDAY INDEPENDENT, 6 February 1972, p. 8.

[69] There was a huge demonstration the following weekend: *Newry Stays Peaceful As 25,000 Hold A Silent March Of Protest*, THE TIMES, 7 February 1972, p. 1. Marches continued in Fermanagh, Derry, Belfast, Armagh, Tyrone; Farrell, *supra* note 2, p. 290.

[70] BOB PURDIE, POLITICS IN THE STREETS: THE ORIGINS OF THE CIVIL RIGHTS MOVEMENT IN NORTHERN IRELAND 247–248 (1990).

[71] NIALL Ó DOCHARTAIGH, FROM CIVIL RIGHTS TO ARMALITES: DERRY AND THE BIRTH OF THE IRISH TROUBLES 283 (1997).

be put on trial for their crimes, or a form of public investigation can be carried out. The format of the criminal trial is familiar – from the Israeli trial of Adolf Eichmann to the Argentinean trials of the former junta. Latterly the model has been employed to address the gross violations arising from the conflicts in Rwanda and the Balkans. However successor trials are relatively rare[72] and although the criminal process may demonstrate the shift to liberal democratic values, there are dilemmas about the application of due process. Other legal models are available and in use – such as public investigation. This is a less obvious but pervasive model, of which two principal variations can be identified – the truth commission and the public inquiry. Public inquiries are a British export, tend to be highly legalistic and are usually narrowly focussed, whereas truth commissions are often a quasi-legal model with a wider ranging remit.

Since the early 1970s, truth commissions have developed as ways of addressing patterns of human rights abuses.[73] Truth commissions are usually, but not exclusively, addressed at abuses committed by the state or by previous regimes exercising state power and usually arise during or as a result of political transition. They are often a way of reconciling the new version of the conflict with the old, although they are sometimes perceived as "victor's justice". The use of the term "truth commission" implies that "the truth" has been denied or covered up and that the purpose of the commission is to find and establish that truth. Truth commissions have taken place all over the world, including South Africa, Guatemala, Chile, Argentina, El Salvador, Bosnia and Sierra Leone. Whilst these are separate and distinct processes with different aims and structures, they are in essence, as Hayner notes, flexible.[74] Truth commissions are thus largely products of political transition and are often perceived as a necessary part of that transition. Public inquiries, on the other hand, are a creation of United Kingdom public law, although they have been exported to other common law countries.[75] They are often very

---

[72] TEITEL, *supra* note 15, at Chapter 2.

[73] See Priscilla B. Hayner, *15 Truth Commissions – 1974 to 1994: A Comparative Study*, 16 HUMAN RIGHTS Q. 597 (1994).

[74] *Ibid.*

[75] Such as Australia (ROYAL COMMISSION ON ABORIGINAL DEATHS IN CUSTODY); Israel (the KAHAN COMMISSION ON THE INQUIRY INTO DEATHS IN THE SABRA AND SHATILA REFUGEE CAMPS); in Canada (*e.g.*, TSUU T'INA INVESTIGATION INTO USE OF LETHAL FORCE BY THE RCMP IN ALBERTA)

formal, and although they are intended to be inquisitorial, they can on occasion become highly adversarial.

The experience of such inquiries is problematic. Inquiries tend to work well when seeking "not to allocate blame but to increase understanding".[76] However, they are often poor at investigating controversial events, where allocation of blame is a necessary element. As Phil Scraton observes, "official discourse, institutional processes and professional interventions within advanced democratic states are expressions of power which construct and legitimate self-serving versions of the truth".[77]

This is official discourse as denial, where law's power is used to serve the interests of the state. This has been the experience in Northern Ireland, where official inquiries have shored up the state's position and denied the existence of abuses.[78] The classic case of this is the Widgery Inquiry, an inquiry whose processes and findings were so flawed and controversial that almost 30 years after the events a second unprecedented inquiry under Lord Saville was set up.[79] Northern Ireland is in a form of political transition and without this transition, it is unlikely that the new Inquiry would have been created. This a harsh political reality, but is also a worrying signal about the possibilities of law outside of transitions.

In some respects the new Inquiry into Bloody Sunday is a hybrid – a public judicial inquiry *and* a truth commission. It is bound by those domestic legal norms which bind other such inquiries, but it is certainly different to other such inquiries in the United Kingdom – demonstrated by, for example, the presence of international judges,[80] who were brought into the structure as a response to the Irish government's call for a completely international inquiry. The Bloody Sunday Inquiry has continually emphasised that its key aim is to find out the truth and all parties involved in it repeatedly speak about "finding the truth", despite the fact that neither the enabling Act nor the parliamentary resolution required by it mention the word "truth" at all. This is patently a different aim than "investigating the events". In fact the purpose of the Inquiry, given the history and context that surrounds it, makes it a form

[76] Mavis Maclean, *How Does An Inquiry Inquire? A Brief Note on the Working Methods of the Bristol Royal Infirmary Inquiry*, 28 J. LAW & SOCIETY 590 (2001).

[77] *Lost Lives, Hidden Voices*, 44 RACE AND CLASS 107, 116 (2002).

[78] See Hegarty, *supra* note 35.

[79] THE BLOODY SUNDAY INQUIRY, *infra* note 122, and accompanying text.

[80] Chief Justice Hoyt of New Brunswick and Mr John Tuohy, a retired Australian High Court judge.

of truth-finding exercise. It is certainly the case that a number of people see the Inquiry as a form of "truth commission", emblematic for them of the need to uncover the truth about other traumatic events and loss of life in over three decades of civil unrest in Northern Ireland. In many respects some public inquiries, those into particular kinds of disputed events, have to serve as both types of process, largely due to the nature of the events they are set up to investigate.

VI. OTHER LEGAL PROCESSESS

There are other legal ways of seeking accountability and a number of these were attempted in the case of Bloody Sunday. The results of these are also testament to the problems encountered when trying to make the state accountable for its actions through the law. There was a police investigation into the case, carried out by the Royal Ulster Constabulary (RUC). The information collected was sent by way of a file to the Director of Public Prosecutions.[81] The investigation was hampered and broke down largely due to the anonymous nature of the military witnesses,[82] who had been granted anonymity by Lord Widgery. This has been key problem in the investigation of Bloody Sunday and remains an issue for the new Bloody Sunday Inquiry, where it has been the subject of a number of judicial reviews of the Inquiry's initial rulings.[83] The Attorney General advised Parliament, by way of a written answer to a Parliamentary Question in August 1972, that no prosecutions would be taken against any of the military personnel and that "in the public interest" none of those civilians charged with riotous behaviour would be prosecuted.[84] At the inquest

[81] The Director of Public Prosecutions for Northern Ireland is responsible for the prosecution of indictable criminal offences in the jurisdiction. The office was established in 1972, on foot of the Hunt Report. For a fuller explanation of the role and scope of the office, see BRICE DICKSON, THE LEGAL SYSTEM OF NORTHERN IRELAND (4th ed., 1998). The office and its operation have been deeply controversial over the years, with allegations of bias and failure to uphold the rule of law in respect of killings by state forces. See JOHANNA KEENAN A BRIEFING PAPER ON THE OFFICE OF THE DIRECTOR OF PUBLIC PROSECUTIONS FOR NORTHERN IRELAND (2000) (available at <http://www.serve.com/pfc/policing/dpp/dppintro.html> (visited 31 July 2001).

[82] The official police report concluded that at least one of those killed was murdered, but that no prosecution was possible because the soldier who committed the offence could not be identified (BLOODY SUNDAY INQUIRY, Main Hearings, Day 47 (20 November 2000), p. 44, lines 20–21).

[83] See *R.* v. *Lord Saville, ex parte A*, [1999] 4 All ER 860.

[84] British Irish Rights Watch, *supra* note 3, at para. 9.2.

into the deaths a year later,[85] the Coroner labelled them "sheer unadulterated murder".[86]

The report of the Coroner bears comparison with that of Widgery. The Coroner felt it appropriate to find that the behaviour of the army was criminal, unlike Lord Widgery. In his view the soldiers "ran amok that day and shot [the victims] without thinking what they were doing".[87] Both inquiries were forms of public investigation, although only civilian witnesses gave evidence to the inquest.[88] Legal representatives for the army were told not to cross-examine those witnesses at the inquest because the Widgery Tribunal had established the facts and the inquest proceedings were mere formalities.[89] Thus, two official inquiry processes came to entirely different conclusions - the inquest supporting the near-unanimous view throughout Ireland and Widgery reinforcing the "official", state version of events: already there were competing histories. There were attempts to make the issue an international human rights law concern. In 1972 the Irish government amended its pre-existing application under the European Convention on Human Rights[90] to include an allegation of a breach of article 2 by the United Kingdom in respect of Bloody Sunday, but this application was rejected on procedural grounds.[91] More than 20 years later, another application would also fail, for similar reasons.[92] There were no other legal actions or attempts to overturn the

[85] See Ní Aoláin, *supra* note 12, at chapter 3. This inquest system has been recently considered by the European Court of Human Rights, which held that it was not adequate to satisfy the procedural aspects of article 2 of the European Convention in respect of investigation of loss of life. *McKerr* v. *United Kingdom*, App. no. 28883/95, *Jordan* v. *United Kingdom*, App. no. 24746/94, *Kelly and Others* v. *United Kingdom*, App. no. 30054/96, and *Shanaghan* v. *United Kingdom*, App. no. 37715/97, Judgment, 4 May 2001.

[86] Statement issued by the Coronor of Londonderry, Major Hubert O'Neill, 21 August 1973.

[87] Report of the Coroner, statement issued 21 August 1973. See also Derek Brown, *Bloody Sunday: The Never-Ending Inquiry*, The Guardian, 27 March 2000 available at http://www.guardian.co.uk/bloodysunday/article/0,2763,184918,00.html.

[88] Christopher Clarke QC, Opening Statement to the Bloody Sunday Inquiry, Inquiry Transcript, *supra* note 50, Main Hearings, day 41, p. 152, line 22.

[89] *Ibid.*, lines 23–25.

[90] *Ireland* v. *United Kingdom*, *supra* note 7.

[91] The European Commission held that, contrary to the procedural requirements of the Convention, all domestic remedies had not been exhausted. For a discussion of this see Dermot Walsh, Bloody Sunday and the Rule of Law in Northern Ireland 287 (2000).

[92] *McDaid and others* v. *United Kingdom*, App. No. 25681/94, (1996) 22 EHRR 29.

Widgery findings until many years later. It appears that this was due to a number of factors.

First, many of the families were in shock and that prevented any coherent campaigning, until around the 20th anniversary in 1992.[93] Second, as Dermot Walsh observes, the domestic legal options were limited: prosecutions had been effectively ruled out by the DPP and a judicial review of Widgery's findings was unlikely to succeed. Third, Northern Ireland was engulfed in the most serious civil unrest and violence: there simply was no opportunity for legal strategies to address the killings. This collapse of political space was exacerbated by the Widgery Tribunal's findings, which was perceived as "the second atrocity".[94] For many people Widgery had been such a negative experience of the law and specifically of "British justice" that there was no merit in considering legal challenges in a British court. Their view was that the rule of law had been so thoroughly abandoned to commit and then to justify the killings that it was therefore unlikely that the law would permit the "whitewash" – as it was routinely referred to – to be exposed. For them law's paradox was resolved: in favour of the state, its supporters and those who wielded power within the state.

Nor was there in 1972, unlike today, a culture of challenging official action by way of legal action. "Cause-lawyering" was relatively rare. The expansion of judicial review was in its infancy in Britain then and was even less developed in Northern Ireland.[95] That culture and the legal expertise and skills which are part of it has developed in the 30 years since then, as British security policy led to further "emergency" measures and as the field of public law in the United Kingdom generally expanded. Finally, as Kieran McEvoy notes, the Republican tradition in Ireland at the time, which was the natural constituency out of which such a campaign might have arisen, "largely ignored the potential of legal challenge as a source of external or objective validation".[96]

It is also the case that there are other narratives than those of the legal process in operation. For example, there are a number of artistic

---

[93] Tony Doherty, *Interview*, in UNFINISHED BUSINESS: STATE KILLINGS AND THE QUEST FOR THE TRUTH 16 (Bill Rouston, ed., 2000).

[94] Daly, *supra* note 54, at p. 211.

[95] On this point generally, see Brigid Hadfield, *Judicial Review in NI: A Primer*, 42 NORTHERN IRELAND LEG. Q. 332 (1991).

[96] Kieran McEvoy, *Law, Struggle and Political Transformation in Northern Ireland*, 27 J. LAW & SOCIETY 542, 550 (2000).

works reflecting the events of Bloody Sunday. As the Saville Inquiry continued its hearings, two new films dramatising the events of Bloody Sunday were made.[97] The production of these two films has driven the debate about what happened about Bloody Sunday back onto the mainstream agenda in Britain in a way that the Inquiry's proceedings, reported sporadically in the British media, has not. Arguably these two films – and the poems, songs and plays about the events – have had a far greater impact upon public consciousness than the Inquiry's proceedings. The films were prompted by the Inquiry but they may actually contribute more to public understanding of the notions of truth and human rights than the legal processes to which they respond.

VII. THE FAILURE OF LAW

From a radical perspective, it was impossible for the truth to have emerged about Bloody Sunday in 1972. The primary mechanism, which purported to deliver that truth, was a fraud. The purpose of setting up the Widgery Inquiry was not, as the state claimed, to find out the truth, but precisely the reverse: it was intended to *prevent* the truth of the events emerging. Without a public inquiry of some sort, the state would have been open to wider condemnation and possibly to further investigation. Politically, the Inquiry was necessary, but control had to be retained. The memo of the meeting between Heath and Widgery records the Prime Minister's view that,

> All the pressures were for a public inquiry ... There was a risk that, if the Inquiry was not held in public, some would condemn it as invalidated on the ground that they had been unable to see and hear what took place. It would be necessary to consider ... how access to the Tribunal's proceedings could be limited.[98]

Other papers disclosed to the second Bloody Sunday Inquiry under Lord Saville confirm the state's view of the uses of public inquiries: "All the ministers agreed that the Army's resistance to special inquiries or official tribunals was well-founded, but they felt that

---

[97] *Bloody Sunday*, directed by Paul Greengrass and made by Granada TV for British commercial television and *Sunday*, written by Jimmy McGovern for Britain's Channel 4 TV. Both were shown in January 2002, coinciding with the thirtieth anniversary of Bloody Sunday.

[98] Downing Street Memorandum, *supra* note 57, supra, at (d).

some sort of independent voice was needed to reassure public opinion".[99]

Sir Edward Heath, in his oral evidence to the Bloody Sunday Inquiry, provided further insight. Speaking about internment, he said, "we had to try to find means of reassuring public opinion and so on and this was one of the ways in which we thought it could be done, with an independent view".[100] In the case of Bloody Sunday, Widgery facilitated the state in fielding any criticism of its actions by providing this talismanic "independent view".

This approach is key to understanding why it is that liberal democratic states bother with the expense and the complexities of public investigations. It is because they understand that the events are sufficiently serious to merit public concern, but rather than seek to account for wrong-doing and seek to avoid it in the future, some wish to deny that wrong was done and to use the law as a way of doing so. Thus the interests of the state and the official discourse of law militated against the truth about Bloody Sunday emerging. In 1972 international human rights law was not then as developed as it is today and the local legal community had little expertise and awareness of it,[101] which meant that it was largely only the domestic legal route that could be explored. The violent crisis into which Northern Ireland was descending made it even less possible for that official discourse to be effectively challenged: Bloody Sunday and the travesty of legal accountability that was Widgery incensed feelings in the nationalist community throughout Northern Ireland against the state and led to further violent civil unrest.

Yet, despite Widgery being the end of the matter so far as the state was concerned, Bloody Sunday remained an issue for the nationalist community in Northern Ireland and its supporters elsewhere. The state continued to insist that Widgery's verdict had laid the matter to rest, but those findings were further undermined and discredited, especially by the discoveries in the Public Record Office of the

---

[99] 'Note of a meeting at Chequers, Thursday, 19 August 1971', Bloody Sunday Inquiry document no G9A.66.1, p. 66.3 (Inquiry Transcript, *supra* note 50, Day 282, pp. 100–101, at lines 20–25 and lines 1–20). The meeting was attended by, amongst others, Heath, Reginald Maudling (then United Kingdom Home Secretary), Lord Carrington (then United Kingdom Foreign Secretary) and Brian Faulkner (Prime Minister of Northern Ireland).

[100] Inquiry Transcript, *supra* note 50, Day 282, p. 102, lines 8–10.

[101] See Livingstone, *supra* note 13, pp. 132–140.

documents kept from the legal representatives of the families of the dead and the wounded.[102]

Bloody Sunday became both an iconic event in nationalist Ireland and, further afield, a status supported and enhanced by the response of artists and communities to it. In any litany of nationalist complaints against the British state it featured significantly and was often referred to as "Britain's Sharpeville".[103] But its effect was even more ruinously significant. It demonstrated that human rights violations were at best an incidental aspect of security policy and at worst a deliberate strategy. Widgery compounded the harm by providing a disturbing illustration of the impunity the state was prepared to afford itself and the power it had to ensure that impunity pertained when committing human rights abuses. As Fionnuala Ní Aoláin notes, Bloody Sunday "represents a watershed in the relationship between minority community and state, cementing a history of coercion and disaffection, compounded by the state's willingness to exonerate the agents responsible for any acts which caused loss of life. The combination of this incident and the ongoing internment process indicated that due process had been entirely abandoned and that the military approach now dominated the political agenda."[104]

The knowledge of this, engendered by first hand experience, drove many in Northern Ireland towards the gun and made appeals to respect the law and observe due process seem hollow. Thus Bloody Sunday and the attempt by the state to contain the truth about it within the sham of a public judicial inquiry catalysed the deterioration in the relationship between the nationalist community and the state, a deterioration which drove the conflict into one of its bloodiest phases. If the Lord Chief Justice of England, one of the most senior law officials in the state, would preside over such a travesty of justice, it was said, how could any faith be maintained in the state to provide justice?[105] It appeared that the legal process, intended to provide an alternative to violence and anarchy, had assisted the state in covering up the killings of unarmed citizens. Thus law was appropriated to further the political will of the state and in that process led to an almost complete alienation from the state of a substantial section of its citizenry.

---

[102] See *supra* note 58 and 59 and accompanying text.

[103] Simon Winchester, *13 Killed As Paratroops Break Riot*, THE GUARDIAN, 31 January 1972 (quoting John Hume).

[104] Ní Aoláin, *supra* note 12, pp. 42–43.

[105] See Eamon McCann, *The Civil Rights Campaigner*, in HIDDEN TRUTHS: BLOODY SUNDAY 50, 51 (Trisha Ziff, ed., 1998).

This response and the subsequent alienation from the state was an inevitable outcome of a policy that was prepared to countenance civilian deaths[106] and to deny the truth about those deaths. It is a sombre warning about believing governments who claim to be neutral in internal conflicts, but who appropriate law in pursuance of a policy that is anything but neutral. Bloody Sunday is an archetypal case of Cohen's theory of official denial, where "magical legalism is a method to 'prove' that an allegation could not possibly be correct because the action is illegal".[107] Thus the law was used to protect the state and the process of public inquiry used to insulate it against domestic and international criticism. Lord Widgery, who should have acted as "the pivotal trustee of the rule of law"[108] instead chose to behave as a participant in a "propaganda war".[109]

VIII. ALTERNATIVES TO LAW

Widgery had another important impact, this one less catastrophic. Its purported version of the truth led eventually to the community most affected by Bloody Sunday finding alternative ways to remember it and to tell its version of the truth, but this did not happen immediately. Having been denied what it regarded as a fair investigation into the events of Bloody Sunday and instead presented with an official version of events that contradicted hundreds of local eyewitnesses, the local community began to commemorate the events of Bloody Sunday in its own ways. There were annual memorials, starting in 1973, on the first anniversary, but as the conflict in the north escalated those commemorations themselves became the subject of dispute and eventually dwindled to an annual march organised by Sinn Fein,[110] which continued to organise the annual commemoration until 1989. Apart

---

[106] The then Prime Minister, Sir Edward Heath, has denied that this was the policy at the time of Bloody Sunday. (See Inquiry Transcript, *supra* note 50, Day 287 (22 January 2003), pp. 107–122), yet documentary evidence shows that civilian deaths were contemplated later in 1972, during Operation Motorman (*ibid.*, at pp. 124–129).

[107] Cohen, *supra* note 26, at p. 108.

[108] The Irish Government's Assessment of the Widgery Report and the New Material Presented to the British Government in June 1997 177 (1998).

[109] "Downing Street Memorandum", *supra* note 57, at p. 270.

[110] The republican movement had split in January 1970, into a faction that recognised the institutions of both the British and Irish states ('the Officials') and one that resolutely opposed it ('the Provisionals'). See Bishop & Mallie, *supra* note 44, at pp. 132–138. Due to the split in the republican movement, there were actually separate marches commemorating Bloody Sunday for a period of some years.

from those commemorations, all impetus to address the events of Bloody Sunday withered, largely a result of the trauma of the events and their aftermath. By the 20th anniversary, however, there was a renewed energy for the case and this led to the creation of a new campaign. It also facilitated the need of the local community to have its "truth" told. This truth was in direct conflict with the state's version and the response of the state to the renewed campaign was to label it "subversive".[111]

In one sense the campaign was of course subversive, in that it sought to have the official version refuted, but in another sense it was anything but subversive: it was about preserving the rule of law rather than perverting it. This demonstrates the important point that that law is not, in reality, the preserve of the state. The defence of the rule of law may involve challenging the state and key to the validity of such a challenge will be the victims of human rights violations. This is why it is a remarkable but defining feature of the Northern Ireland conflict that those who seek accountability for loss of life have been so widely derided. That it is the state they seek to call to account is the key factor. There is a hierarchy of victims in Northern Ireland[112] in which those killed by the state have been relegated to relative invisibility. The British media in particular tend to treat those killed by the state as third-class victims.[113] This was acutely obvious in the early stages of the renewed Bloody Sunday campaign, where the establishment media and others lambasted those involved. One prominent columnist's denunciation of the twenty-fifth anniversary commemorations resulted in a libel action, later settled by the newspaper.[114] More recently films dramatising the events and based upon eyewitness testimony have been described in the mainstream conservative British press as a "fantasy".[115]

The process begun around the twentieth anniversary was an alternative way of "telling the truth", through community activity, but also

---

[111] For example, the premises of the newly created Bloody Sunday Initiative were raided by the police force and those who worked for it, including the son of one of those killed on Bloody Sunday, were arrested but later released without charge. See Doherty, *supra* note 93.

[112] "All Truth Is Bitter; A Report of Dr. Alex Boraine's Visit to Northern Ireland", Community Relations Council for Northern Ireland, p. 24.

[113] Roy Greenslade, *supra* note 4.

[114] *Para Chief 'Sorry' for IRA slur on Relatives*, IRISH NEWS, 10 July 1999, reporting the settlement by THE IRISH TIMES of a libel claim by organisers of the Bloody Sunday commemorations. The libel claim arose after remarks in the paper by columnist Kevin Myers.

[115] Ruth Dudley Edwards, *When the Real Victim is Truth*, THE DAILY MAIL, 8 January 2002.

through art, drama, poetry and oral history. The events of Bloody Sunday had already inspired a number of prominent writers and artists, including a song by John Lennon, two plays – *The Freedom of the City* by Brian Friel and *Carthaginians* by Frank McGuinness – and a number of poems, one by Seamus Heaney and *The Butchers Dozen* by Thomas Kinsella. Many of those who had witnessed the events of Bloody Sunday found themselves telling and re-telling their stories and they became absorbed into a local mythology of the events. It is sometimes said that one of the functions of myths is to provide a form of communal memory.[116] They are constructed because there is no agreed version of the truth and communal story-telling – itself very important in the Irish cultural tradition – is one way in which a form of truth was agreed, at least by the community to whom Bloody Sunday had happened. Inevitably, as with all myths, there are elements that become exaggerated or distorted.

IX. FROM ABANDONMENT TO INTERVENTION

The effect of this alternative process was important. For something that had begun as an abandonment of law, it led people back into the legal process. It culminated in a re-opening of the case and the institution of a second inquiry, but it had also raised the consciousness and the capacity of those involved. Most significantly of all it led them to expect that the new inquiry would operate much more as a truth commission than an orthodox public inquiry and that there would be less investigation of the events and rather more exposition of the local version. It had long been the "received wisdom" in Derry that the people of the city knew what happened on Bloody Sunday. The process leading to the new inquiry came about therefore not because people needed to *be told the truth*, but rather because people needed *the truth to be told.* As Eamon McCann observes, "[t]he long campaign for a new inquiry to repudiate the finding of the Widgery Tribunal in 1972 did not arise from a need to know the truth, but from the fact that, knowing the truth, we needed to have it acknowledged. And, that done, and just as important, to know why."[117]

Consequently, the expectation of the families and of the local community was that the new inquiry would look much more like a

[116] See JOSEPH CAMPBELL, THE POWER OF MYTH (1988).

[117] Eamon McCann, *If innocent citizens were deliberately killed by servants of the State we all need to know*, THE SCOTSMAN, 17 January 2002, available at http://www.thescotsman.co.uk/s2.cfm?id=59322002.

truth commission than a public inquiry. This expectation was fuelled in part by the unprecedented nature of the inquiry and by the presence of international judges, but it was not an expectation that was shared by the United Kingdom political and military establishments. Nor was it the belief of the Inquiry itself. This fundamental difference of opinion and expectation of the role of the Inquiry has created an unhappy tension in its proceedings and demonstrates the difficulties inherent in trying to make truth-finding both closure and accountability mechanism. A process that confirms a new, fully formed version of the truth must inherently be a different process to one that investigates events and comes to some objective conclusion about them.

X. THE SECOND BLOODY SUNDAY INQUIRY

This Inquiry is chaired by Lord Saville of Newdigate, but the three member panel was completed by judges from outside the United Kingdom: Chief Justice William Hoyt from New Brunswick in Canada and Sir Edward Sommers, a retired New Zealand High Court judge. In late 2000, Sir Edward retired for health reasons and was replaced by a retired Australian judge, John Tuohy. The presence of non-British judges is a precedent in United Kingdom law and says much about its uniqueness. The Inquiry first sat in public in The Guildhall in Derry on 3 April 1998 and began oral hearings on 27 March 2000. The Inquiry finally ended on the 23rd November 2004, with a two-day closing statement from Counsel to the Tribunal. The Inquiry is not expected to report until 2005.

The Inquiry is a Tribunal of Inquiry, set up under the Tribunals of Inquiry (Evidence) Act 1921 and as such is subject to the relevant administrative law and practice, such as the Salmon Principles.[118] It is subject to judicial review by the English High Court and has already had a number of its rulings overturned by both the English Divisional Court and Court of Appeal.[119] It is the largest and most complex public inquiry in United Kingdom legal history, sitting for 434 days. It collated around 525 volumes of evidence, 41 audiotapes and 62 videotapes having been circulated to interested parties.[120] It is

[118] Formulated by the Royal Commission chaired by Lord Salmon (REPORT OF THE ROYAL COMMISSION ON TRIBUNALS OF INQUIRY (1966), Cmnd. 3121).

[119] See *infra* notes 120–130 and 154–160 and accompanying text.

[120] The Bloody Sunday Inquiry, 'Frequently Asked Questions', paras 23–25, at < http://www.bloody-sunday-inquiry.org > (visited 30 June 2004).

expected to cost £155 million.[121] Over 1,700 civilians, clergy, journalists, photographers, current and former military personnel have been interviewed and have given statements and 919 of these witnesses gave oral evidence.[122]

The purpose of a Tribunal of Inquiry is to "inquire into a definite matter of urgent public importance".[123] It is charged with finding out the truth and with carrying out a public investigation. The very existence of a second inquiry suggests that whatever the official view of events, public confidence in Widgery – where it had existed – had eroded. One might therefore infer that the state has now accepted that the official version promulgated in Widgery is now no longer valid. As the Prime Minister said in his statement to the House of Commons, "a new inquiry can be justified only if an objective examination of the material now available gives grounds for believing that the events of that day should be looked at afresh, and the conclusions of Lord Widgery re-examined".[124]

This means that the new Inquiry has the difficult task of laying to rest the ghosts of Widgery, despite its insistence that it is "not an investigation into how Lord Widgery conducted his Inquiry. We are not sitting as a court of appeal from the Widgery Inquiry."[125] As it got underway, it was clear that it had to balance the competing demands of public confidence in Ireland and public confidence in Britain and that it would have to do so whilst being regularly criticised by a largely hostile British media and political establishment.[126] In its initial statement and approach, the Inquiry demonstrated considerable sensitivity and skill in doing this. But it had to combat a welter of negative factors. The sheer size and amount of the information uncovered by the Inquiry is a testament to its thoroughness, but it has consequently made the entire process much slower and

[121] *Ibid.* See also *Bloody Sunday inquiry set to cost £100m*, IRISH TIMES, 17 December 2001.

[122] *Ibid.*, para. 14. Many relevant documents, including daily transcripts of the oral proceedings, ruling, judgments, press notices and other information are available on the Inquiry website, <http://www.bloody-Sunday-inquiry.org>.

[123] S. 1(1) of the Act.

[124] HANSARD, H.C. DEBS., 29 January 1998, col. 502.

[125] Bloody Sunday Inquiry, Opening Statement of Lord Saville, 3 April 1998, available on the Inquiry website, *supra* note 122.

[126] See Don Mullan, *British Establishment Guns Trained On Bloody Sunday Inquiry*, IRISH TIMES, 18 June 1999; Inquiry Transcript, *supra* note 50, Preliminary Hearings, 27 September 1999, pp. 117–118.

more expensive than might have been anticipated.[127] It has also made some errors. For example, the first ruling on the application for complete anonymity by military witnesses[128] in which the Tribunal ruled that the names of those soldiers involved in Bloody Sunday should be publicly disclosed, was legally flawed[129] and allowed a damaging judicial review to succeed. This confirmed prejudices and fears on both sides – the families believing that once again the British "establishment" was obstructing the truth of Bloody Sunday emerging and the soldiers and their supporters making the case that the Inquiry was fundamentally flawed. This application for judicial review was to be the first in what has become a continuing and parallel legal process running in the English courts, in which the rights of military witnesses have trumped the rights of the families of the dead and of the wounded to an independent, fully public and accessible inquiry.

XI. WHAT IS THE PURPOSE OF THE INQUIRY?

The simple answer to this question might be provided by examining the enabling statute, the debate in parliament when the Inquiry was set up or even the inquiry's own statements on the matter. However, whilst those certainly reveal much of what the purpose of the inquiry is, they do not tell the full story. Crucial to a successful outcome for the Inquiry is the support of the various sections of society to whom it is addressed, chief amongst whom are the families of those killed and those who were wounded on Bloody Sunday. This is confirmed by an examination of the Prime Minister's remarks in the course of the debate in Parliament that followed the announcement of the new Inquiry. He said

> As for the suggestion that people may want a type of verdict that convicts the "British army of occupation" and all the rest of it, and they are not going to get it, and that will be a problem for them, I am not setting up the inquiry for those people. I am setting up the inquiry because the relatives of those who died that day have the

[127] The series of judicial reviews has also slowed down the Inquiry proceedings and added to its cost. See Sir Louis Blom–Cooper, *The Cost of Bloody Sunday*, THE OBSERVER, 20 January 2002.

[128] *R.* v. *Lord Saville of Newdigate, Rt. Hon. Sir Edward Somers, Hon. Justice Hoyt (The Members of Tribunal Sitting as Bloody Sunday Inquiry)*, ex parte *"B", "O", "U" and "V"*, [1999] EWHC Admin 232 (Q.B.D.).

[129] *Ibid.*, paras 12(3) and (4).

right to expect us, their Government – the British Government – to try to establish the truth of the events of that day. *I am interested in their interests, their concerns and their sense of grievance*, not in the sense of grievance of people who have engaged in terrorist acts.[130]

Thus the Prime Minister signalled from the outset that the constituency to whom the Inquiry should have first regard was the relatives of the dead. Yet that has been made quite difficult by the approach of his own government and others, which has placed the constituency of the soldiers and their supporters at the same or even at a higher level than the Bloody Sunday families.

The purpose of the inquiry may be said to be to examine afresh the evidence of what happened on Bloody Sunday, to come to a reasoned set of findings and to do so in a manner that secures public confidence in the rule of law. Clearly, therefore, the Inquiry's findings are important, but the process by which it arrives at those findings is also vital. It only exists because the first inquiry failed to secure confidence in the rule of law. There are long-standing allegations that the state deliberately covered up the truth about Bloody Sunday, an iconic event in a long history of contested and controversial activities by the state in Northern Ireland. The Inquiry's task therefore is to achieve "not only a sense of justice, but the elimination of a sense of injustice".[131]

When the Inquiry began, it devoted some thought to how to balance the sometimes competing considerations of fairness, justice and truth.[132] A significant decision early in the Inquiry's deliberations was the securing of an undertaking from the Attorney General in relation to information supplied by witnesses to the Inquiry.[133] The undertaking meant that no evidence or information supplied by a witness to the Inquiry in relation to the events of Bloody Sunday could be used in the prosecution of that witness – but crucially not that of others – for a criminal offence. This meant that witnesses would be reasonably free to discuss their own behaviour on Bloody Sunday, without fearing that their disclosures would lead to prosecution. So, for example, some civilian witnesses

---

130 HANSARD, H.C. DEBS., 29 January 1998, col. 517 (emphasis added).

131 M. Cherif Bassouni, *Searching for Peace and Achieving Justice: The Need for Accountability*, 59 LAW & CONTEMPORARY PROBLEMS 9, 23 (1996).

132 Christopher Clarke, Counsel to the Inquiry, considered this in his Opening Statement: Inquiry Transcript, *supra* note 50, 27 March 2000, p. 6, lines 7–13, p. 7, lines 2–22, p. 13, lines 7–18, pp. 15–18.

133 *Ibid.*, at pp. 15–16.

have been able to admit to riotous behaviour[134] or to IRA membership at the time[135] and some military witnesses have been able to admit to lying at the time, both to the military hierarchy[136] and to the Widgery Tribunal.[137] This assurance, at first perceived by some relatives of the dead as conferring a form of immunity on the soldiers involved in the shootings, has been key in persuading a number of witnesses to give detailed accounts to the Inquiry.

The struggle for truth through law and the question of whether it can be achieved remains unresolved in the case of the current Bloody Sunday Inquiry. Until the Inquiry produces its final report, no complete judgment can be made about the success or otherwise of its process. However, the difficulties faced by the Inquiry are demonstrative of the problems created when trying to make the state face up to its culpability in human rights violations and the tension inherent in a process which is meant to be investigatory but which is also intended to provide closure for victims. In several key aspects of the Inquiry thus far these difficulties and tensions can be observed.

XII. THE CONCEPT OF PUBLIC JUSTICE

It is an accepted principle of public law that inquiries should be open and accessible.[138] It is also a requirement of the European Convention on Human Rights that, where the right to life is concerned, "there must be a sufficient element of public scrutiny of the investigation or its

---

[134] See, for example, the statement of Paul McDaid and his oral evidence to the Inquiry (Inquiry Transcript, *supra* note 50, 12 March 2001, p. 134, lines 12–18, p. 135, lines 19–25).

[135] See, for example, the statement of Martin McGuinness to the Inquiry (admitting to being the adjutant (second in command) of the Derry Command of the Provisional IRA at the time); Colin Blackstock, *Leak Confirms McGuinness' IRA Role During Bloody Sunday,* THE GUARDIAN, 23 January 2002; the statement of Reg Tester to the Inquiry (admitting to being the Quartermaster of the Derry Brigade of the Official IRA at the time, Inquiry Transcript, *supra* note 50, 4 April 2000, p. 62, lines 6–9).

[136] See, for example, Inquiry Transcript, *supra* note 50, 11 April 2000, p. 14, lines 7–25.

[137] See, for example, David Pallister *Key Bloody Sunday Witness Found – Former para. To Testify Against Ex-Colleagues In Return For Security Deal*, THE GUARDIAN, 19 August 2000; *Soldier Fired Rubber Bullet Into Car*, DERRY JOURNAL, 12 October 2001.

[138] REPORT OF THE COMMITTEE ON ADMINISTRATIVE TRIBUNALS & INQUIRIES (Cmnd. 1432, 1957) ("The Franks Committee").

results to secure accountability in practice as well as in theory".[139] As the European Court of Human Rights has remarked, "[p]roper procedures for ensuring the accountability of agents of the State are indispensable in maintaining public confidence and meeting the legitimate concerns that might arise from the use of lethal force".[140]

It is acknowledged by all the interested parties that the Tribunal should sit primarily in public. As the Tribunal itself has noted, "[t]he statute under which we are acting allows us to exclude the public or any portion of the public from any part of the proceedings, if we consider that it would be in the public interest for us to do so, but we shall need very strong grounds indeed to take that course..."[141]

The Tribunal sat in public because it is in the interests of public justice to so do. However, "sitting in public" means more than that the events may be covered in a newspaper – it means that the public should both have access to and be able to scrutinise the proceedings. The purpose of public hearings is to ensure accountability, primarily to the families of those killed and those wounded, but to all of those against whom offence has been committed. Dozens of people were arrested and many of them have alleged that they were violently and brutally assaulted by soldiers on Bloody Sunday.[142] Many more witnessed the murder and wounding of people they regarded as innocent. The Inquiry, arguably, has a duty to consider the effect upon them. As the European Court of Human Rights has noted, "there must be a sufficient element of public scrutiny of the investigation or its results to secure accountability in practice as well as in theory".[143] It added: "Proper procedures for ensuring the accountability of agents of the State are indispensable in maintaining public confidence and meeting the legitimate concerns that might arise from the use of lethal force."[144] On the other hand, the Inquiry, which is a part of the United Kingdom legal system, naturally seeks to retain the confidence of the British public in general. This should be distinguished from the confidence of various interested elements of the state, unionist and conservative politicians and the conservative media. The latter had long maintained

[139] *McKerr* v. *United Kingdom*, *supra* note 35, at para. 114.

[140] *Ibid.*, para. 160.

[141] Bloody Sunday Inquiry Opening Statement, 3 April 1998.

[142] See Inquiry Transcript, *supra* note 50, day 188 (11 February 2002), pp. 1–7.

[143] *McKerr* v. *United Kingdom*, *supra* note 35, at para. 114

[144] *Ibid.*, para. 160.

that the actions of the army and the state on Bloody Sunday were justifiable.[145] Their confidence had not been undermined by the events themselves nor by the Widgery Tribunal, nor even by the new evidence. As Dermot Walsh notes,

> It is a sad fact of life in Northern Ireland that there is a section of public opinion which would not be unduly concerned whether the Army had fired on unarmed civilians in the Bogside. There is an even larger section who would simply refuse to believe that the British Army would do any such thing. There are also those who would be only too willing to believe it irrespective of the evidence. It is axiomatic that these sections of the public are not going to be profoundly influenced by the contents of the Tribunal's Report one way or the other. The success of the Report cannot be judged by the extent to which it mollifies or confirms their prejudices.[146]

Trying to balance these competing tensions has been very difficult and the Inquiry has been forced into a protracted series of legal arguments, played out in the United Kingdom courts, where the outcome has consistently favoured the state. In this, the matter of public confidence is at the heart of the Inquiry's difficulties. For example, there has been a dispute over where the military witnesses, including former soldiers, should give their evidence. The Inquiry ruled that they should do so in Derry, taking the view that, "the chances of this Inquiry restoring public confidence in general and that of the people most affected in particular ...would be very seriously diminished (if not destroyed) by holding the Inquiry or a major part of the Inquiry far away and across the Irish Sea, unless there were compelling reasons to do so".[147]

It had to address competing concerns on this point. On the one hand, if the military witnesses were to be permitted to give their evidence in a different venue, whilst anonymous and perhaps even from behind screens,[148] then public confidence in the Inquiry might well be very deeply undermined. On the other hand, the military witnesses argued that without such protections they were at risk[149]

[145] See, by way of illustration, HANSARD, H.C. DEBS., 29 January 1998, col. 504 (Mr. Trimble's remarks that "The basic facts of the situation are known and not open to dispute"); col. 513 (Mr. Wilkinson's assertion that "Lord Widgery produced an exemplary report, which was remarkable for its clarity and objectivity").

[146] Dermot Walsh, *supra* note 58, at p. 72.

[147] Inquiry Ruling on Venue, 1 August 2001, para. 5.

[148] According to Mr. Clarke, 42 witnesses were screened in one fashion or another. See BS Inquiry Transcript, DAY 433, P1, at line 16. All but one of these were military, police or security service officers.

[149] And that in particular their rights under article 2 of the European Convention on Human Rights are at risk. See *R.* v. *Lord Saville, ex parte A*, *supra* note 83, at paras. 39, 68(5) and (9).

and could not themselves have confidence in the Inquiry. This latter point was accepted by the English Court of Appeal, which seemed to fundamentally misunderstand the nature of public confidence and its relevance in a Tribunal of Inquiry.[150] The quashing of the Inquiry's initial ruling by the English courts prompted concerns about the independence of the process.[151] Giving judgment for the court, the Master of the Rolls, Lord Phillips said

> ... we would hesitate long before taking a step that would be likely to rob [the Inquiry] of credibility. We also sympathise with the desire of the people of Londonderry and, in particular the families, for the whole of this Inquiry to take place in their city. In their shoes we would share their emotion. But in our judgment the risk posed in Londonderry to the soldier witnesses by dissident Republican terrorists does constitute a compelling reason why their evidence should be taken in a venue other than Londonderry. In these circumstances we do not see why, should we direct a change of venue for these witnesses, this should threaten the credibility of the Tribunal or confidence in their Inquiry. *The fairness and objectivity of this Tribunal must by now be quite clear to all in Londonderry.*[152]

But the court did not reflect upon its capacity to make such an assessment and upon the effect that *its* judgment, as an English court, might have upon public confidence in Derry. Nor did it consider the context of mistrust of the state in Northern Ireland and the particular history of Widgery and Bloody Sunday. Similar sentiments had been asserted over the years about the "fairness" and "objectivity" of Widgery: asserting them did not make them any more widely believed.

The new Inquiry is obliged to balance these competing pressures, whilst adhering to the strictures laid down by the courts' interpretation of the relevant Human Rights Act provisions. It may well be that this is an impossible task. It seems that the substantive article 2 rights of the military witnesses are always going to trump the "procedural" article 2 rights of the relatives of the dead because of the manner in which the English courts have chosen to apply the Human Rights Act 1998.[153] A

---

[150] *Ibid.*, paras. 29, 68(1) and (4).

[151] See, for example, Robert Verkaik *Soldiers will not attend Bloody Sunday inquiry* THE INDEPENDENT, 20 December 2001; Seamus McKinney, *British courts could 'stall Saville truth'*, IRISH NEWS, 20 December 2001, both quoting legal representatives and family members expressing concern that repeated interventions by the English courts would prevent the truth emerging.

[152] *Ibid.*, at para. 56 (emphasis added).

[153] See *R.* v. *Lord Saville of Newdigate & Ors* ex parte *A & Ors.*, [1999] 4 All ER 860 (CA); *Lord Saville of Newdigate & Ors* v. *Widgery Soldiers & Ors*, [2001] EWCA Civ 2048 (CA).

re-thinking of the source of the procedural right to life may be necessary, but the English courts throughout their consideration of the issues raised in the Bloody Sunday judicial reviews have struggled to understand the extent and the application of the European Court of Human Rights jurisprudence.[154]

The matter is further complicated by the consistent unwillingness of the United Kingdom courts to unpack the reasons for the findings by the security services that the military witnesses are at a greater risk if they give evidence in Northern Ireland than in London. Little weight seems to have been given to the fact that the security services are themselves an interested party before the Inquiry. There appears to be scant comprehension that a security assessment emanating from the Ministry of Defence, which supports the position taken by its former employees, will be regarded with great suspicion in large parts of Northern Ireland and that consequently might impact on the level of public confidence in the Inquiry. In fact the assessments provided reasons for the court to accede to all of the requests for judicial reviews on these issues by those representing the military and former soldiers. As one judge observed, "[t]he conclusion that there was no objective reason for fear on the part of the officers would itself have been perverse in the light of the intelligence evidence".[155]

12.1. *The Meaning of "Public Confidence"*

Tribunals of Inquiry are set up to address a crisis in public confidence.[156] But what exactly is the nature of that crisis in public confidence? It is evident that the crisis of confidence that prompted this particular Inquiry was not a crisis of confidence of the general public in Britain, which generally accepted the Widgery version of events. Nor, very obviously, was it a crisis of confidence of members of the military or of the political establishment, who promoted the Widgery version, which reflected their accounts and largely rejected those of the civilians. It can therefore be argued that the crisis of confidence this Inquiry was created to address was primarily that of the general public in Derry and throughout Ireland, most of which had never accepted the official version of the event. Implicitly acknowledging

---

[154] See Hegarty, *supra* note 35.

[155] *In the Matter of an Application by the Next of Kin Of Gerard Donaghy for Judicial Review and in the Matter of a Decision of the Bloody Sunday Inquiry*, [2002] NICA 25B, *per* Girvan J.

[156] REPORT OF THE ROYAL COMMISSION ON TRIBUNALS OF INQUIRY, *supra* note 118, para. 28.

this, the Inquiry chose to sit in Derry. It might also be argued that it was in the interests of general public confidence in the rule of law that serious allegations of murder by the state be fully and properly addressed by the state, not least because article 2 of the European Convention on Human Rights requires it. As the European Court of Human Rights said in *McKerr* v. *United Kingdom*, "[t]he right of the family of the deceased whose death is under investigation to participate in the proceedings requires that the procedures adopted ensure the requisite protection of their interests, which may be in direct conflict with those of the police or security forces implicated in the events".[157]

Deciding what "public justice" means has been a crucial aspect of the inquiry's proceedings, but the definition remains unclear. For the judiciary, public justice does not mean entirely open proceedings, taking the view that

> [t]here is a danger ... in conflating the concept of the public nature of the inquiry with the asserted need for witnesses to be identified and visible. The latter is relevant to the degree of confidence that people may have in the outcome of the Inquiry but the public nature of the proceeding is not eliminated by allowing witnesses to give evidence from behind screens. Put shortly, the Inquiry still takes place in public although the proceedings are not as open as before.[158]

Yet public inquiries are held partly because the public has to be reassured about controversial events that have undermined confidence in the rule of law. They are also one mechanism by which law can access truth and dispense justice, provided that they are carried out in way that does not serve the interests of the state. Thus the manner in which an inquiry is conducted will be crucial to its success. An inquiry that takes place in public and which is unfettered by limitations that serve the interests of the state, is one way in which that confidence may be restored. Confining the extent to which that inquiry is conducted in public and limiting its investigations will inevitably lead to suspicions that a "cover-up" is taking place. Yet this happened with both Bloody Sunday inquiries. The confidence of the key stakeholders in the process, those for whom the Inquiry was explicitly set up, seems to have weighed little in the judicial equation. The limitations upon the public nature of the second inquiry are taking place at the behest and for

---

[157] *McKerr* v. *United Kingdom*, *supra* note 35, at para. 148.

[158] *In the Matter of An Application by Mary Doherty for Judicial Review*, 19 February 2002 (Northern Ireland High Court), para 15, *per* Kerr J.

the benefit of those who are alleged to have been involved in the unlawful killings of 14 civilians and the wounding of 14 others. These limitations reflect those imposed at the Widgery Inquiry, where soldiers gave evidence anonymously and partly disguised, and which led to allegations of an official cover-up. It is precisely because the outcome of *this* second Inquiry must inspire confidence, where the previous inquiry did not, that the proceedings should be as open as possible. There are three significant limitations on the inquiry's "openness" – the anonymity of the military witnesses, the change of venue to London and the screening of police officers and others. Individually, these are challenges to the Inquiry's capacity to carry out its task fully, but taken together they say something very significant about the approach of the state to public justice and its attitude when confronted with allegations of its misdeeds.

Comparisons may be drawn with other public inquiries in the United Kingdom, where witnesses alleged to have been involved in the killing of civilians were compelled to give evidence, despite serious civil unrest actually taking place at the venue of the Inquiry hearings. After the murder of Stephen Lawrence[159] and the subsequent controversial police investigation a public inquiry was established under section 49 of the Police Act 1996.[160] Amongst those who were required to give evidence to it were the five men suspected of the murder. The five had already had charges against them dropped and a private prosecution against them, taken by the family of Stephen Lawrence, had failed. Nonetheless, they objected to their summons to give evidence[161] and challenged it

[159] Stephen Lawrence was a black teenager who was killed in a racist knife attack in Eltham, South London on 22 April 1993. His murder was unsatisfactorily investigated by the Metropolitan police and became a *cause célèbre* and a defining moment in the public discourse about racism in Britain. See BRIAN CATHCART, THE CASE OF STEPHEN LAWRENCE (2000).

[160] The Inquiry was chaired by Mr Justice William McPherson and his report was published as THE STEPHEN LAWRENCE INQUIRY: REPORT OF AN INQUIRY BY SIR WILLIAM MACPHERSON OF CLUNY, Cm 4262-I (February 1999) (available at <http://www.archive.official-documents.co.uk/document/cm42/4262/4262.htm> (visited 30 June 2004). He found, *inter alia*, at para. 46.1, that "[t]he investigation was marred by a combination of professional incompetence, institutional racism and a failure of leadership by senior officers".

[161] The applicants initially challenged the legality of the summons, but later changed their challenge to simply one to the propriety of the questions the Inquiry proposed to ask.

unsuccessfully in the courts.[162] They subsequently gave their evidence, openly and without the benefit of screens, despite the fact that hostile public demonstrations were taking place outside the hall where the Inquiry was sitting. Roads were blocked and the Metropolitan Police fired CS gas canisters.[163] At one juncture, the room in which the Inquiry was sitting was invaded by demonstrators, causing its adjournment for three hours.[164] Nonetheless, the Inquiry proceeded to hear the evidence of the five witnesses. Nothing remotely as disruptive occurred at or during the Bloody Sunday Inquiry.

XIII. WITNESSES AT THE INQUIRY

The Inquiry emphasised from the start that it was an inquisitorial process, not an adversarial one. As Lord Saville noted

> The Tribunal, unlike the families and the wounded (or indeed those with opposing views), does not start with any beliefs at all. Those held by the families and the wounded are clearly genuinely held and may prove to be justified, but the Tribunal alone is in a position to collect, collate, analyse and present all the available evidence, with no pre-conceived views at all, and with only its desire to seek the truth. That indeed is the duty of the Tribunal.[165]

This inquisitorial approach has had consequences for the manner in which civilian witnesses are treated.[166] Whilst the Inquiry regards itself as inquisitorial, the oral hearings are in fact highly adversarial, with the consequence that some witnesses have had the disadvantages of both approaches and the advantages of neither. Generally, public inquiries in the United Kingdom must carry out the difficult task of satisfying two well-established principles in relation to inquiries. First, witnesses must be treated fairly.[167] The definition of "fairness"

---

162 *R.* v. *Chairman Of Inquiry Into Matters Arising From Death Of Stephen Lawrence* Ex Parte *Neil A'court, Jamie A'court* & *David Norris*, [1998] EWHC Admin 647 (QBD, Div. Ct).

163 See *Lawrence Suspects Deny Involvement*, THE GUARDIAN, 30 June 1998.

164 David Pallister & Rory Carroll, *Lawrence Inquiry Fiasco*, THE GUARDIAN, 30 June 1998.

165 Bloody Sunday Inquiry Ruling, 24 July 1998.

166 See *infra* note 178 and accompanying text.

167 See L. Blom Cooper, *Witnesses and the Scott Inquiry*, [1994] PUBLIC LAW 1; L. Blom Cooper, *Witness Before Public Inquiries: an Example of Unfairness*, [1996]. PUBLIC LAW 11; G. Howe, *Procedure at the Scott Inquiry*, [1996] PUBLIC LAW 445; R. Scott, *Procedures at Inquiries - The Duty to Be Fair*, 11 L. QUARTERLY REV. 596 (1995).

is to be found in the six Salmon Principles, which lay down how witnesses before Tribunals of Inquiry are to be treated.[168] Second, the inquiry must conduct its work "with efficiency and as much expedition as is practicable".[169] One criticism that might be levelled at the Bloody Sunday Inquiry is that it has been fairer to some witnesses than to others, creating further doubts about the power balance in legal processes where the state is being challenged about its actions on its own territory.

For example, a number of civilian witnesses have been questioned in detail by counsel for the Inquiry and for the soldiers as to knowledge they may have about the membership of various wings of the IRA.[170] The Inquiry has taken this approach as it is of the view that there was no other avenue open to it in its investigation of the events of Bloody Sunday.[171] A number of witnesses have refused to name anyone they thought to have been in the IRA, to the consternation and objections of the Inquiry and of the legal representatives

---

[168] The six principles are:

1. Before any person becomes involved in an inquiry, the Tribunal must be satisfied that there are circumstances which affect him or her and which the Tribunal proposes to investigate.
2. Before any person who is involved in an inquiry is called as a witness, he or she should be informed of any allegations which are made against him or her and of the substance of the evidence in support of them.
3. He or she should be given adequate opportunity of preparing his or her case and of being advised by legal advisers; his or her legal expenses should normally be met out of public funds.
4. He or she should be given the opportunity of being examined by his or her own solicitor or counsel and of stating his or her case in public at the inquiry.
5. Any material witnesses he or she wishes called at the Inquiry should, if reasonably practicable, be heard.
6. He or she should have the opportunity of testing by cross-examination conducted by his or her own solicitor or counsel any evidence which may affect him or her.

[169] THE SCOTT REPORT, RECOMMENDATIONS ABOUT INQUIRY PROCEDURES (Part 4, Section K, Chapter 1), at para. K1.2.

[170] See, for example, the questioning of Gerry Duddy, day 59 (11 December 2000), pp. 153–154; of Charles McDaid, day 60 (12 December 2000), pp. 131–137; of Eamon McCann, day 87 (6 March 2001), pp. 113–120; of Denis Bradley, day 140 (12 September 2001), pp. 97–110.

[171] Lord Saville has remarked, "it is our basic duty to discover the whole truth if the only way we can do that, unsatisfactory though that is, is to ask questions about rumours and who knew who and so on". Inquiry Transcript, *supra* note 50, day 87, p. 7, lines 11–14.

of the military witnesses.[172] Some of those witnesses were journalists who took the view that disclosure of names would be a disclosure of sources and thus contrary to their professional ethics.[173] The vast majority of civilian witnesses most likely do not know who was in the IRA, which is a secret and covert organization.[174] Thus, most of those being cross-examined about the matter probably do not have certain knowledge of who was in the organisation and therefore any response they give may be little more than repeated gossip or speculation. Approaching witnesses like this may also infringe the Salmon principles.[175] It is being alleged that witnesses know the identities of members of the IRA, an organisation that is proscribed under United Kingdom law and has been pursued by the authorities for its activities, which amount to criminal offences. Possession of such information may amount in law to knowledge of a criminal conspiracy and refusal to supply such information may amount to a criminal offence under section 89(2)(c) of the Terrorism Act 2000.[176] In order for witnesses to be properly legally advised as to their responses to questions like this, they should probably be notified of these questions in advance of their oral testimony. This is something the Inquiry itself has taken a view upon, stating that '[i]f any of the interested parties seek to make an allegation against any of the Inquiry's witnesses they must give details to the Inquiry of the allegation that they intend to make. None of the interested parties will be allowed, without the permission of the Tribunal, which is unlikely to be given save for very good reason, to pursue an allegation against any of the witnesses unless it has been the subject of a notice given to the Inquiry in good time..."[177]

Yet both counsel for the Inquiry and counsel for the various soldiers have persisted in questioning a number of witnesses on this issue, implying that they believe the witness may have such

[172] Submissions on behalf of the clients of Mr Anthony Lawton, May 2003.

[173] Such as Eamon McCann, Peter Taylor and Mary Holland.

[174] The IRA is a secret organisation. Its rules on knowledge and disclosure of membership are fairly specific. See Ed Moloney, *supra* note 44.

[175] Principle 2 of which states: "Before any person who is involved in an inquiry is called as a witness, he should be informed of any allegations which are made against him and of the substance of the evidence in support of them."

[176] In Part VII, which applies only to Northern Ireland and which preserves a section from the previous incarnations of the Northern Ireland (Emergency Provisions) Acts.

[177] Bloody Sunday Inquiry, Rulings and Observations, 13 October 1999, para. 101 (i) and (v).

information and few, if any, of the local civilian witnesses have received any advance notice of this. Counsel for many of the soldiers lodged an application to the tribunal, seeking it to recall a number of such witnesses and to be compel them to provide names of alleged IRA personnel to the Tribunal, arguing that the interests of the military witnesses would be prejudiced if it did not.[178]

When senior members of the military and of the government of 1972 came to give evidence they had a less arduous experience than many of the civilians.[179] Counsel for one of the families, Michael Lavery QC, took the unusual step of addressing the Inquiry directly on the matter, when he raised with it the manner in which Sir Edward Heath's oral evidence had been handled. Noting that Sir Edward had refused "to answer a large number of questions" he said that "on no single occasion has the Inquiry, as far as I could see from reading the transcript, indicated to Sir Edward that it is not really appropriate to abuse Counsel; and I have to say that the latitude that this witness has been given is completely outside my experience..."[180]

Sir Edward's counsel, who robustly defended his client, specifically rejected Mr Lavery's remarks[181] and this illustrates one of the factors causing this problem. Whilst local civilian witnesses were entitled to legal representation when giving their written statements, it has been extremely rare for such a witness to be accompanied by counsel.[182] In the Inquiry's view, all witnesses are the Inquiry's witnesses and as such need no specific legal representation, unless they are granted it by the Inquiry. The formality and shape of this particular legal process has made judgments as to how certain categories of witnesses are to be represented and will not bend even when it is clear that those witnesses are at a disadvantage.

[178] See Christopher Walker, *Army QC calls on media to name IRA men*, THE TIMES, 31 May 2003, available at <http://www.timesonline.co.uk/article/0,,2-697855,00.html>

[179] Eamon McCann, *Saville Too Soft on Heath*, IRISH NEWS, 27 January 2003.

[180] Inquiry Transcript, *supra* note 50, day 286 (21 January 2003), p. 100, lines 11–16.

[181] *Ibid.*, Mr Mackie, at p. 102, lines 17–25; p. 103, lines 1–25.

[182] Indeed when one civilian witness asked for representation by counsel he was refused. His experience in giving evidence was such that he wrote to the Inquiry to complain about that treatment and the refusal to grant him full legal representation. (Interview with Dr. Raymond McClean, Transcripts of Interviews conducted for Bloody Sunday Trust, 'Witness: The Civilian Experience of The Bloody Sunday Inquiry', Video Production, 30 January 2002.)

All of the military witnesses, even those who did not fire a shot on Bloody Sunday and whose involvement in it may have been peripheral, are fully legally represented. They are deemed to be "interested parties" and are quite properly entitled to such legal representation because of the serious nature of allegations against some of their number. It is also because they and their supporters have the support of government to assert those rights.[183] Civilian witnesses who have allegations put to them that they knew members of an unlawful organisation are not similarly supported, because they are deemed not to be "interested parties" and do not have the backing of the state. Thus both the formality of law and the balance of power in the state advantage the state's witnesses. It may just be a design flaw, but if the purpose of law is to find truth and achieve justice, such an advantage is a fundamental one. On the other hand, if law's purpose is to serve the state in denying responsibility, such an imbalance is crucial in delivering that end.

A demonstration of this issue and the confusion on the part of the Inquiry itself on the matter arose when Lord Saville responded to a question from a civilian witness.[184] In the course of his answer to that question, he said "there are plenty of barristers in this room acting for the interested parties, the families and so on who I am sure would be the first to raise the matter with us if they felt we had not treated the citizens of this city properly".[185] In response to this counsel for the families pointed out that they were not instructed by nor would they be able to defend civilian witnesses. As Mr Mansfield put it, "[w]e do not represent witnesses other than the families we are personally responsible for".[186]

The civilian witnesses therefore remain the sole province of the Inquiry, whose eagerness to seek the truth may conflict with the interests of some of those civilian witnesses, who are not independently legally represented. Local witnesses also found their credibility challenged because they had relatives killed by the state or because they became involved in paramilitary activity after Bloody Sunday.[187]

---

[183] The Ministry of Defence, for example, has made legal submissions in support of the soldiers' application for anonymity and are paying for their legal team, through The Treasury Solicitor. See *infra* note 194 and accompanying text.

[184] Inquiry Transcript, *supra* note 50, day 86, at p. 169, lines 1–11.

[185] *Ibid.*, lines 14–18.

[186] *Ibid.*, day 87 at p. 9, lines 13–15.

[187] Interviews conducted for Bloody Sunday Trust, '*Witness: The Civilian Experience of The Bloody Sunday Inquiry*', Video Production, 30 January 2002.

This caused great apprehension amongst many of the civilian eyewitnesses and made what was a difficult experience all the harder.[188] One important issue therefore is the *effect* first-hand experience of legal truth finding has upon victims and survivors of human rights abuses. In truth processes, cross-examination of witnesses is highly unusual. In such proceedings, the purpose of the oral evidence is for the story, the experience to be heard, acknowledged and honoured. But law will not always bend to hear those stories. As Julie Mertus has observed, "[t]he legal process is inherently counter-narrative; it opens and closes, letting in only enough information to prove the issue at hand".[189]

For many of the civilian eyewitnesses testifying before the Bloody Sunday Inquiry, the experience has been a traumatic, terrifying one. They are unable to come and simply "tell their story": they are interrupted by questions and confronted by transcripts of interviews given years ago. Their incomplete memories, the differences however slight from statements made at the time or years later to journalists, are subtly proffered as reasons to disbelieve their evidence. Some have left the Inquiry feeling worse than before. If the experience of giving evidence leaves people less confident about the legal process than before, then, one might wonder, how is the purpose of "restoring confidence in the rule of law" achieved?

XIV. CONCLUSION

The task undertaken by the Bloody Sunday Inquiry is an extraordinarily difficult and complex one, not least in the meeting of the expectations and needs of its different audiences, but it has already faltered in being forced to recalibrate its priorities. The key audience for it ought to have been the families of the dead and the survivors, who have good reason not to trust the British government and the state. Yet they are no longer its primary constituency. Substantial sections of the military witnesses are opposed to the inquiry and they have successfully challenged decisions taken by the Inquiry. This has been compounded by the visceral hostility of some politicians and

---

188 *Ibid.*

189 In *Truth In A Box: The Limits of Justice Through Judicial Mechanisms*, in THE POLITICS OF MEMORY: TRUTH, HEALING AND SOCIAL JUSTICE 144 (Ifi Amadiume & Abdullahi An-Na'im, eds., 2000).

sections of the media.[190] All of this is taking place against the background of a fluctuating political climate, where the contours of the terrain are continually shifting and where the very existence of the Inquiry itself is an element of that climate.

The inquiry has been required by law, practice and court-rulings to become a very formal, complicated process and is as a result, overly legal. Whilst inquiries are legal processes, they are intended to be of a different nature, inquisitorial, rather than adversarial. The Bloody Sunday Inquiry has become the longest, the most expensive and the most complex public inquiry in United Kingdom legal history. This may an inevitable consequence of the complex and controversial nature of the material the Inquiry is investigating, coupled with deep mistrust amongst the parties which has led to a plethora of legal representation. The contrary expectations of the Inquiry has led to strains between the Inquiry and its "client" group – the families, their lawyers and civilian witnesses who survived Bloody Sunday. The circumstances that led to the second Inquiry created specific expectations amongst that "client group" that it would be some form of truth commission. However, this was not the expectation, nor indeed the intention of the Inquiry.

Some of its aspects, such as the presence of international judges and its interpretation of its remit send out signals that this is something other than an ordinary public inquiry. For example, the length of time spent in Christopher Clarke's marathon opening statement on the social and historical context of Bloody Sunday indicate that the Inquiry sees itself as examining a broader context, which fits with the idea of it as a truth-finding process. But this truth-finding function has been obstructed by the delays and challenges explored above. It may be that the highly formal model of a Tribunal of Inquiry is not the correct format for such a truth-finding exercise. That is, of course, provided that the Inquiry is intended to be such an exercise. It is, after all, the ongoing contestation of truth that is the real reason for the delays and the difficulties and that may betray the real aims of the state.

What then, was the expectation of the state, which had set the Inquiry up? The view of the Prime Minister, who announced the establishment of the Inquiry to Parliament, was that "the aim of the inquiry is not to accuse individuals or institutions, or to invite fresh

[190] Indeed, one newspaper went so far as to describe the Inquiry as "a gesture of appeasement to the IRA". See Mary Holland, *Demand For Anonymity Threatens Peace Hopes*, IRISH TIMES, 10 June 1999 (which describes such newspaper editorials).

recriminations, but to establish the truth about what happened on that day, so far as that can be achieved at 26 years' distance". He added, "I believe that it is in everyone's interests that the truth be established and told. That is also the way forward to the necessary reconciliation that will be such an important part of building a secure future for the people of Northern Ireland".[191] Thus he, like the families of the dead and the wounded, saw the role of the inquiry as a form of truth process which would assist in reconciliation. However, it seems that not all of his government shared this view.

The United Kingdom government's official line, repeated in Parliament, is that "as the Inquiry is independent, its working practices are a matter for it to decide for itself; therefore, it would not be appropriate for the Government to comment".[192] Yet other parts of the United Kingdom government take a different position. The Ministry of Defence, for example, "made a submission in support of anonymity and ... are also funding the soldiers' lawyers".[193] It is clear from media coverage of the judicial reviews that parts of the government support the soldiers' position.[194] When the first legal challenge to the Inquiry's position on anonymity succeeded, the Prime Minister's office "welcomed" it.[195] It seems curious that a government would set up an inquiry into events, believing that the "only course that will lead to

---

[191] Tony Blair MP, Prime Ministerial Statement, HANSARD, H.C. DEBS., 29 January 1998, col 503.

[192] Marjorie Mowlam MP, then Secretary of State for Northern Ireland, in response to a written question from Norman Godman MP, HANSARD, H.C. DEBS., WRITTEN ANSWERS, 15 February 1999, col 483.

[193] John Spellar, MP, Undersecretary of state for Defence, Briefing By The Under Secretary Of State For Defence, Mr. John Spellar Mp And The Assistant Chief Of The Defence Staff (Operations), Rear Admiral Simon Moore, 28 MAY 1999 (<http://www.kosovo.mod.uk/brief280599.htm>, visited 30 June 2004).

[194] A response by the Prime Minister's Office to the first successful judicial review by the soldiers suggests that some policy was at work. (Richard Ford, *Bloody Sunday Soldiers Are To Withhold Names*, THE TIMES, 18 June 1999, reporting that "[t]he Prime Minister's office said: 'This is very welcome news for the soldiers'." A number of other news reports record that Mr Robertson, the then British Defence Secretary, was "sympathetic" to the soldiers' case (*e.g.*, Nicholas Watt, *Plea To Name Bloody Sunday Soldiers*, THE GUARDIAN, 29 May 1999).

[195] Seamus McKinney, *Support For Paras Angers Families*, IRISH NEWS, 28 May 1999, noting that relatives of the dead and inured were angered when the then "British Defence Secretary George Robertson backed an establishment campaign for the soldiers to be granted anonymity when they give evidence at the new inquiry". The report goes on to record however that "a Downing Street spokesman last night stressed that the government had not adopted any official policy on the matter".

public confidence ... is to set up a full-scale judicial inquiry"[196] but subsequently permit parts of that government to behave in ways which could reasonably be described as obstructive. The government's position is in even more doubt since Home Secretary Jack Straw condemned the Inquiry in a recent debate in Parliament with the remarks that "we sometimes make a mistake in investing quite the faith that we do in appointing a judicial figure to chair an inquiry of this kind".[197]

This apparently contradictory approach can be explained if the Inquiry is viewed as a consequence of a political deal that emerged out of a long campaign for truth and in the wake of a peace process, but where there was a fundamental mismatch of expectations as to the likely outcome of the inquiry. Significant parts of the state did not appear to envisage that the scope or operation of the Inquiry would be radically different to that of Widgery, even if it were a possibility that the new Inquiry might come to a different conclusion.

Thus, the Bloody Sunday Inquiry is impeded by the continuing official denial of the events it was set up to investigate. The truth of those events may never emerge in a domestic process, where the state is still in a position to use law to further that denial, although changes to legal and political culture have made it more difficult. It may have been naive to assume that the state would allow a full accounting of discovery of its activities, given its record in Northern Ireland. It may be that it is only when the mechanism employed to seek truth is in all its important elements truly independent of the state that the truth about human rights abuses committed by the state may emerge. As Bernadette Devlin-McAliskey pithily put it when she came to give evidence to Saville: "This [inquiry] should be somewhere else, where the accused is not running the party".[198]

However, there was a general sense when the Inquiry was announced, that the state, in creating it, was preparing to abandon its defence of its version of Bloody Sunday. This is clearly not the case. The state's current version of events may be different to the one it espoused in 1972, but it still declines to accept blame and the official version appears at the moment to be that whilst all those who were killed were

---

[196] Tony Blair MP, Prime Ministerial Statement, HANSARD, H.C. DEBS., 29 January 1998, col. 502.

[197] HANSARD, H.C. DEBS., 4 June 2003, col. 200. Mr Straw was rejecting calls for a public inquiry into the United Kingdom government's handling and use of intelligence on 'weapons of mass destruction' in Iraq.

[198] Inquiry Transcript, *supra* note 50, 15 May 2001, at p. 70, lines 11–12.

innocent, the army were firing at IRA snipers who escaped.[199] It may be partly because the Provisional IRA was initially largely unwilling to co-operate with the Inquiry.[200] This initial unwillingness of the IRA's Army Council to sanction co-operation with the Inquiry may in turn be partly a product of the unwillingness of the state to co-operate fully with the Inquiry.[201] Both state and paramilitary seem significantly unwilling to surrender their mythology.

The real question is, of course, which mythology is closer to the truth. That is the question that the inquiry was set up to answer and which it has yet to do. That task is a vital one. The problem may be that a Tribunal of Inquiry is simply not equipped to deal with the vortices of emotion, distrust and history that are the legacies of Bloody Sunday. The discourses of British law and political culture may be incapable of confronting the colonial past and their culpability in it.

---

[199] Edwin Glasgow, QC, Opening Statement to the Bloody Sunday Inquiry.

[200] This apparent reluctance prompted a call by the Chair of the Inquiry, Lord Saville, for co-operation. See Bloody Sunday Inquiry Transcript day 224, pp. 158–159 (20th June 2002).

[201] Martin McGuinness, who was the deputy Officer Commanding the Derry Brigade of the Provisional IRA in 1972 gave first a written statement and then oral evidence to the Inquiry about the IRA's activity on the day and other former IRA members followed suit (*More Provos expected to testify over Bloody Sunday*, THE GUARDIAN, 20 September 2002). See also Mr Clarke's remarks on 19 September 2002 (Inquiry Transcript, *supra* note 50, day 236, p. 162, lines 1–7) that three witnesses had indicated that they were prepared to make a statement and that "one of them may be from the Official wing and two of them may be from the Provisionals". In fact, by the end of oral evidence to the Inquiry, more than 30 former IRA members had given evidence, including the Officer Commanding the Provisional IRA on Bloody Sunday. Other former members of the IRA have testified but as witnesses to the events, rather than as members of the organisation (see, for example, Raymond McCartney's evidence to the Inquiry, 5 September 2002, (Inquiry Transcript, *supra* note 50, Day 228, pp. 2–76). He joined the IRA after and possibly as a result of Bloody Sunday.

CASE LAW

*SPECIAL COURT FOR SIERRA LEONE**

Prosecutor v. Sam Hinga Norman (Case No. SCSL-2003-08-PT), Decision on Appeal by the Truth and Reconciliation Commission for Sierra Leone ("TRC" or "The Commission") and Chief Samuel Hinga Norman JP Against the Decision of His Lordship, Mr Justice Bankole Thompson Delivered on 30 October 2003 to Deny the TRCs Request to Hold a Public Hearing with Chief Samuel Hinga Norman JP, 28 November 2003.

Justice Geoffrey Robertson, President, Special Court for Sierra Leone

I. THE PRESIDENT OF THE SPECIAL COURT FOR SIERRA LEONE ("THE SPECIAL COURT"): NOTING THE SUBMISSIONS OF THE PARTIES HEREBY DECIDES AS FOLLOWS:

1. The matter comes before me in the form of a joint application by Chief Sam Hinga Norman and the Truth and Reconciliation Commission ("TRC"). It arises from a decision of His Honour Judge Bankole Thompson, delivered on 29 October 2003, in which he refused a TRC request to conduct a public hearing with this indictee.[1] Judge Thompson entertained the request by virtue

*The special Court of Sierra Leone was established on 16 January 2002 by an Agreement between the United Nations and the Government of Sierra Leone pursuant to Security Council resolution 1315 (2000) of 14 August 2000.

[1] *Prosecutor v Norman*, Case No. SCSL-2003-08-PT, Decision on the Request by the Truth and Reconciliation Commission to Conduct a Public Hearing with Samuel Hinga Norman, 29 October 2003.

Criminal Law Forum **15:** 247–272, 2004.
© 2004 *Kluwer Academic Publishers. Printed in the Netherlands.*

of his position as Presiding Judge of the Trial Chamber, given jurisdiction to do so by Rule 5 of the Practice Direction on the procedure following a request by a State, the TRC or other legitimate authority to take a statement from a person in the custody of the Special Court.[2] Rule 5 of that Direction provides that once it is proved that an indictee has given informed consent to questioning by the TRC, a joint request "will only be rejected if the Presiding Judge is satisfied that a refusal is necessary in the interests of justice or to maintain the integrity of the proceedings of the Special Court". An appeal against rejection shall be decided by the President if it is made expeditiously and jointly by the detainee and the requesting authority.

2. The appeal having been made expeditiously and jointly by notice filed on 1 November 2003[3] (Grounds of Appeal following on 4 November 2003[4]) I convened an oral hearing on the next day, 5 November, in which the Applicants and the Prosecution were fully represented and joined in a helpful discussion of what is, on any view, a novel and difficult question and one that is likely to recur for other indictees and in other post war situations where the local and international community considers that the establishment of both a Special Court and a Truth Commission will assist in the restoration of peace and justice. For this reason, I have consulted with others who have relevant experience, especially of the TRC process. Because of the significance of the matter I permitted subsequent submission in writing from all parties over the fortnight following the hearing.
3. Although the decision takes a judicial form, it inevitably embodies a balancing of values and interests that I have undertaken in my role as President of the Special Court – a role which encompasses administrative and representative responsibility relevant to

[2] This Practice Direction was adopted on 9 September 2003 and amended on 4 October 2003.

[3] Appeal by the Truth and Reconciliation Commission for Sierra Leone ("TRC" or "The Commission") and Chief Samuel Hinga Norman JP against the Decision of His Lordship, Mr. Justice Bankole Thompson delivered on 30 October 2003 to Deny the TRC's Request to Hold a Public Hearing with Chief Samuel Hinga Norman JP, 1 November 2003.

[4] Grounds of Appeal by the Truth and Reconciliation Commission ("TRC" or "The Commission") and Chief Samuel Hinga Norman against the Decision of His Lordship, Mr. Justice Bankole Thompson ("The Decision") delivered on 30 October 2003 to Deny the TRC's Request to Conduct a Public Hearing with Chief Samuel Hinga Norman JP, 4 November 2003.

co-operation with other institutions like the TRC. It is not normally appropriate for one judge to review another's exercise of discretion, so I have not treated this appeal as a judicial review of the decision of Judge Thompson or strictly as an appeal from his decision, by rather as a fresh hearing in a context where as President, I have the flexibility to explore alternative solutions. It was the thinking behind the amendment of Rule 5 (which had originally provided that the decision of the Presiding Judge would be final) to allow the President to take a broader view about an indictee's contacts with third parties and institutions, a role he is in any even give by the Rules of Detention.[5]

1.1. *Historical Background*

4. The TRC was an express product of the Lomé Accord, which was signed on 7 July 1999.[6] The Act to establish the Commission was itself passed by Parliament in February 2000.[7] That was well before the Treaty which established the Special Court, agreed by the United Nations on 16 January 2003[8] and ratified by the Sierra Leone government on 29 March 2002.[9] So the Special Court, which has an overriding duty to try those accused of bearing greatest responsibility for the war, was not in prospect when the TRC was given statutory form. In consequence, the provisions of the TRC Act do not envisage that indictees may testify to it or any basis upon which they might do so. The Special Court was given, by Article 8 of its Statute, a primacy over the national courts of Sierra Leone (and, by implication, over national bodies like the TRC). It has overriding duty to prosecute those alleged to bear the responsibility for the war, with which duty the Government

[5] See Rule 48(c) of the Rules governing the detention of persons awaiting trail or appeal before the Special Court for Sierra Leone or otherwise detained on the authority of the Special Court for Sierra Leone, 7 March 2003, as amended 25 September 2003.

[6] Peace Agreement between the Government of Sierra Leone and the Revolutionary United Front of Sierra Leone, 7 July 1999.

[7] The Truth and Reconciliation Act 2000, February 2000.

[8] Agreement between the United Nations and the Government of Sierra Leone on the Establishment of a Special Court for Sierra Leone, Freetown, 16 January 2002.

[9] The Special Court Agreement, 2002 (Ratification) Act, 2002, Sierra Leone (as amended), implementing legislation passed 19 March 2002, Presidential assent received 29 March 2002.

bound itself to cooperate.[10] There was nothing in the Court's Agreement or Statute which required the Court to compromise its justice mission by deferring to local courts or national institutions.

5. The expectation of the United Nations in this respect is set out in the report of the Secretary General at paragraph 8:

> The present report... does not address in detail specifics of the relationship between the Special Court and the National Truth and Reconciliation Commission. It is envisaged, however, that upon the establishment of the Special Court by the appointment of its Prosecutor, arrangements regarding cooperation, assistance and sharing of information between the respective courts would be concluded and the status of detainees awaiting trail would be urgently reviewed. In a similar vein, relationship and cooperation arrangements would be required between the Prosecutor and the National Truth and Reconciliation Commission, including the use of the Commission as an alternative to prosecution, and the prosecution of juveniles, in particular.[11]

6. The Spirit of cooperation envisaged by the Secretary General had in fact resolved all problems without the need for any formal agreements, until this particular issue concerning whether indictees should give public testimony to the TRC arose late in October 2003. The Office of the Prosecutor, which has substantially more resources than the TRC, has followed a different and independent process of investigation. The Prosecutor even announced that he would not use any evidence collected or heard by the Commission, although this undertaking was made at a time when it was not envisaged that any indictee would testify (and the Prosecutor has made clear that he will not be constrained from using indictee testimony). Even so, this was a very considerable compromise by an organ of the Special Court: if crucial evidence against an author of a crime against humanity were to surface at a TRC hearing, one would expect the Prosecutor to obtain it (if a document) or to subpoena the witness, certainly if the testimony was given in public. Nonetheless, the Prosecutor is entitled to make agreements or announce self-denying ordinances and "no go" areas, and he gave this undertaking precisely to avoid any

[10] See Article 17 of the Agreement between the United Nations and the Government of Sierra Leone on the Establishment of a Special Court for Sierra Leone, 16 January 2002.

[11] Report of the Secretary General on the Establishment of a Special Court for Sierra Leone, 4 October 2000, UN Doc. S/2000/915; Archbold (International Criminal Courts), Appendix E2.

possible conflict with the TRC process. What he cannot do, of course, is bind defendants: if evidence vital for their defence is given at a TRC hearing, then the Trial Chamber would not be prevented from entertaining a defence application to obtain it.[12]

7. The TRC report is due in February 2004, just before the Special Court trails are due to start. Judicial notice might be taken of it, and it might provide considerable assistance to the Court and to all parties as an authoritative account of the background to the war. It will recommend to the government reforms designed to prevent re-ignition of violence. But the TRC has not, significantly, given any undertaking to suspend judgement on individuals awaiting trail in this court. Should any statement of fact or opinion in the TRC report be challenged by either side, the Court would have to make up its own mind on the evidence presented to it. Bishop Humper (the TRC Chairman) joined me on 4 December 2002 in expressing the hope that the Commission and the Court would complement each other, with mutual goodwill and an understanding of our separate responsibilities.
8. There were a number of concerns expressed in 2002 about possible problems in having a TRC and a Special Court in operation at the same time: none has come to pass. Ironically, the question of an indictee's public testimony did not appear to be problematic, if only because it was not envisaged that the TRC would, or could properly, seek to obtain it. The initial expectation in this respect of informed persons well-disposed to both processes was expressed in an illuminating report by the International Centre for Transitional Justice ("ICCTJ"):

> In the case of persons indicted by the Special Court, the TRC should decline to interview them altogether until the proceedings against them are concluded.[13]

This absolute position (which the ICTJ authors no longer maintain) at least gave full force to the universal value that nothing should be done to endanger a fair trial. The TRC, by this application, wishes to go towards the other extreme: it seeks not only to interview

[12] The issue is discussed by one Commissioner, William A. Schabas, in *The Relationship Between Truth Commissions and International Courts: The Case of Sierra Leone*, 25 Human Rights Quarterly 1035 (2003).

[13] Marieka Wierda, Priscilla Hayner and Paul Van Zyl, "Exploring the Relationship between the Special Court and the TRC of Sierra Leone, *ICTJ* (New York: 24 June 2002), p. 18.

indictees, but to do so in public, in a courtroom over several days, in a form that will permit them to broadcast live to the nation, and then face sustained questioning shortly before their trial.

1.2. *Judge Thompson's Decision*

9. This application was refused by Judge Thompson in a carefully considered decision delivered on 29 October 2003. His starting point was that "it is the unquestionable expectation of the international community that judges of the Special Court should discharge their judicial functions independently and impartially free from pressures (institutional, societal, political, or otherwise). (Article 13(1) of the Court's Statute.)"[14] His concern was that the TRC Statute only permitted public testimony and impartially free from "victims of abuses and violators; perpetrators of abuses and violations and interested parties" none of which three categories properly described an indictee. He feared, from this aspect of the Act and from the Commission's claim that "the accused did play a central role in the conflict in Sierra Leone",[15] that he would testify under the rubric of a "perpetrator", contrary to the presumption of innocence and in a forum where his rights could not be protected. Notwithstanding, the societal interest in the TRC process, "the accused's right to a fair and public trial always prevails".[16] It prevails, in Judge Thompson's judgement, even over the indictee's own decision to waive his due process rights: the Court in effect was to be judge of where his best interests lay:

> It is incontrovertible that what is at stake here is the accused's right to a fair and impartial trial before the Special Court where he can enjoy ample opportunity, with all the judicial guarantees and procedural safe-guards, to vindicate himself. Nothing should be done to deprive him of that opportunity or unduly burden prematurely exercise of that right.[17]

---

[14] Decision on the Request by the TRC to Conduct a Public Hearing with Samuel Hinga Norman, para. 9.

[15] See request SHN 001/submitted on 07 October 2003 by the Truth and Reconciliation Commission for Sierra Leone to conduct a public hearing with Chief Samuel Hinga Norman JP in terms of the Special Court for Sierra Leone Practice Direction adopted on 9 September 2003, as amended on 4 October 2003, para. 9.

[16] Decision on the Request by the TRC to Conduct a Public Hearing with Samuel Hinga Norman, para. 14.

[17] Decision on the Request by the TRC to Conduct a Public Hearing with Samuel Hinga Norman, para. 16.

10. I do not sit judicially to review this decision for reasons that I have already explained.[18] The applicants point out that "playing a central part" in the conflict does not necessarily entail the commission of human rights abuses and that President Kabbah and other ministers have testified, neither as "victims" nor as "perpetrators" bus rather (I suppose) as "interested parties". The presumption of innocence, to which the Judge attached much weight, is really a rule which places the burden of proof on the Prosecution at trial; it is not a straitjacket which insulates an indictee, against his wishes, from all forms of questioning prior to his trial. The applicants say that the decision failed to take into account the importance of an indictee's autonomy and his freedom of speech or to note the presumption which paragraph 5 of the Practice Direction sets up in favour of an application which comes with the indictee's informed consent.
11. Irrespective of these submissions, however, it remains the fact that Judge Thompson, Presiding Judge of the Chamber which must accord a fair trial both to this defendant and to other defendants and to the Prosecution, finally concluded that the integrity of such a trial would be undermined were he to grant the application in the form in which it was presented. He was not asked to consider alternatives, but I have sought to find a compromise that will maintain the integrity of the Special Court process while permitting the TRC to fulfil its statutory mandate and allow an indictee (but only if he wishes) to have his say. That solution must be capable of application not only to this indictee but to others who wish to testify and capable of replication elsewhere in circumstances where courts and truth commissions operate in tandem.

1.3. *The TRC*

12. The object of the TRC is set out in Section 6(1) of its Act. It is

> to create an impartial historical record of violations and abuses of human rights and international humanitarian law related to the armed conflict in Sierra Leone, from the beginning of the conflict in 1991 to the signing of the Lomé Peace Agerement; to address impunity, to respond to the needs of victims, to promote healing and reconciliation and to prevent a repetition of the violations and abuses suffered.

[18] See para. 3 above.

This is a broad mandate, although I pause at this juncture to note that it is to report only on the period from 1991 to the Lomé Accord of July 1999. The Special Court jurisdiction is to try those accused of the greatest responsibility for war crimes from November 1996, the date of the failed Abidjan Accord, (which ironically also contained a provision for a TRC) to the end of the conflict, which broke out again after Lomé and continued until early 2002. If the TRC mandate had been limited to end with the Abidjan Accord, there would be no difficulty, but there is an overlapping period until July 1999, which will be the subject of scrutiny both by the TRC, and in the different context of a criminal trial, by the Special Court.

13. The TRC functions may broadly be divided, in accordance with its title, into those of providing an historical record ("truth") and those of assisting victims to come to terms with their perpetrators ("reconciliation"). The "truth" functions, described in Section 6(2)(a) of its Act,[19] could be interpreted as permitting findings about individual responsibility – the prime function of the Special Court. The "reconciliation" functions, described in Section 6(2)(b) are not so problematic, so long as they invite victims to reconcile with perpetrators who do not bear great responsibility and are not Special Court indictees.[20] IT is possible to envisage an indictee pleading guilty and then going before the TRC to beg his victims' forgiveness, and subsequently asking for any such forgiveness to be taken into account by the Court in mitigation of his sentence. But that is not the case and no indictee has yet evinced any intention to plead guilty. It is the "truth" aspect, which is of most concern, together with the "reconciliation" procedures which the TRC wishes to adopt (or adapt) to hear evidence from indictees.

[19] Section 6(2)(a) reads: "to investigate and report on the causes, nature and extent of the violations and abuses referred to in subsection (1) to the fullest degree possible, including the antecedents, the context in which the violations and abuses occurred, the question of, whether those violations and abuses were the result of deliberate planning, policy or authorisation by any government, group or individual, and the role of both internal and external factors in the conflict".

[20] Section 6(2)(b) reads: "to work to help restore the human dignity of victims and promote reconciliation by providing an opportunity for victims to give an account of the violations and abuses suffered and for perpetrators to relate their experiences, and by creating a climax which fosters constructive interchange between victims and perpetrators, giving special attention to the subject of sexual abuses and to the experiences of children within the armed conflict".

14. The Act does not lay down any procedure for TRC reception of information or evidence. Section 7(1) of the Act is couched in very general terms.

> 7. (1) The Commission shall, subject to this Act, solely determine its operating procedures and mode of work with regard to its functions which shall include the following three components:
> (a) undertaking investigation and research into key events, causes, patterns of abuse or violation of the parties responsible;
> (b) holding sessions, some of which may be public, to hear from the victims and perpetrators of any abuses or violations of from other interested parties;
> (c) taking individual statements and gathering additional information with regard to the matters referred to in paragraphs (a) or (b).

There are other, very general, powers-to require that statements be taken on oath, to hold private interviews, or to arrange for information to be given in confidence, which "the Commission shall not be compelled to disclose".[21] There is in effect a power to prosecute for perjury those who testify so any indictee who does so would in theory face people jeopardy.[22] It may be significant that the Act itself does not give "public sessions" any special importance or prominence, or treat them as central to the functioning of the Commission. "Sessions" are merely permitted, "some of which may be public".

15. The TRC was to have completed its work and submitted a final report by October of this year: it has obtained an extension of time until the end of December. A representative was recently reported as telling the International Crisis Group that its final product "will be a report on the causes of the war (including an historical narrative) that attempts to offer a road map with recommendations on a range of reforms necessary to prevent a new conflict".[23] This would be unexceptional, and obviously helpful to the country and to the Court. But there is no guarantee that its "historical narrative" will not include a judgement on the responsibility (even the guilt) of individuals indicted by

---

[21] Section 7(3).

[22] See Section 9(2) which reads: "Any person who wilfully obstructs or otherwise interferes with the Commission or any of its members or officers in the discharge of the Commission's functions under this Act, commits an offence and shall be liable on conviction to a fine not exceeding one million leones or to a term of imprisonment not exceeding on year or both such fine and imprisonment".

[23] "Sierre Leone: The State of Security and Governance", *ICG Africa Report No. 67*, (Freetown/Brussels: 2 September 2003), p. 12 (ICG interview with TRC representative, May 2003).

the Special Court. I was told at the hearing by TRC representatives that the Commissioners are preparing to make some assessments of responsibility, and I have been given no assurance that indictees awaiting or undergoing trial will not be "judged" guilty or innocent by the Commissioners (who are not qualified judges), whether or not they testify to the TRC. The TRC has made no "self-denying ordinance" in this or any other respect that is comparable to the decision of the Special Court Prosecutor to refrain from using evidence presented to the TRC. If its report carries any conclusion about the criminal responsibility of an indictee, then the professional judges of the Special Court will have to ignore the premature judgement, as indeed they are trained to do. But its publication may create expectations and anxieties among prospective witnesses and other defendants and prove indirectly damaging to either Prosecution or Defence. For the very reason that it would necessarily be a premature judgement, it might be shaken or reversed after all the evidence is heard and exposed to the test of cross-examination at the trial. Any such result might discredit the TRC report, but the Court must take no account of this: its judges remain committed by oath to reach their verdicts according to the evidence before them.

16. One solution to the problem could be for the TRC to issue a preliminary report in February and then suspend its operations until the trial process has been completed, when it would reconvene to consider the trial evidence and prepare and publish a final report, incorporating the results of the trials. But I am told that no such course can realistically be contemplated.

1.4. *The Indictee*

17. In these circumstances, a competent lawyer would be unlikely to advise an indicted client to run the risk of testifying before the TRC. There are no procedural safe-guards; he might make damaging admissions under questioning from the counsel to the Commission or from the Commissioners themselves and these admissions could be used by the Prosecution, whose self-denying ordinance does not extend to indictee testimony; he might be condemned in the Commission's report in a way which would create an expectation of his conviction by the Special Court and in consequence frighten off potential defence witnesses. When the TRC first approached a number of indictees, earlier in the year,

they all declined a chalice that they were doubtless advised was poisoned. There came a point, however, when this applicant changed his mind. In a letter dated 26 August 2003 to his lawyer, copied to the TRC and the Court, Chief Sam Hinga Norman refers to legal advice given him in June to the effect that his appearance before TRC would be inappropriate. But since, almost 6 months after his arrest, "there is no news about the start of the trial... I would prefer to be heard by the people of Sierra Leone and also be recorded for posterity". He refers to the fact that President Kabbah has testified, as have other ministers of the Government.

18. I have considerable sympathy with Chief Hinga Norman's concerns about his trial fixture. He expected a speedy trial but after 6 months in custody there was not yet a trial date. He is himself a Minister of Government and political leader. He heard broadcast testimony from the President and he too wanted to make his appeal to "the people". He thinks that it is discriminatory not to permit him to do so. He possesses, even as an indictee remanded in custody, a qualified right to freedom of speech. That right must be capable of assertion, in some meaningful way, to answer, if he wishes, any allegations that have been made against him in another forum: particular resonance attaches to free speech when it is sought as a "right of reply". He is entitled to set out his own account for posterity. The practical question concerns only the method by which this should be done whilst he awaits his trial.
19. To these claims of the indictee must be added the claim of the TRC itself to be put in a position to decide where the truth lies. The Commission states in paragraph 9 of its Application

> The TRC perceives Chief Samuel Hinga Norman JP to have played a central role in the conflict in Sierra Leone. The Commission's report – insofar as it purports to present an impartial historical record – would not be complete without hearing from Chief Hinga Norman the particular details of his role in the conflict and his insights and views into its causes, course and character.[24]

As will appear, I endorse this claim, so far as it goes. The TRC certainly can have the indictee's evidence, if (and only if) he is prepared to take the risk of volunteering it. The crucial question, again, is the form in which the evidence may be secured.

---

[24] See Request SHN 001/submitted on 07 October 2003, para. 9.

1.5. *The Special Court Practice Direction*

20. The Special Court was first approached by letter from the Executive Secretary of the TRC sent on 3 September 2003, peremptorily requesting that the indictee be made available for interview in the unit where he is being detained on 4 September – the very next day. Significantly, this was a request for a *private* interview, lasting two days, with several TRC investigators. It was not a request for a public hearing.[25] On any view the timing of the request was impracticable, but the Registrar immediately consulted with me, the Vice President and the Presiding Judge of the Trial Chamber, and a Practice Direction was produced with great urgency in an effort to co-operate with the TRC.[26] The Practice Direction was promulgated on 9 September 2003.[27] The chief concern of the judges was that indictees should know what they were letting themselves in for it they gave interviews to the TRC, and to ensure that in the event they would be given every reasonable protection against self-incrimination. Thus any prisoner who agreed to participate in the process had to signify his agreement in writing, confirmed by a lawyer who had advised him about it; he had to be provided with a list of written questions and told he was not obliged to answer any particular one; he had to be informed that his answers might be used against him by the Prosecution and that no "finding" by the TRC about him would sway the Court. Any interview had to be supervised by a lawyer appointed by the Registrar and had to be held in the presence of a lawyer for the indictee.
21. It must be understood that these were protections laid down not to obstruct the TRC but to provide fundamental protection for men facing charges alleging heinous crimes which if proved could lead to long years of imprisonment. That protection was essential where they were facing impromptu questioning by a skilled counsel for the TRC and by the commissioners themselves. There was not, indeed never has been, any inhibition against an indictee

[25] Letter dated 3 September 2003 from Franklyn Kargbo to Robin Vincent, Registrar.

[26] The suggestion by Schabas (para. 12) that the Special Court actually opposed indictee testimony is incorrect although his article was apparently written before the Practice Direction and its amendment.

[27] Practice Direction on the Procedure to Take Statements from a Person in the Custody of the Special Court for Sierra Leone, 9 September 2003.

volunteering or communicating information to the TRC in writing, either directly or through his lawyers. The indictee retains freedom of speech to this very considerable extent that he can write a book, if he wishes, about "his role in the conflict and insights and views into its cause, course and character" and have it sent to the TRC – by his lawyers, who will sensibly vet it first. It is surprising that the TRC does not appear to have requested information in *written* form from this indictee. It is also surprising that it has shifted its request from a two-day private interview with investigators to a full-scale public hearing broadcast "live" to the nation.

22. The Practice Direction was the result of earnest consultation, and marks an important shift from the principle initially endorsed by the ICTJ and set out at paragraph 8. This shift was made a part our of a willingness to co-operate with the TRC, subject to iron-clad protection of indictees' rights, and in part to reflect the recent common-law recognition that prisoners retain a certain core freedom of speech. Nonetheless, the promulgation of the Practice Direction was followed by TRC objections that it would infringe its powers to take evidence in confidence – powers that it seemed to want to use in respect of Chief Hinga Norman. There was correspondence and further meetings with the Registrar before an amended Practice Direction was adopted on 4 October, precisely to meet TRC objections to the first practice direction and to permit them to apply for a confidential hearing. For the purposes of the record, I set the current Direction out in full:

The Registrar of the Special Court for Sierra Leone,

NOTING that a State, the Truth and reconciliation Commission (TRC), or other legitimate authority may on occasion request the assistance of the Court to take evidence for the purposes of their proceedings from a person who is in the custody of the Special Court or who is in the custody of another authority based on an order or request of the Special Courts;

HEREBY issues this Practice Direction in consultation with the President of the Special Court pursuant to Rule 33(D) of the Rules of Procedure and Evidence of the Special Court, setting out the procedure governing such requests:

1. A request by a State, the TRC, or other legitimate authority for assistance to question or take evidence from a person who is in the custody of the Special Court or who is in the custody of another authority based on an order or request of the Special Court ("detainee") shall be transmitted

to the Registrar. In addition, all correspondence between the detainee a State, the TRC, or other legitimate authority shall be copied to the detainee's counsel.

2. Requests shall be in writing and shall contain:

(a) details of the authority ("requesting authority" making the request;
(b) the name of the detainee to whom the request relates;
(c) details of the purpose of the request and a summary of the reasons for there quest;
(d) a description of any offences or suspected offences charged or likely to be charged or under investigation by the requesting authority;
(e) any relevant dates, such as the date of the trial at which the evidence is required, or any cause for special urgency (as appropriate);
(f) details of any caution which should be given to the detainee under the law of the requesting authority;
(g) a list either of specific questions or of subject areas about which questions are to be asked; and
(h) a description of any person from the requesting authority seeking to be present at the questioning and a description of the facilities which will be required for recording and transcribing the questions

3. The Registrar shall notify the President of any request. The request shall be forwarded to the Presiding Judge as appropriate, and to the Prosecutor and the Defence Office.

4. The Registrar shall inform the detainee and the detainee's counsel of the request. The Registrar shall ensure that the detainee has ample opportunity to take legal advice before deciding whether or not to agree to the questioning and is made aware:

(a) that the detainee is not obliged to agree to the questioning, or if he does, that he is not bound to answer any particular questions;
(b) that the questioning will be transcribed and the transcript filed with the Court Management System;
(c) that a copy of the record may be made available, upon order by the Presiding Judge, to a party or defence counsel for potential use in proceedings before the Special Court unless the questioning is covered, in whole or in part, by a confidentiality order, statute, or protocol, in which case a party or defence counsel may apply to the appropriate chamber for an order that the record of the questioning shall be disclosed in the interests of justice (which may include the interests of justice with respect to other suspects or accused before the Special Court); and
(d) that no decision, judgement, conclusion, or comment by the requesting authority will be allowed to influence the Special Court in determining the detainee's guilt or innocence.

5. In the event that the detainee agrees to the questioning (such agreement having been signed in writing by the detainee and confirmed by the detainee's

counsel), the Registrar shall inform the parties and place the request before the Presiding Judge. The Presiding Judge shall instruct the parties and the detainee's counsel on the procedures to be followed on making representations concerning the request. After such representations are made the Presiding Judge shall grant approval (conditional or otherwise) if the said judge is satisfied that the detainee agrees to the questioning and has been fully advised in terms of paragraph 4 above. In such circumstances, the request for questioning will only be rejected if the Presiding Judge is satisfied that a refusal is necessary in the interests of justice or to maintain the integrity of the proceedings of the Special Court. An appeal against rejection shall be decided by the President if it is made expeditiously and jointly by the detainee and the requesting authority.

6. Once the Presiding Judge has approved the request, the Registrar shall make appropriate arrangements for the questioning to proceed on a date convenient for the detainee's counsel to be present. The Registrar shall ensure that the detainee has the services of an interpreter if required.

7. The questioning shall be supervised by a legal officer nominated by and acting on behalf of the Registrar. This officer shall have the authority to stop the questioning if it goes significantly beyond the scope of the questions notified pursuant to paragraph 2 (g) above and/or if any conditions imposed by the Presiding Judge (e.g., as to identification or protected witnesses) are not observed.

23. The Practice Direction again relates only to the taking of oral evidence and in no way prohibits or obstructs written correspondence. At the TRC's request, it makes provision for a confidential process of receiving information. Most importantly, paragraph 5 sets up a presumption that the Presiding Judge will grant a TRC request if satisfied that the indictee has given an informed consent, unless "satisfied that a refusal is in the interests of justice or to maintain the integrity of the Special Court".

1.6. *This Joint Application*

24. The TRC duly brought before the Presiding Judge an application which complied with these protocols and was joined by Chief Hinga Norman. The TRC supplied a list of some 32 fairly broad subject areas they wished him to cover. They further requested at least two days occupancy of the Special Court courthouse, for a public hearing which would be broadcast live to the nation with edited highlights on the evening television news. I quote extracts from the TRC application to the Court:

Chief Hinga Norman will be required to take an oath prior to making any statement before a hearing of the TRC... In consultation and agreement with his legal representatives the Commission will determine in advance the scope of the hearing and the ambit of the questions that will follow his initial statement to the Commission. Chief Hinga Norman's legal team will be at his side throughout the hearing and will be permitted to intervene at any time on their client's behalf... The TRC would suggest that the courthouse on site at the Special Court compound be used for the public hearing... The hearing will be presided over by five commissioners (possibly six) ... Selected representatives of the public will be in attendance ... The TRC's public hearings are normally broadcast live. We accordingly request that two telephone connections be made available to enable SRBS and UNAMSIL radio to broadcast the hearing. In terms of facilities the TRC will supply its own transcribing and video equipment and support staff who will manage the recording. The TRC will also employ a photographer for the purpose of taking still photographs of the hearing. With regard to the time required to conduct this public hearing, the Commission requests that two full days be reserved. It is envisioned that the first session on the first designated day will commence at 10 a.m. and conclude by 5 p.m.[28]

25. I asked the TRC head of investigation, Mr. Howard Varney, some questions to elicit further details of the proposed procedure. He thought the indictee could read from a prepared script, face-to-camera as it were, for the first day, although he agreed that it might be possible for his counsel to "lead" him though his evidence as would be the case at trial. Then the following day the indictee would be questioned by the Commissioner's counsel, an experienced barrister, then by his own counsel, and by each of the Commissioners in turn, who would be sitting in the courtroom on the judges' bench. Bishop Humper (who is not of course a judge or trained lawyer), would preside and would determine the procedure to be followed as the hearing progressed. It would be desirable to have some victims present and indeed preferably to have the whole hearing in a town hall where many victims could be present. The hearing would be broadcast live on SRBS radio and Radio UNAMSIL and television would show "snippets" in the evening. The indictee would be given the opportunity to make an "uninterrupted presentation" for as long as he required. There was not written or settled procedure. Mr. Varney confirmed that there was nothing in the Act to prevent findings of fact against individuals and he understood that the TRC would indeed make findings on the role of factions and of certain individuals. There would be no standard of proof in respect of such findings as Mr. Varney correctly observed: "The TRC is not a court".

[28] Request SHN 001 / submitted on 7 October 2003, paras 16–17, 19–24.

26. The Prosecution opposes the joint application, despite admitting that the availability of evidence on oath from the defendant at an open hearing "had a certain appeal" – for reasons that are obvious. Nevertheless, it asserted that such a hearing would undermine the integrity of the Special Court, imperil the security situation in the country and could serve to intimidate witnesses given that the indictee has a large following, even if this was not his intention. The latter claim is always easy for prosecutors to make and often difficult for defendants to refute. It could have been discounted, but the TRC's warning that if the Chief did not testify then his supporters might cause unrest and "unleash powerful emotions" against the Special Court. This comment, made on behalf of the TRC at the hearing, indicates that the prosecution concern may have some foundation. Mr. Tim Owen, for the Chief, immediately disassociated himself from this TRC argument and I accept his statement that unrest is the last thing his client would wish to stir up. (That is evident from his very first statement to his followers after his arrest, in which he made it clear he would co-operate with a process which he believed would establish his innocence). But the danger of unintended consequences, in a society where factions still have access to arms and where the war ended only last year, must be born in any judicial mind. To allow any accused to testify live-to-air, for several days in an uncontrolled environment may be asking for unpredictable trouble.
27. Following the hearing I received written submissions from all parties, which I carefully considered but do not think they much advance the arguments made at the hearing.[29] The prosecution again draws attention to the "fragile equilibrium"[30] in the country and to the potential for destabilisation where the forces which the indictee commanded are still active association and interested in securing his freedom, although there is no evidence that they intend to do so by unlawful means, much less that Chief Hinga

[29] See Letter with enclosures from David Crane, Prosecutor, to Judge Geoffrey Robertson, President, dated 11 November 2003; Letter from Howard Varney, Head of Investigations at the TRC to Judge Robertson, President of the Special Court, dated 13 November 2003; Additional Submissions on behalf of Chief Hinga Norman on his application to appear before the Truth and Reconciliation Commission of Sierra Leone, dated 12 November 2003, filed on 27 November 2003.

[30] Letter with enclosures from David Crane, Prosecutor, to Judge Geoffrey Robertson, President, dated 11 November 2003.

Norman is likely to encourage such a course. There is frustration on all sides, because his trial date has not yet been fixed, a matter to which I shall have to revert.

28. I have had to remind myself of the legitimate interests of others who have not been represented. There are other indictees, many from factions, which fought against Chief Hinga Norman and against whom he might well testify any TRC hearing. It would hardly be fair to them to be subjected to public attacks, which they could not answer. It would place pressure on them to give evidence to the TRC, waiving their right against self-incrimination, perhaps with disastrous results. An interesting indication of just how dangerous is the road down which the TRC would draw indictees is provided by its application in the case of Augustine Gbao, an indictee from a different faction.[31] This application was also refused by Judge Thompson, albeit on different grounds.[32] What strikes me is the extent and detail of the conditions upon which his testimony was offered to, and apparently accepted, by the TRC. These include:[33]

(i) That the Chairman of the Commission provide a written assurance to Mr. Bao's defence counsel that he will retain full control of the proceedings and, acting in good faith, will fully brief the participants in the proceedings of these conditions and the importance of them, and that he will not permit any breaches of these or other conditions and will generally protect Mr. Bao from any intervention which might serve to prejudice Mr. Bao's future trial.

(ii) That Mr. Bao be permitted to retain his right to silence at all times and that he be permitted to withdraw from the proceedings at any time.

(iii) That Mr. Bao's legal team be permitted to sit with him throughout the proceedings and to have rights to audience for the purpose of intervening at any stage where it becomes necessary to protect Mr. Bao's right and in particular his right to a fair trial before the Special Court.

[31] The TRC Application is contained in: Request AAB 002/Submitted on 10 October 2003 by the Truth and Reconciliation Commission for Sierra Leone to conduct a public hearing with Mr. Augustine Ato Bao in terms of the Special Court for Sierra Leone Practice Direction adopted on 9 September 2003, as amended on 4 October 2003.

[32] *Prosecutor v Gbao*, Case No. SCSL-2003-09-PT, Decision on the Request by the Truth and Reconciliation Commission of Sierra Leone to Conduct a Public Hearing with the Accused, 3 November 2003.

[33] See Defence Agreement and Response to Truth and Reconciliation Commission of Sierra Leone request to conduct a public hearing with Mr. Augustine Ato Bao in terms of the Special Court for Sierra Leone Practice Directio nadopted on 9 September 2003, as amended on 4 October 2003, 17 October 2003.

(ix) That Mr. Bao's legal team be permitted an opportunity to remedy any inadvertent damage which may have been caused to Mr. Bao's right to a fair trial before the Special Court.

(iv) That any transcripts or recordings produced by the Truth Commission should not be passed onto any third party expect with the written consent of Defence Counsel for Mr. Bao or by order of a judge of the Special Court.

(v) It is to be noted that the Defence for Bao reserve the right to take any legal action necessary to remedy any prejudice to a fair trial caused by any of the activities of the Truth Commission linked to these proceedings. To this end, it is requested that any findings or conclusions of the Truth Commission intended to be published in its final report concerning Augustine Bao's role in the former conflict be copied to counsel for Augustine Bao at least 14 working days before the publication of that report. Defence counsel for Mr. Bao undertakes to respect the confidentiality of any such statements save for the purpose of presenting the nature of such statements to a judge for the purposes of any legal proceedings designed to protect Mr. Bao's right to a fair trial, should that become necessary.

29. Conditions of this kind – different for each indictee who testifies, depending one supposes on the advice of their different lawyers – need only be set out to be recognised as recipes for endless disruption and litigation, in the TRC itself, in national courts and in the Special Court. Allowing an application to permit public testimony along the lines suggested by this application would – as these conditions demonstrate – run risks of the fair trial rights of an indictee being jeopardised at a hearing before the Bishop in the Special Court building. This could lead to an application for an injunction in the Supreme Court of Sierra Leone, or an application before the Special Court for protective measures. Suppose counsel for Mr. Gbao takes exception to a passage in the draft TRC report: will he apply on the basis of this agreement with the TRC to injunct it in the national courts, or seek a right to refute it, or apply for protective measures before the Trial Chamber? The prospects of litigation – and consequent diversions and delays to Special Court trials – are endless.

II. DISCUSSION

30. What is actually proposed by this application may be described in different ways: it may appear as a spectacle. A man in custody awaiting trial on very serious charges is to be paraded, in the very court where that trial will shortly be held, before a Bishop rather than a presiding judge and permitted to broadcast live to the nation for a day or so uninterrupted. Thereafter for the following day or days, he will be examined by a barrister and then

questioned from the bench by the Bishop and some five or six fellow Commissioners. In the immediate vicinity will be press, prosecutors and "victims". His counsel will be present and permitted to interject but there are no fixed procedures and no Rules of Evidence. The event will have the appearance of a trial, at least the appearance of a sort of trial familiar from centuries past, although the first day of uninterrupted testimony may resemble more a very long party political broadcast. It is not necessary to speculate on the consequences of this spectacle: there may be none. There may be those the Prosecution fears which could lead to intimidation of witnesses and the rally or dormant forces. There may be those that doubtless informed the original advice of his lawyers against testifying – namely fodder for the Prosecution, an adverse effect on public perceptions of his innocence and a consequent disheartening of potential defence witnesses. There will probably, I fear, be this consequence, namely intense anxiety amongst other indictees, especially from rival factions, and concerns over whether they should testify to the TRC as well, or in rebuttal. The spectacle of the TRC sitting in court may set up a public expectation that it will indeed pass judgement on indictees thus confronted and questioned, whose guilt or innocence it is the special duty of the Special Court to determine.

31. I cannot believe that the Nuremberg Tribunal would have allowed its prisoners to participate in such a spectacle, had there been a TRC in Germany after the war, or that the International Criminal Tribunals for the Former Yugoslavia or Rwanda would readily permit indictees awaiting trial to broadcast in this way to the people of Serbia or Rwanda. If it is the case that local TRC's and international courts are to work together in efforts to produce post-conflict justice in other theatres of war in the future, I do not believe that granting this application for public testimony would be a helpful precedent.

32. The applicants have not satisfactorily explained their insistence on *public* testimony. There are many other ways for the TRC to receive information, and its own Act suggests that public hearings might be an exception not the rule. It has never explained why it has shifted first from its initial request for a two-day private interview – a request which might well have been granted – to a request for permission for a confidential interview (which might also have been granted) to an application for the televised spectacle described above. It may have been unduly influenced by Chief Hinga Norman's insistence that he will only give evidence at

a public hearing – a legitimate position on his part, but one which cannot bind the Court, no matter how much it may have shaped the TRCs application.

33. Let me return to first principles. Truth Commissions and International Courts are both instruments for effectuating the promise made by states that victims of human rights violations shall have an effective remedy.[34] Criminal courts offer the most effective remedy – a trial, followed by punishment of those found guilty, in this case of those who bear the greatest responsibility. TRC reports can assist society to move forward and beyond the hatreds that fuelled the war. Truth commissions offer two distinct prospects for victims – of truth, *i.e.* learning how and why they or their loved ones were murdered or mutilated, and of reconciliation, through understanding and forgiveness of those perpetrators who genuinely confess and regret. It seems to me that these are separate and severable objectives.

34. In what has been termed "transitional justice" periods, truth commissions may be the only option for weak governments. In this context they were common in South America in the 1980s – in Bolivia, Chile, El Salvador, Haiti, Argentina and so forth. They were usually accompanied by blanket amnesties and were not permitted to "name names" of those who might be identified as perpetrators of crimes against humanity, not to avoid prejudice to trials (which were not in prospect), but to avoid political embarrassment. The reports nonetheless shed light on abuses – in some cases, as with "Nunca Mas", very great light. They achieved a degree of truth, but without justice and in many cases without reconciliation – see the recent public demands in these countries to vacate the amnesties and prosecute the perpetrators. The Lomé Accord of 1999 offered both a blanket amnesty and a TRC: only after that agreement was comprehensively violated did the international community deploy its muscle to insist on the prosecution of those bearing the greatest responsibility for the war.

35. The Sierra Leone TRC may have emerged from a dishonoured agreement, but it took on a statutory form that does not preclude its co-existence with the subsequently established Special Court. It was modelled to some extent on the South African TRC although it must be understood that this body offered what were in effect plea-bargains: those who testified were only absolved from

[34] Article 2(3) of the International Covenant on Civil and Political Rights, GA res. 2200A (XXI), 21 GAOR Suppl. No. 16 at 52.

criminal liability if they testified truthfully and were prepared if need be to repeat that testimony in court against others. This plea-bargaining aspect has not been replicated in Sierra Leone's TRC statute. It has had to operate in a society where some major players in the war are indicted in the Special Court.

36. In the case, as here, of Truth Commissions coinciding with court trials of alleged perpetrators, there is a dearth of precedent. In East Timor, a Memorandum of Understanding has been drawn up between the Office of the General Prosecutor (OGP) and the Commission (CAVR) which provides that:

> The OGP is able to provide information to the CAVR that is relevant to its truth-seeking function only in circumstances where this does not prejudice ongoing investigations or prosecutions or the confidentiality of witnesses or victims and is consistent with the mandate of the OGP.[35]

This does not address the specific issue of indictee testimony, although it demonstrates that in balancing the interests of the two processes, the value of fair trial must be overriding.

37. There is some assistance to be drawn from the experience of Peru, where the issue has arisen in relation to testimony by members of *Shining Path* who were awaiting trial. The TRC chose, I am told, to hear any testimony offered by such indictees in private, so as not to impact on their trial, even though the trial process there was to be inquisitorial rather than adversarial. This may be a helpful pointer to the desirability of finding a compromise solution which involves information volunteered to a TRC in a form that cannot reasonably affect ongoing trials. I note also that the TRC in that case wrestled with the difficulty inherent in public hearings for convicted perpetrators, namely that this can provide a "soap-box" or platform for justification of their crimes. It declined to provide such hearings for persons whose testimony (which it saw in written form in advance) was either self-promoting or at odds with other credible information it had gathered. This is not an issue here, but it does demonstrate how public hearings can be problematic for TRCs even when those who testify are not awaiting trial. Despite some well-publicised confessions at

---

35 Memorandum of Understanding Between the Office of the General Prosecutor (OGP) and the Commission for Reception, Truth and Reconciliation (CAVR) Regarding the Working Relationship and Exchange of Information between the Two Institutions, 4 June 2002, para. 9.

the South African TRC, I am informed that it is rare for perpetrators, whether alleged or convicted, to use public hearings to make confessions: these are more likely to be forthcoming in private hearings. For that very reason, of course, private hearings cannot be fully immunised from prosecution scrutiny: the compromise adopted by this court is found in Practice Direction paragraph 4(c).

38. As I have explained, the TRC is not *required* to hold public hearings. It has many powers to obtain evidence in different ways – even through confidential processes. It has held some meetings at which victims have been able to confront perpetrators. It has held a few public hearings at which ministers and even the President have spoken. It is entirely understandable that it should seek information from Chief Hinga Norman and from other indictees who are "central figures" whether or not they are guilty of war crimes. It is understandable – although I wonder whether it is really necessary – that the TRC should wish that information to be stated on oath. This course would, at least in theory, make the indictee vulnerable to a perjury prosecution in the national courts, and I do not consider it right or fair that he should be exposed to such double jeopardy. This prospect would without endangering the integrity of the Special Court, then it is right that the TRC should have it in that fashion and no other.

39. It would clearly not be right that the TRC apply its "reconciliation" processes of public hearing, confrontation with victims, live broadcast and so on to Special Court indictees who have not pleaded guilty. This would, for the reasons given above, be wholly inappropriate. It might conceivably be permitted for an indictee whose guilty plea had been entered and accepted by the Court and by the Prosecution, but that is not this case. I have to decide how to effectuate the wish to testify of an indictee who, his counsel tell me, intends to plead "not guilty" and to vigorously defend the legality of his actions in putting down an insurrection by use of what he will contend was reasonable force. His free speech entitlement may only be restricted – like his freedom of movement – to the extent that is consonant with his present status as an indictee.

40. That status does not only restrict his speech in the interests of security. It carries with it a host of considerations about ensuring the fairness of his trial (and "fairness" includes fairness to the Prosecutor and its witness) and fairness to other indictees who

face trial. At common law, a prisoner retains all the rights other than those taken away expressly or by necessary implication: *Raymond v Honey*[36]; *Ex parte Simms*.[37] These cases were pressed by counsel for the indictee, although they establish that convicted prisoners retain rights to urge the wrongfulness of their convictions (but not to engaged a political debate).[38] Although the indictees here may well wish to discuss political issues, the important distinction is that he is unconvicted and may to the extent be accorded more freedom. But that freedom is bounded, nonetheless, by the requirements to exercise it compatibly with his status as an indictee, which for present purposes means in a manner that gives rise to no real apprehension that it will disturb the fair trial process which he and others are obliged to go through. The argument, whether viewed as a free expression claim by an indictee or a concomitant claim to receive that expression by the TRC, cannot permit the applicants to dictate the manner in which the Special Court must effectuate it.

III. CONCLUSION

41. In my judgment, Chief Sam Hinga Norman is entitled to testify to the TRC upon condition that he has been fully apprised and advised of the dangers of so doing. I am satisfied that he has been expertly warned. His testimony must, however, be provided in a manner that reduces to an acceptable level any danger that it will influence witnesses (whether favourably or adversely) or affect the integrity of court proceedings or unreasonably affect co-defendants and other indictees. This in my judgment can be achieved by evidence prepared by him in writing (with the benefit of legal advice) and sworn in the form of an affidavit. I direct that if he wishes to take this course the Registrar should arrange for the swearing of the affidavit within the Detention Unit in the presence of a TRC official, and permit the original affidavit to be handed over to the TRC, on condition that it gives an undertaking not to bring or assist any other person or agency to bring a prosecution for perjury under S9(2) of its Act. What public use, if any, is made thereafter of

---

[36] [1983] 1AC 6.

[37] [1999] 3 WLR 328.

[38] *Ibid.*, p. 337.

that affidavit will be a matter for the TRC and for the detainee and his lawyers. Should counsel for the TRC have any further questions, these may be put to the indictee in writing and his answers may be sword and delivered in the same way. There shall be no public hearing of the kind requested or of any other kind prior to the conclusion of the trial. This is without prejudice to his right, if so advised, to make *unsworn* written statements to the TRC. IT is without prejudice to his right to meet with commissioners in the Detention Unit, if they apply for that purpose, or to his right to meet them for a confidential session, if a joint application is made for that purpose.

42. This solution means that the TRC is put in the position of receiving sworn testimony on every subject it wishes to explore, so long as the indictee is prepared to volunteer it. All that it is denied is a public hearing, an event more conducive to its reconciliation work (which cannot apply to indictees who plead not guilty) than its business of constructing an historical record. So far as the indictee is concerned, he can put anything he wishes before the Commission, and on oath. Mr. Tim Owen made the point that an affidavit would not be so beneficial as a radio broadcast in getting his message across to his followers, because many of them cannot read. But this begs the question of the legitimate purpose of the TRC hearing, which must be to get information across to the Commissioners for the purpose of their request, rather than to permit indicted political leaders to get messages to their followers. What is important is that followers should know that their leaders have been given an opportunity to put forward their version of events in full detail, and this is achieved by the affidavit method. The indictee will shortly address the Court either to have the seven charges against him dismissed (if his Preliminary Motions fail[39]) or else to refute them by his own defence which he will be given every opportunity to develop under procedures that have been scrupulously lad down to achieve fairness. The time for him to give public testimony will be if and when he exercises his right to give evidence on oath.

---

[39] *Prosecutor v Norman*, Case No. SCSL-2003-08, Preliminary Motion based on Lack of Jurisdiction: Lawfulness of the Court's Establishment, 26 June 2003; Preliminary Motion based on Lack of Jurisdiction: Judicial Independence, 2 June 2003; Preliminary Motion based on Lack of Jurisdiction: Child Recruitment, 26 June 2003.

43. In an application for a change in conditions of detention to a form of "house arrest"[40] I note that he appreciated this point and indeed offered as a condition that he would undertake not to speak at all to the media – a position that would be undercut were I to grant a TRC application involving his speech through the media over several days. What really matters – as I pointed out in my Decision on that application[41] – is that the Court should effectuate his right to a speedy trial. It would appear that he only changed his mind and volunteered testimony to the TRC at the end of August, in frustration because by that time no trial date had been fixed. At the hearing, in early November, both Prosecution and Defence claimed to be ready for trial, although the Prosecution said it wanted to apply for joinder of another defendant who was only arrested in July. The Appeals Chamber has in a recent decision emphasized the importance in this Court of speedy trial[42], and this very application illustrates one of many reasons for the importance. The Trial Chamber will have this in mind in dealing with any application which has the consequence of delay.

44. The work of the Special Court and the TRC is complementary and each must accommodate the existence of the other. The TRC is not in a position to suspend its work once trials begin in order to issue a final report when they are over, taking the evidence and verdicts into account. It would be seemly if the report that the TRC is (I am told) to issue in February refrains from passing concluded judgement on the criminal responsibility of any person who is detained to face trial in this Court. Should comment or conclusion be passed, it will of course have absolutely no effect on the minds of the judges of this Court who sit to provide a fair trial according to international standards. That said, the Special Court respects the TRC's work and will assist it so far as is possible and proper, subject only to our overriding duty to serve the interests of justice without which there may not be the whole truth and there is unlikely to be lasting reconciliation.

---

[40] *Prosecutor v Norman*, Case No. SCSL-2003-08-PT, Motion for Modification of the Conditiosn of Detention, 23 July 2003, para. 9(f).

[41] *Prosecutor v Norman*, Case No. SCSL-2003-08-PT, Decision of Motion for Modification of the Conditions of Detention, 26 November 2003, para. 16.

[42] *Prosecutor v Norman*, Case No. SCSL-2003-08, *Prosecutor v Kallon*, Case No. SCSL-2003-07, *Prosecutor v Gbao*, Case No. SCSL-2003-09, Decision on the Application for a Stay of Proceedings and Denial of Right to Appeal, 4 November 2003.

GPSR Compliance

The European Union's (EU) General Product Safety Regulation (GPSR) is a set of rules that requires consumer products to be safe and our obligations to ensure this.

If you have any concerns about our products, you can contact us on ProductSafety@springernature.com

In case Publisher is established outside the EU, the EU authorized representative is:

Springer Nature Customer Service Center GmbH
Europaplatz 3
69115 Heidelberg, Germany

Batch number: 10823959

Printed by Printforce, the Netherlands